PIRATES & OUTLAWS OF CANADA 1610-1932

PIRATES & OUTLAWS
OF CANADA 1610-1932

**Harold Horwood
& Edward Butts**

1984
Doubleday Canada Limited, Toronto, Ontario
Doubleday & Company Inc., Garden City, New York

Library of Congress Catalog Card Number: 82-45542

FIRST EDITION

Printed and bound in Canada by T. H. Best Printing Company
Limited
Typesetting by ART-U Graphics Ltd.

Canadian Cataloguing in Publication Data

Horwood, Harold, 1923   Butts, Edward, 1951
Pirates and outlaws of Canada

Includes index.
ISBN 0-385-18373-9

1. Pirates — Canada — Biography.   2. Outlaws — Canada —
Biography.   I. Butts, Edward, 1951-   II. Title.

FC161.H67 1984   364.1′64′0922   C84-098187-2
F1026.H67 1984

For JoAnn and Melanie

CONTENTS

ACKNOWLEDGEMENTS

THE AUTHORS WOULD like to thank the following institutions: The Public Archives of Newfoundland, Nova Scotia, Prince Edward Island, Ontario, Saskatchewan, and British Columbia; the Glenbow Institute, the Public Archives of Massachusetts; the Public Archives and National Library of Canada; the British Public Records Office; the Arts Library, University of Waterloo, Gosling Memorial Library, St. John's; the Conception Bay Museum, Harbour Grace; the Maritime Museum, Boston; the Newfoundland Historical Society; Metropolitan Toronto Police Museum, Library of Congress, Confederation Life Art Collection, Toronto; Remington Art Museum, Ogdensburg, New York; the New York Historical Society; New York Central Library; the Public Libraries of Metropolitan Toronto, Owen Sound, Sault Ste. Marie, (Ontario), Kitchener, Hanover, and Goderich. A special note of thanks to Mr. Dwight Girty.

PIRATES & OUTLAWS
OF CANADA 1610-1932

INTRODUCTION

PIRACY AND BRIGANDAGE are older than history. The ships of Ancient Egypt had to defend themselves against sea rovers; caravans went armed for fear of raids by desert nomads. Pirates seized the young Julius Caesar and held him for ransom. They played a major role—perhaps the decisive one—in bringing to an end the great Norse venture to Greenland and America in the five centuries before Columbus. The Greenland colonies, founded so long before by Eric the Red, were repeatedly sacked early in the fifteenth century by English and Scottish pirates who carried off Greenlanders to be sold as slaves in the Moslem lands of North Africa.

The great age of piracy in the Atlantic coincided with the colonizing of the New World by Europeans. The Spanish colonies, in particular, were little more than centres for the gathering of loot from older and richer civilizations such as those of the Incas and the Aztecs. Since this loot had to be convoyed across the Atlantic to Spain, and since the English, French, and Dutch had by that time learned to build ships that were faster, nimbler, and better armed than anything owned by the Spaniards, the Spanish treasure ships offered a tempting and easy target for pirates and privateers from northwestern Europe.

The distinction between a pirate and a privateer was simply that the privateer sailed with the blessing of his government

1

to capture enemy ships either in wartime or in a part of the world that his government regarded as no-man's-land, while the pirate sailed under no greater authority than that of his own guns. The privateer carried letters of marque authorizing him to prey on the ships of certain nations. England, in the sixteenth and seventeenth centuries, made the curious distinction that even when she was at peace with Spain she might still be at war with the Spanish colonies in the New World. After all, the Spaniards were in the Caribbean by authority of the Pope, and the Pope, in newly Protestant England, had *no* authority. So the reasoning went—an excuse for allowing Drake, Hawkins, and their successors to prey on Spanish ships and Spanish colonies even when Spain and England were not at war.

Hard on the heels of the Spanish thrust into Central America came the English, French, and Portuguese fisheries in Newfoundland and Nova Scotia. The fisheries quickly mushroomed into an immense industry, employing hundreds of ships and tens of thousands of men and women in a land with no government closer than Europe and no authority higher than that of the "fishing admirals"—the first captain to arrive at a port in the spring became "admiral" of that port for the year. So Newfoundland became the very nest from which pirates were hatched. The pirate captains set up forts, careenages, docks; recruited shipwrights, sailmakers, ironworkers, deckhands by the thousands; then sailed south, well equipped to deal with the merchant ships of all nations, including their own.

Although the taking of the Spanish treasure ship was the grand slam of piracy, other smaller victories were welcomed —French cargoes of wine, English cargoes of shore-cured fish, and, a little later, cargoes of furs from Hudson Bay and the St. Lawrence River. The dukedoms of southern France ran a massive black market. One could sell anything, including captured ships, in the French "free ports." One could do almost as well, with no greater risk, in Ireland and western England, where robber barons commanded armed castles only loosely attached to the English Crown. These barons became the great outfitters and protectors of the English pirates, investing in pirate voyages without risk to themselves and having the means to dispose of whatever cargoes the pirates brought home.

As civilization marched across the continent of North America, the outlaw—simply a pirate without a ship—gradually replaced the sea rover as a central fact of North American life. He operated along the edge of the European conquest—in the "wild west" or the wild north. Therefore, outlaws were still flourishing in British Columbia one hundred years after piracy had finally been suppressed in Newfoundland.

The Canadian establishment has admitted rarely that Canada has a violent history. They have created the myth of the "rule of law" right from the day General Wolfe "planted firm Britannia's flag on Canada's fair domain," allowing them to look down their long blue noses at the barbaric Americans. We shall show in the pages that follow how the rule of lawlessness survived in Canada for over three hundred years.

The arch-pirate Peter Easton is a folk hero in Newfoundland. A monument has been erected to his memory on the site of his old fort. In their time, Avery and Bellamy were also folk heroes. Such men who preyed on rich and poor impartially as the opportunity arose acquired the Robin Hood image because the masses of poor and dispossessed badly needed to believe that the filthy rich got their comeuppance, at least sometimes, from a rebel, an outcast, or a leader to whom they could relate if only in fantasy.

Such fantasies are the origins of the outlaw-hero myth. Among the outlaw-heroes of history, beginning with Spartacus in Rome, have been Italy's Angelo Duca, Mexico's

Pancho Villa, Australia's Ned Kelly, and a whole string of American cut-throats immortalized in American movies: Jesse James, Billy the Kid, Pretty Boy Floyd, Bonnie and Clyde. In Canada we seem to prefer as our folk heroes men who have made war against the State in a more or less formal way. One of our prime ministers was proud to trace his ancestry to William Lyon Mackenzie, who escaped from the country with a price on his head after trying to raise an armed rebellion. Louis Riel, who many strongly believe was insane, has been cannonized and enshrined on a Canadian stamp. Gabriel Dumont, a far more dangerous rebel than Riel (and who was most definitely sane and an astute tactician) has achieved hero status in the past quarter-century or so. But we are beginning to run out of rebels to exalt. The myths we have been weaving in the past ten or fifteen years have centred around such lone-wolf outlaws as Almighty Voice and the Mad Trapper of Rat River, Albert Johnson. Prominent among those weaving such myths has been the novelist Rudy Wiebe.

Whether a real Robin Hood, who robbed the rich to enrich the poor, has ever existed may well be questioned. But outlaws were usually free spenders who paid well for services and by this means tended to spread their loot among the underprivileged. The popularity of Duca and Billy the Kid was based on the their habit of spending money like drunken sailors. But this by itself does not fully explain the outlaw's popularity. As recently as the 1960s, Newfoundlanders at Beachy Cove have sheltered and fed penniless gunmen on the run from the police. In any game of cops and robbers, the robber was the natural ally.

No amount of "participatory democracy" that we have yet seen has done anything to change the fact that authority is the servant of the rich, the oppressor of the poor, and that the poor will make heroes out of any who dare to challenge authority with violence. If the real-life outlaws are somewhat less than heroic, then the myths that are created around them will soon clothe them in heroism. Jesse James, who in real life gunned down defenceless bank clerks and beat up helpless train passengers, becomes, in legend, the hero who saves a poor widow about to lose her house to the villainous banker with a mortgage. Almost identical stories are told of Robin Hood, Pancho Villa, and Butch Cassidy—not one of them supported by a shred of evidence.

Even outlaws for whom no such legends were invented managed to claim the sympathies of the common people so long as they confined their attacks to the rich and powerful. In the early 1900s when the bandit Bill Miner was robbing CPR trains in British Columbia, one resident told a newspaper reporter, "Hell, old Bill Miner ain't so bad. He only robs the CPR once every two years. The CPR robs us all every day." Miner was no man of the people but a lone wolf who was never known for committing an act of generosity in a long and useless life.

The glittering reward, the great hope that lured men into piracy and banditry, was wealth, with its attendant power and ease. In the seventeenth century, when the story of piracy and outlawry in Canada begins, the annual wage for a working man ranged from five to ten pounds sterling. But the payoff at the end of a pirate voyage was often a thousand pounds or more—enough to buy an estate or, prudently invested, to support one's family in comfort for life. A common pirate might rise from deckhand ("scum," as their officers called them) to country squire. A pirate captain might rise much higher. Three of the Newfoundland pirates bought their way into the European nobility.

Piracy was a much more complex trade than mere brigandage. To practise it successfully one needed a ship, preferably well armed, a navigator, and a large crew. Pirates captured their prizes, as a rule, by sheer weight of numbers. A merchant crew facing a boarding party that might outnumber them ten to one had little choice but to surrender. If they surrendered without a fight, their lives would usually be spared. Often they would have the choice of joining the pirates or sailing away naked in an empty ship.

The pirates depended upon constant recruitment, often at sea. Bristol, in the seventeenth and eighteenth centuries, was the world capital of both piracy and the slave trade, a port that eclipsed even London in the volume of its commerce. But even there a pirate captain could not boldly recruit a crew of a hundred fighting men and clear "for the high seas." Rather, he left on a peaceful trading or fishing voyage and then "went on the account." This phrase, meaning "turned pirate," was derived from "going off on your own account," in other words, working for yourself instead of for a shipowner.

Merchant ships carried only a handful of men and boys— ten to twenty—depending on the size of the ship. Fishing ships might carry twice that number, including two or three women and several "Irish youngsters" shipping out as servants in the fishery. So, when a captain and crew went on the account, the first thing they needed was more men—hence the everlasting recruitment of fishing crews and the astonishing numbers of Newfoundland fishermen reported to have sailed away as pirates.

There was always the risk of being caught and hanged— pirates *were* still sometimes hanged in the seventeenth century —but the risk was no longer a very grave one. Governments, especially of Great Britain, often issued general pardons to allow wayward seamen to come home and man the fleets once more. If war broke out, as it frequently did, whole flotillas of pirates would volunteer as privateers, with all past sins forgiven. Anyone rich enough could almost always buy immunity from the tolerant kings of England or France or even Spain—the Spaniards were not above hiring foreign pirates to help them compete in their losing struggle for maritime supremacy with their northern rivals. But the one thing one had to avoid if one was a common jack pirate with no saleable skills was to fall into the hands of the Spaniards, who had a nasty habit of burning pirates alive as heretics or working them to death as plantation or galley slaves. It was a young man's game. Most pirates ranged between the ages of eighteen and thirty. A few older men went on the account, but most either died or retired before middle age. Boys as young as ten were repeatedly listed as members of pirate crews and sometimes escaped hanging because of their youth (only to be sent to the plantations as indentured labour or, in one case, to be reprieved from hanging and imprisoned for ten years). The pirates, too, seem to have pitied these waifs of the high seas. In one shareout of pirate plunder, all boys under the age of sixteen were allotted one hundred pounds each "to enable them to apprentice themselves to an honest trade ashore."

By the late seventeenth century the major pirate black markets had shifted from the old world to the new. Ireland, Cornwall, and the Riviera now gave place to the capitals of the English overseas colonies. Sir David Kirke, who captured Quebec from Champlain and was awarded the governorship of Newfoundland, made his capital, Ferryland, into a free port for the sale of pirate loot and a major centre in the rum trade.

The Navigation Acts that, in effect, tried to force the British colonies to trade with Britain alone encouraged smuggling and piracy. By the 1670s, colonial governors from New England to the Carolinas were outfitting pirates and openly entertaining them in their mansions and, at times, even issuing letters of marque (for which they had no authority) to protect the pirates from any king's ship they might chance to meet. Such governors were often recalled by outraged British officials, but just as often were replaced by men equally corruptable—the pirates found that almost every governor had his price.

Although commissions for the suppression of piracy date back at least to 1620 in Newfoundland, no really effective remedy was found until the Royal Navy began patrolling the high seas with fast sloops-of-war especially fitted out for capturing pirates. This action, carried out in the latter part of the eighteenth century, was effective for a while, until the American War of Independence, the Wars of Napoleon, and the War of 1812 set off privateering on a massive scale, with many of the privateers slipping into piracy when their letters of marque expired. Piracy in the Atlantic was not finally suppressed until well into the second half of the nineteenth century. In Canada the last hanging for piracy was in Halifax in 1809, but other Canadian pirates were hanged for murder or retired. One didn't die until 1870, long after piracy had disappeared from Canadian seas.

This was just about the time that the outlaw in his modern guise was becoming common in Canada, following the march of empire westward to the Pacific. But outlaws of another breed had been with us almost from the beginning. *Coureurs de bois*, proscribed by the laws of New France for illegal trading with the Indians, were adventurers who sold their services impartially to England and France in the struggle for the fur trade of Canada. Deserters from the Royal Navy and the fishing plantations formed the band of Masterless Men in Newfoundland.

Such men, sometimes heroic, sometimes pitiable, sometimes unrelievedly vicious, are the substance of this book, their lives wrapped up in the blood, the violence, and the terror that have been edited out of Canada's past.

It is interesting to question just who should and who should not be classed as a pirate or outlaw. In Spain *El Draco* is remembered as the most vicious pirate in all history, the Ghengis Khan of the freebooters; in England he is remembered as Sir Francis Drake, the greatest hero of the Elizabethan Age. So fine is the distinction between pirate and privateer (the latter being a *licensed* pirate) that there is still a lively debate among historians as to whether Captain Kidd was ever guilty of piracy at all.

With outlaws the distinctions are even more various. Étienne Brûlé, Pierre Radisson, and Sieur des Groseilliers are all given an honoured place in Canadian history—at least as it is written by English Canadians. The fact that they all worked for English interests against the interests of New France might have something to do with this. Our decision to include Brûlé as one of the earliest Canadian outlaws rested partly on the fact that he was defined as an outlaw by the French and partly because he was the founder of the great outlaw tradition of the *coureurs de bois*. As for Radisson and Groseilliers, they were bandits by anyone's definition—not only outlaws but outlaws on the grandest scale, leaders of private expeditions that engaged in acts of warfare during time of peace. The English government simply found it convenient to deal with them, and English historians have honoured them because this pair of traitorous rogues founded the Hudson's Bay Company.

Outlawry is a way of life, chosen either as a career (Radisson) or adopted in desperation (Almighty Voice). Individual acts of lawlessness, such as the barn burnings said to have been committed by the Black Donnellys of Lucan, Ontario, do not make outlaws of those who commit them. The Donnellys were probably arsonists. They were massacred by a vigilante mob. But neither they nor their killers were outlaws in the sense that they were living beyond the law. Criminals, yes. Outlaws, no.

Here, then, is the record of some of the Canadians who, during the past four centuries, have lived outside the law. We shall follow their story from the days of first settlements in Newfoundland, Nova Scotia, and Quebec, through the wilderness of northern Ontario where outlaws seized and held entire communities against all comers, across the Prairies, and into the western forests where boy bandits, train robbers, and the Mad Trapper of Rat River helped create the myth of the Mountie who always (well, nearly always) gets his man.

CHAPTER 1

THE GREAT EASTON

IN THE YEAR 1611 Samuel Champlain was struggling to
found his tiny colony at Quebec, Henry Hudson was adrift
in a boat, cast away by his mutinous crew in the great bay
that would later bear his name, and Port Royal, in southern
Nova Scotia, was languishing, virtually abandoned, because
the colony was bankrupt.

But in the land that would later become Canada, trade
and commerce were booming in at least one place. In Newfoundland some ten thousand men (and a few women) with
three hundred and fifty to four hundred ships carried on the
greatest fishing enterprise the world had ever seen.

The New Founde Land (which then included Labrador,
the Gulf of St. Lawrence, and most of Nova Scotia) was
claimed by England but was host to the ships of several
nations. St. John's, its principal harbour and centre of
commerce, was a free port where Basques, Portuguese,
French, and English traded their goods and refitted their
ships.

In those days even the humblest fishing ship went armed
with at least a few cannons or swivel guns, since dried and
salted fish was an immensely valuable cargo. A shipload
might sell for a thousand pounds sterling at a time when one
pound was a generous month's wages for a tradesman. So
there was constant danger that both ship and cargo would

11

be hijacked and sold in the French free ports, the independent dukedoms of the Riviera which at that time ran the world's largest black market and carried on a lively trade with the Moslem kingdoms across the Mediterranean in North Africa.

Into the anarchy of the Newfoundland fishery there descended, in the summer of 1611, an agent of law and order who recognized no authority higher than his own but had both the force and the will to impose a kind of government. This was Captain Peter Easton, the pirate admiral in command of ten strong ships of war, who flew from the masthead of his flagship, the *Happy Adventure*, not some fanciful rag of a skull and crossbones later flown by minor cutthroats like Blackbeard, but the red and white cross of St. George, the flag that Drake and Raleigh and Gilbert had carried across the oceans a few years before.

Easton was an English gentleman and from an old family that had produced a bishop in the twelfth century. The Eastons had fought in the Crusades and, much later, against the Spanish Armada. In the great days of Queen Elizabeth I they had taken to seafaring, like so many other prominent families, and one of them had been master of the *Sunshine*, flagship of the Davis expedition that sailed in search of the Northwest Passage in 1585.

Peter Easton had visited Newfoundland as early as 1602, when Elizabeth was still on the throne of England and was still engaged in hit-and-run warfare at sea with the King of Spain. Much of this warfare and some of the convoy duty for England's commercial fleets was carried on by privateers, ships owned and fitted out by private citizens, most of them wealthy aristocrats, and carrying the Queen's commission to prey on the shipping of her enemies.

On that occasion Easton sailed as convoy for the Newfoundland fishing fleet, and on the outward voyage he liberated from a Dutch privateer an Irish girl named Sheila O'Connor, known in Newfoundland ever since as "the Irish Princess" or "Sheila Nagira." ("Nagira" is not a surname, but a corruption of an old Gaelic word meaning "The Beautiful.") Sheila had married one of Easton's lieutenants, a young man named Gilbert Pike. They became planters at the settlement of Mosquito, now called Bristol's Hope, and founded the very large family of Newfoundland Pikes.

A planter was not someone who planted crops but someone who planted a business enterprise of some kind in a colony—in the case of Newfoundland, planters owned fishing premises and boats and employed either servants or sharemen in the shore fishery.

On that first visit to Newfoundland Peter Easton had the legal right to requisition stores, munitions, even seamen if he needed them, from the fishing fleets. On his second visit he behaved in the same way with not a shred of legal authority. The privateer had become the world's most powerful pirate.

There had been a massive transition from privateering to piracy in 1603 when Elizabeth died and was succeeded by King James I. He promptly made peace with Spain, cancelled all letters of marque carried by privateers, and laid up the vessels of his own fleet. Men who had served in the navy kept their rank but ceased to draw pay from the royal exchequer. Men who had served as privateers and had lived by legal plunder now found themselves unemployed and wholly unfitted for a life of honest toil. Many of them turned to piracy. This happened, for example, with the captains who had sailed in the fleets of Elizabeth's favourite, Sir Walter Raleigh. They are euphemistically described as "erring captains" by the chroniclers of James's reign.

There were three classes of such pirates—those who attacked only the ships of their former enemies, the Spanish (and perhaps the Dutch, who were Spanish vassals), those who attacked ships of any foreign power, and those who attacked anything, including the ships of England.

Easton seems to have belonged to the third class. He wielded such power that he rarely had to shoot it out with anybody, but he certainly took supplies and seamen, if not cargoes, from English shipping and seems to have levied fees for free passage through the English Channel—at least, that seems to have been the complaint of the West Country merchants in a petition to the Lord Admiral explaining that they were forced to pay "protection" money, a kind of toll, to ensure safe passage in and out of such ports as Poole and Bristol.

By 1610 Easton commanded a fleet of forty ships that controlled all traffic through the English Channel. Just how firm a control he exercised over this fleet is open to question. Most of the pirate captains must have been fairly independent, but they were beholden to aristocratic patrons ashore, especially to the Killigrews, the "Robber Barons of Land's End," who were financiers and brokers for the pirates and gave them safe haven in the fourteen miles of navigable water that lay inland from their great fortress, Pendennis Castle, in Cornwall. The Killigrews, in turn, regarded Easton as their principal agent at sea, and he was, if not exactly a pirate admiral, at least the recognized leader of a loose federation of pirates.

The Killigrews were always well connected at court. One of them had been Elizabeth's Foreign Minister. Another was Groom of her Bedchamber. A third was Master of the Revels (to James), and a fourth became a desk admiral. But their loyalty to the Crown was loose and self-serving. One of the Killigrews even tried to sell England to the Spanish invaders for ten thousand gold crowns and was tried for treason but was eventually acquitted and restored to favour.

In 1610 the Bristol merchants presented a petition to Lord Nottingham, head of King James's paper navy, begging for relief from Easton's depredations. Nottingham replied by commissioning a daring young man named Henry Mainwarring (pronounced "Mannering") to go in pursuit of Easton and bring him to London.

Mainwarring, aged twenty-three, was a scholar, soldier, sailor, lawyer, and politician, an aristocrat a step higher on the social scale than Easton—a typical Elizabethan born a generation too late. When he discovered that the ships offered to him by Nottingham were worm-eaten and unseaworthy from seven years of disuse, he fitted out his own squadron, headed by his own ship, the *Princess*, presumably at his own expense and at the expense of his friends.

This gave Easton plenty of time to decide what to do. He had news, through the Killigrews, of everything that went on in government, and they doubtless advised him to make a foreign voyage. Giving battle to Mainwarring within the "Narrow Seas" might be interpreted as making war on the King, treason within the realm, as it was called. So he sailed for the Coast of Guinea—the long bight of Africa that was the source of ivory, gold, and slaves—and thence to Newfoundland, where he arrived in 1611 with ten ships of war "well furnished and very rich," as Sir Richard Whitbourne described them in his *Discourse and Discovery of the New-Found-Land.*

Whitbourne, who spent his working life in Newfoundland from 1579 to 1619, rising from a ship's mate to a Vice-Admiralty Court Judge and finally to a knighthood, was fishing admiral of the port of St. John's when Easton arrived and the closest thing Newfoundland had to a colonial governor. The pirate invited Whitbourne to visit him, and: "I was kept eleven weeks under his command, and had from him many golden promises, and much wealth offered to be put into my hands as is well known."

Whitbourne was entertained lavishly on Easton's flagship. They ate and drank in the comfort of the "great cabin" built at the stern between the main deck and the quarterdeck. It was the only decent living quarters anywhere on the ship, furnished with rugs, chairs, tables, cabinets, great lamps hung in gimbals, and instruments of navigation. There may also have been a glass-fronted case with books and a Bible. We do not know whether Easton carried a library in his ship, but other gentlemen-navigators of the time did and liked to sit on the quarterdeck in fair weather with a book of poetry in hand.

He is described as a dark man of athletic build and medium stature, but no portrait of him survives. He dressed like all gentlemen of his period, in doublet and hose, silver-buckled shoes, with fashionable cloak, sword, lace cuffs, and, more than likely, a feather in his hat.

The men who worked his ships loved and admired him — he was regarded as a great and generous leader. But between him and them there was a vast gap in status, appearance, and lifestyle. The seamen had no living quarters. They slept between decks among the guns, in a space where you couldn't stand straight because of lack of headroom. If they had hammocks, they slung them wherever they could. Otherwise, they slept on the deck boards.

They were universally barefooted and ill-clothed. Unlike gentlemen, who affected knee-breeches and silk stockings, the sailors wore trousers and little else. The trousers and a coarse shirt or jerkin were often made of sail canvas and were sometimes tarred to make them weatherproof. Pirates of a later day dressed in the captured clothing of their victims, but it seems unlikely that the tightly disciplined sailors who served under the aristocratic pirates of Easton's time did so.

The *Happy Adventure* was a ship of about 350 tons, double-decked and three-masted. In naval terms she might have been called a frigate, meaning something lighter than a full war galleon, with a rig similar, but not identical, to that of a merchant ship. She probably mounted thirty to forty full-sized cannons and any number of smaller swivel guns designed not for wrecking ships but for killing or maiming their crews when armed with canister and grapeshot and other such devilish devices. She would need about 150 men to work her properly in battle.

She was rigged with square sails, except for a large fore-and-aft or lateen sail at the stern. The advantage of the large

fore-and-aft sail was that it made the ship more manoeuvr-
able than a full square-rigger and better able to sail close-
hauled against the wind. In an age when fore-and-aft sails
were still uncommon except on single-masted ships, the
pirates had discovered and adopted this mixed rig, later to
become standard on all the seven seas.

We might wonder why Captain Whitbourne, holding a
Vice-Admiralty commission for the suppression of piracy
(the first ever issued outside the realm of England), would
allow himself to be "kept under the command" of a man like
Easton. The answer lies in the bred-in-the-bone attitudes of
the seventeenth century. Whitbourne, for all his authority
among the fishing fleets, was a mere merchant who had
risen from the working class, while Easton was an aristocrat,
born to rule. Commoners crossed such men at their peril.
They might be out of favour with the King this year but
one of his trusted councillors the next.

Easton's main purpose in Newfoundland was to recruit
men, repair and reprovision his ships, and capture arms and
ammunition, especially from French and Basque fishing
ships, most of which would carry a few guns but not nearly
enough to put up a fight against Easton's squadron. But
while he was about this more serious business, he also took
cargoes of salt fish from French and Portuguese ships and
at least one cargo of French wine. Sir William Vaughan,
who tried to found a colony near Cape Race, estimated that
Easton's ships took out of Newfoundland 100 pieces of
ordnance and 1500 mariners or fishermen, "to the great hurt
of the Newfoundland plantations."

One of the letters from John Guy's colony at Cupids,
dated 1612, reports Easton at Harbour Grace "trimming
and repairing his shipping, and [hath] taken munitions, etc.
together with about 100 men out of the bay, he purposeth to
have 500 out of the land before he goeth."

The numbers recruited for pirate crews may seem exaggerated until we remember that Easton manned his ships

with 180 men each (as reported by Guy) compared with the crew of 28 employed by Whitbourne at fishing.

But the London and Bristol Company that had founded the colony at Cupids was glad enough to accept the pirates' protection when it came to their stores. Fishery salt was always in short supply because the English had to get it in trade from France or Portugal, and in winter or early spring, when the colony was undermanned, their supplies would be vulnerable to thieves or raiders. So on October 12, 1612, John Guy's colonists landed at the pirates' fort in Harbour Grace and gave their fishing supplies, including fifteen tons of salt, into Easton's keeping for protection until the following spring.

Although Newfoundland was his home base from 1611 to 1614, Peter Easton's main interests lay far to the south where he could prey on Spanish shipping and even on English ships that he caught trading with the Spaniards. One such ship belonged to Captain Rashley of Foy in Cornwall. Easton captured it "upon the coast of Guinnie" where it was loading slaves for the Spanish colonies and took it to Newfoundland as a prize. But Whitbourne persuaded him to restore it to its owner, secured a freight for the vessel, and sent it home, "never having so much as thanks for my pains."

Easton's greatest coup during this period was a successful raid on the Spanish colony at Puerto Rico, with its supposedly impregnable fort, Moro Castle, that had withstood an attack by Sir Francis Drake. Easton apparently took the colony by surprise and decamped with whatever stockpiles of gold had been smelted from its famous mines. He also brought home to Harbour Grace a Spanish ship, the *San Sebastian*, reportedly stocked with treasure. This daring raid gave him a reputation for invincibility that he enjoyed ever afterwards.

On returning from his Caribbean cruise, Easton found Harbour Grace in the hands of French Basques who had captured his fort during his absence. The Basque fleet, led by a ship named the *St. Malo*, sailed out to give battle. As with all of Easton's engagements, we have no details of the ensuing fight—only the results. The Basque ships were sunk or captured, and the *St. Malo* herself was stranded on a small islet near the entrance to Harbour Grace, subsequently known as Easton's Isle (later corrupted to "Eastern Isle" and now to "Eastern Rock"). The pirates then landed and recaptured their fort. They lost forty-seven men in the battle, burying them at Bear Cove, just north of Harbour Grace, in a place still known as "The Pirates' Graveyard."

They gutted, stripped, and burned the *San Sebastian* at Ship's Head, Harbour Grace. A large anchor of Spanish design was recovered there by Captain William Stevenson in 1885—perhaps the only relic found from the treasure ship.

In 1612, while maintaining the fort at Harbour Grace, Easton moved his personal headquarters to Ferryland and there built "a great house" on a place called Fox Hill. This harbour, later the headquarters of Sir David Kirke, had obvious advantages. It was on the open ocean, near Cape Race and major shipping routes. Its entrance was guarded by the steep and easily fortified Isle au Bois. In all its long history, Ferryland was never successfully attacked by sea. A tiny inner harbour called "The Pool" could be used as a sort of dry dock. A steep hill called "The Gaze" rose above the beach and gave a wide view of the ocean in every direction.

Easton was now wealthy by any reasonable standards and willing to retire, so he began negotiating with King James for a pardon. Such pardons could be bought from the King if the price was right, as reported in the journal of Jean Chevalier of Jersey, a contemporary and friend of the pirates and a supporter of the Stuart monarchy. Chevalier names no figures but says English pirates paid "considerable sums of money" for their pardons.

Easton sent off at least three appeals for a pardon by three separate routes, one of them by Whitbourne, who agreed to take his letter to the Killigrews who in turn would become "humble petitioners to Your Majesty for his pardon." Whitbourne, as always, carried out his commission with dispatch: "And so, leaving Easton, I came for England, and gave notice of his intention, letting pass my voyage that I intended for Naples, and lost both my labour and charges: for before my arrival there was a pardon granted, and sent him from Ireland."

Guy, in fact, had earlier reported that Easton was sending a Captain Harvey in a ship to Ireland with his request for a pardon. But King James, obviously scenting gold, pardoned Easton *twice*. Both pardons are preserved in the British Public Records, the first dated February 1612, the second, November 1612.

The Public Records also has an estimate of Easton's depredations in Newfoundland: from English ships, 100 cannons, victuals and munition to the value of 10,400 pounds, "besides 500 fishermen of His Majesty's subjects taken from their honest trade of fishing (many being volunteers) but the most enforced...," from the French, 25 ships, from the Flemish, one "great ship," from the Portuguese, 12 ships.

All this helped to keep the pirate corporation, with its thousands of employees, afloat, but the real wealth came from Easton's private war with Spain, which he continued vigorously even while waiting for the King's pardon. He must have known that the pardon had been issued even if, as Whitbourne suggests, he never actually received a piece of parchment with the royal seal. Whitbourne, indeed, was subtly chiding the King for his choice of messengers. Easton, he says, "was hovering with those ships and riches upon the coast of Barbary, as he promised, with a longing desire and full expectation to be called home," but "lost that hope by a too much delaying of time by him who carried the pardon." If only the King had sent one of his multiple pardons by Captain Whitbourne!

Judging by Easton's subsequent career, he couldn't have cared all that much about the King's pardon. He remained at Ferryland until he received word that the Spanish Plate Fleet was preparing to sail from the West Indies by way of the Azores for Spain. This was an annual convoy by which the Spanish transferred their loot from Central America to their home treasury. It was a complex operation that involved using donkey trains on the Isthmus of Panama, making up ships' cargoes under armed guard, and assembling a fleet, all of which took many weeks. Meanwhile, word from paid informers could be passed to trading ships which in turn could sell their information to Spain's enemies. This form of betrayal had happened in the past, and now it happened once again.

Easton had boasted as early as 1612 that he would intercept the Spanish Plate Fleet. Now, in 1614, he did it. He sailed for the Azores with fourteen ships and deployed them in a wide arc to the south and west of the islands. Sure enough, the Spaniards sailed right into the ambush. Again, we have no details of the battle. We only know that Easton arrived off the Barbary Coast with four Spanish treasure ships containing the annual loot of an empire and was entertained as a conquering hero by the Bey of Tunis, who was said (with what truth no one can determine) to have offered him command of his fleet and a share in his kingdom.

In any case, the Great Easton remained for less than a year with the Moorish prince. By 1615 he had made a deal with the Duke of Savoy and had moved to Villefranche on the Riviera. There he purchased a palace, adopted the title Marquis of Savoy, and, in Whitbourne's phrase, "lived rich." Contemporary accounts estimate Easton's personal fortune at two million pounds sterling.

There is no way to translate this fortune accurately into contemporary terms—the values of too many things have changed. But a penny in Easton's time could buy many of the same things that a dollar can buy today (a dollar, originally, was exactly one fifth of a pound). So, in 1984 purchasing power it might be fair to say that Easton retired with a fortune in the neighbourhood of four hundred to five hundred million dollars.

He became Master of Ordnance for the Duke of Savoy, with whom he took part in at least one military campaign—an attack on the Duchy of Mantua, during which he "distinguished himself by the management and placement of his guns." After that, his career ends in silence.

But there is a monument to him at Harbour Grace, erected by the Government of Canada, with a bronze plaque giving a brief account of his career. Across Conception Bay from Harbour Grace lies the settlement of Kellegrews, named, at many years' remove, for members of the family who sponsored Easton in England. Around the shores of that bay where he fought the Basques, he is remembered in legend and admired as a leader of free spirits in an age of servitude. Did he set free the black slaves whom Captain Rashley was preparing to sell to the Spanish colonies? It would suit his legend if he had.

A town is named for the *Happy Adventure*, but it is only one of many Newfoundland places named for pirate ships. Others include Heart's Content, Heart's Desire, and Black Joke Cove.

In Conception Bay today there are hundreds of people with the surname "Easton." It is, actually, one of the commonest names in that part of Newfoundland. Did some of their ancestors, back in the seventeenth century, follow the old custom of adopting the name of a patron? It is certainly possible. No one knows for sure, but we are free to speculate that many of them may be descended from the "volunteers" whom Easton recruited into his crews—humble fishermen without surnames who followed him to his triumph over the Spanish fleet, took part in the shareout of the wealth, then

returned to the colony with money enough to become planters, adopting their captain's name in his honour.

CHAPTER 2

HENRY MAINWARRING

WHILE EASTON WAS still at Ferryland preparing for his great venture against the Spanish Plate Fleet, Henry Mainwarring arrived, less like an avenging angel than a disciple following the master's steps. The Public Records for 1614 record the event:

> Captain Maneringe with divers other captains arrived in Newfoundland the 4th of June having eight sails of warlike ships...from all the harbours whereof they commanded carpenters, maryners, victuals, munitions.... Of every six maryners they take one.... From the Portugal ships they took all their wine and other provisions save their bread; from a French ship in Harbour Grace they took 10,000 fish; some of the company of many ships did run away unto them.... And so they departed the 14th September having with them from the fishing fleet about 400 maryners and fishermen, many volunteers, many compelled.

Mainwarring, somewhat more the aristocrat than Easton, always acted like one born to rule. The squadron he outfitted in 1612 to run down and capture Easton consisted of just three ships. Clearing from the Thames he made straight for

Falmouth Bay near Land's End in Cornwall, where the Killigrews had their headquarters (their connection with the pirates being an open secret), and there learned that the quarry had flown.

This presented a problem. Mainwarring had almost certainly been backed by a corporation of aristocrats, fitting out three ships of war being a costly job, and had counted on laying claim to his share of Easton's loot. He called a conference of the ships' masters in his great cabin, and they agreed that since there was no prospect of catching pirates, the best way to make the expedition pay would be to go off after some Spaniards.

Unlike Easton, Mainwarring had direct access to Court. His family had been prominent in the Crusades and in the Wars of the Roses. Some of them were scholars and courtiers under Elizabeth. He had been admitted to Oxford at the age of twelve, had his first degree at the age of fifteen, served briefly in the army, and was received at Court at the age of twenty-two.

Mainwarring applied to the King for an enlargement of his letters of marque to allow him to prey upon Spanish shipping. Though England was at peace with Spain, this commission was granted, with the stipulation that his acts of war must be confined to the western seas and not committed in European waters. But Mainwarring must have received assurance from the King or from Nottingham, the King's desk admiral, that any harassment of Spain would be viewed with tolerance, for he was hardly under weigh for the second time before he called his captains together and announced that they would capture Spanish ships whenever and wherever they had the chance.

Instead of heading west, they went south to Marmora on the Barbary Coast of Africa and began intercepting Spanish ships near the Strait of Gibraltar. While in North Africa Mainwarring was received by the Bey of Tunis and was vastly impressed with Moorish civilization. In the Bey's dominions he could walk abroad without weapons by day or by night, for there were none of the thieves, footpads, pickpockets, and cutpurses that infested every city and town in England.

Since the North African Moslems were permanently at war with Spain, their harbours provided excellent bases from which pirates could prey on Spanish ships. Some seventeenth-century writers credit Easton and Mainwarring with teaching the Moslems their seamanship—hardly true, since the Barbary corsairs had centuries of seamanship behind them. What they did teach the Moslems was the superiority of the new sailing ship over the galleys and lateen-rigged luggers of the Mediterranean and the superiority of modern cannons over the bronze antiques still used by the Moorish princes. Mainwarring became a sort of admiral or captain-general of the port of Marmora and was able to offer protection to English shipping trading into Italy.

He also negotiated an English peace with Salee, then an independent sultanate famous for its own brand of pirates—the Salee Rovers. He secured from Salee the release of some hundreds of English prisoners held there as slaves, many of them serving in the galleys where they would have died without his intervention.

Mainwarring, despite his indiscretions, may never have fallen completely out of favour with King James. He consistently acted like an English ambassador at large. No warrant was ever issued against him from London, and it is to be noted that Whitbourne always spoke of him with respect. Nevertheless, he is listed in the English Public Records among the pirates and was certainly so regarded not only by the Spanish, French, and Portuguese, but also by English merchants and colonists.

Mainwarring's move to Newfoundland was prompted by the need for crewmen and for refitting his squadron which had been on the move for two years. Of the eight ships that arrived with him, five probably belonged to independent pirate captains in temporary alliance under his leadership.

In an address to the King written several years later, he described Newfoundland as the best place in the world for outfitting pirate ships, as it had plentiful stores and munitions, ships' gear, maritime tradesmen of every sort, and experienced seamen *more than willing to join pirate crews as volunteers.* He flatly denied that he had "enforced" any of his men. On the contrary, his decision to allow only one man in six to volunteer was made so as not to interfere too severely with the proper employments of the fishery.

His arrival in Newfoundland was widely reported and discussed. His flagship, the *Princess*, caused a good deal of comment on her own account because she was perhaps unequalled by anything afloat for her combination of speed, handiness, and firepower.

Although she lacked the towering, top-heavy, castle-like look of the great Spanish ships, she had extra decks fore and aft, allowing her to mount extra guns in banks, one row above the other. Her three masts were rigged with square sails up to and including what were later called "royals," permitting more flexibility than either the merchant or warships of her time. She had a large fore-and-aft mainsail for tacking in close quarters and on her bowsprit a series of spritsails including a tiny spritsail topsail mounted at the very tip, nearly useless for speed but a neat little gadget for making very fast turns.

In fair weather the *Princess* was steered by a whipstaff—a long lever that went down through the upper deck to a pivot, then to an iron ring connected to the tiller, so that if you moved the whipstaff one way, the tiller moved the other. It provided extra leverage, but not enough to manage the ship in a storm. At such times she was steered with the aid of ropes running through pulleys to the tiller, several men to each rope. No one had yet thought of attaching the ropes to a wheel!

The *Princess* was fitted with cast-iron guns, the latest product of the gun foundries on the Sussex Wold. They had longer range, more accuracy, and could be reloaded and fired more rapidly than any other guns of the time. Some of them, test-fired at the foundries, could hit targets dead centre at ranges of half a mile or more. A few years later, such guns would revolutionize naval warfare. Mainwarring was also using a new tactic—the line of battle. His ships sailed in line and concentrated their fire, broadside, on a target. Perhaps Easton had used this technique before him. In any case, it was an invention of the English pirate admirals, soon to be adopted by the world's navies and employed for the next three hundred years.

Mainwarring's ship (he was absolutely in love with her) stood out like a flower among the drab fishing fleet. She was painted a dazzling sunshine yellow, with numerous brass fittings that he kept shining like gold. Moreover, real gold leaf was applied generously to scroll work at the bow and stern. She undoubtedly also had a gilded figurehead, although he never mentioned it in his writings—possibly a mermaid or a unicorn both of which were popular at the time.

While in Newfoundland Mainwarring plundered French and Portuguese ships indiscriminately, probably without meeting the slightest resistance. The captains of these ships complained to their governments, and these, in turn, complained to King James, but there the matter ended—bills for damages were sometimes presented but were never paid. Mainwarring took over Easton's fort at Harbour Grace and may have built a careenage for cleaning and repairing ships. Like Easton, he entertained Captain Whitbourne and may have used him as a messenger to the King, although on precisely what mission Whitbourne prudently neglects to say: "He caused me to spend much time in his company, and from him I returned into England; although I was bound from thence to Marseilles, to make sale of such goods as I had, and other employments etc."

Mainwarring does not mention Whitbourne or any of his dealings with the government during the years of his "indiscretions," but he does say that the Bey of Tunis offered him command of his fleet, agreeing that he might remain a Christian and return to England whenever he chose. He did not accept this offer. Instead, with his newly recruited crews of Newfoundland fishermen he sailed back to Marmora and renewed his profitable war with Spain.

By now Mainwarring had become such a problem that the Spaniards fitted out a squadron of five warships especially to deal with him. They caught him off the coast of Portugal in the summer of 1615. According to his own account, the battle took place on "Mid-Summer's Day," but his descendant and biographer, G.E. Mainwarring, says it was in July. This probably means July 4, "Mid-Summer's Day" by the pre-Gregorian calendar, although twelve days after the solstice.

The battle lasted "throughout all the daylight hours." Mainwarring was outnumbered, but the Spanish ships were outsailed and outgunned. They still relied on the old tactic of sailing up to individual ships, hammering away at point-blank range, and then boarding them (using grappling hooks) for hand-to-hand combat. Mainwarring, with his superior guns and better sail plan, was able to stand off, perhaps completely out of range and certainly beyond the reach of accurate fire from the Spaniards, while raking their decks with repeated broadsides. When they realized that they were no match for the pirate, they fled into Lisbon harbour and took shelter under powerful shore batteries that Mainwarring could not approach. The arrival of the defeated Spanish squadron was observed by the Venetian ambassador, who sent home a gleeful report to his government.

Spain sued for peace. They sent an envoy to Villefranche, where Mainwarring had taken up temporary residence, and offered him twenty thousand gold ducats to enter the Spanish naval service. But by now Mainwarring was hoping for a similar invitation from England, so he refused the Spanish offer, adding that he did not need the help of the King of Spain to secure twenty thousand pieces of Spanish gold.

The Spanish ambassador in London then obtained the support of the French ambassador, and together they made a presentation to King James, the substance of which was that they would consider the tripartite peace between the three governments to have been violated unless England stopped Mainwarring or declared him an outlaw and issued orders for his arrest.

So James, in turn, sent an envoy to Villefranche with the offer of a pardon, an invitation to Court, and the promise of a commission in the Royal Navy. Mainwarring accepted. The pardon was issued under the Great Seal of England, dated June 9, 1616. It included a general amnesty for all the captains and crews serving in Mainwarring's squadron. Mainwarring then returned to England bearing "a large sum of money" which he presented to the King. Jean Chevalier, who records the event and doubtless knew just how much Mainwarring paid for his pardon, says no more than that.

The pardoned pirate was still under thirty years of age, but had established himself as, with the possible exception of Easton, the foremost seaman of his time. James gave him a knighthood and the command of Dover Castle, England's principal fortress on the North Sea. He was elected to parliament from Dover and rose through a succession of commands in the Royal Navy until he became a Vice-Admiral.

He now turned his mind to the suppression of piracy and the safety of the seas. He wrote a short treatise on the origins and suppression of piracy in which he had the gall to counsel the King to desist from the policy of pardoning pirates. He also wrote a brief account of his own life and a manual of seamanship—the *Seaman's Dictionary*—which became the foundation of all subsequent seaman's manuals in English.

Under his influence the government began issuing commissions for the capture of pirates, making such captures financially rewarding by offering their holders forty percent of the "prize money" realized from the sale of ships and cargoes. Such a commission was issued to John Mason, the governor of the Colony at Cupids, Newfoundland, from

1616 to 1626 (and afterwards founder of New Hampshire). Mason, in turn, issued commissions to others and succeeded in taking a number of pirate prizes, among them the large and picturesquely named *Heart's Desire*.

By 1620 the government, under Mainwarring's influence, was not only commissioning privateers to take pirates as prizes, but was putting the ships of the Royal Navy back into service. By 1621 they ordered a mass impressment of sailors to man these ships. The action had the effect of setting off a new wave of piracy. Few men would serve voluntarily in the navy of the time, where they were herded about the decks by bo'suns with rope's-ends and officers with canes and hanged if they fought back. To escape impressment, many sailors who had served on trading and slaving ships shipped out to Newfoundland with the fishing fleet that year—far more than could find employment in the fishery. Most of these men turned pirate.

Through this policy Sir Henry Mainwarring encountered his most troublesome successor, John Nutt of Lympston, Devonshire. Nutt was no sooner in Newfoundland in the summer of 1621 than he formed a conspiracy with other refugees from the press gang to seize a French ship and fit her out as a pirate. They promptly captured two large trading vessels, one French and one English, and took their loot to Ferryland, where they were welcomed and entertained by the governor of the Ferryland colony, Sir George Calvert, who was almost certainly a broker for pirated goods.

Nutt and his companions plundered the Newfoundland fleets for the rest of that summer, then sailed back to England and set up as Channel pirates, using the Killigrews as intermediaries. The King issued a warrant for Nutt's arrest and at the same time, against Mainwarring's advice, let it be known that a pardon might be considered if the price was right. The Killigrews sent word back that Nutt was willing to discuss a deal, and Vice-Admiral Sir John Eliot went to negotiate with him.

Eliot and Nutt agreed to a price of five hundred pounds. Then Eliot tricked Nutt into going ashore without a safe-conduct and had him clapped into irons, planning to have him hanged and to seize his ship. But by this time Calvert (later Lord Baltimore, founder of Maryland) had returned to England and he intervened on Nutt's behalf. A payment for Nutt's release was agreed on (doubtless higher than the one Nutt had negotiated with Eliot), and Nutt promptly went off to Ireland where he collected a new fleet and began preying on shipping bound in and out of the Bristol Channel.

This time Mainwarring fitted out an armed squadron under Captain Plumleigh to arrest Nutt, but Plumleigh found the pirate in command of a fleet of twenty-seven ships and was lucky to escape without having his own ships taken as prizes. Nutt was never brought to justice. He retired wealthy and disappeared from history.

Mainwarring was the chief architect of the new Royal Navy under James I and remained actively involved when James was succeeded by Charles I. He fought for King Charles in the English Civil War, spending whatever fortune remained to him from his days as a pirate in the losing fight against Oliver Cromwell. His last military action was the defence of Pendennis Castle, the old stronghold of the Killigrews in Cornwall. There he withstood a five-month siege by the Roundheads after the rest of the country had capitulated.

But it was hopeless. In the end Mainwarring and some companions escaped to the Isle of Jersey, where they took refuge with Jean Chevalier, the royalist and diarist whose journals reveal some of the details of the intimate relationship between pirates and governments that were a feature of the Stuart dynasty.

Cromwell never did take the Channel Islands, but in 1651 Sir Henry Mainwarring petitioned for a pardon and for permission to return to England. He was almost destitute.

His estate was valued at eight pounds, consisting only of a horse and some clothing. According to the public records, his fine was fixed at one-sixth of his estate and was paid on December 18, 1651, in the amount of one pound, six shillings, and eight pence.

Mainwarring died a year and a half later and was buried at St. Giles's Church, Camberwell, on May 15, 1653.

For some reason—perhaps because he was too much the aristocrat—Mainwarring never enjoyed the popularity that Easton did in Newfoundland, and there has never been any move to erect monuments to his memory. But in other respects his reputation has fared better than that of his older rival. G.E. Mainwarring went some way toward rescuing him from undeserved oblivion with his two-volume treatise, *The Life and Works of Sir Henry Mainwarring*, handsomely published by the Jersey Historical Society.

Mainwarring is often quoted by marine historians but is otherwise generally neglected. He lived in troubled times and had the misfortune to serve the Stuarts rather than the Tudors. Otherwise his name might well stand beside that of Sir Francis Drake as one of the true founders of Britain's rulership of the seas.

CHAPTER 3

ÉTIENNE BRÛLÉ AND THE COUREURS DE BOIS

WHEN SAMUEL DE CHAMPLAIN founded the colony of
Quebec in 1608, he brought with him from France a young
lad who became the greatest explorer and pathfinder of
early Canada. Throughout most of his life Étienne Brûlé
was an outlaw only in the eyes of the Church, but in the end
he also became an outlaw in the eyes of the State, a traitor
to his country, and, finally, the *pièce de résistance* at a
cannibal feast.

Brûlé spent a quarter of a century in the Canadian
backwoods, visited dozens of Indian tribes, and saw most of
the territory between Lake Superior and Chesapeake Bay.
He was the official discoverer of two of the Great Lakes and
probably visited at least four of them.

Except for one or two youths from Port Royal in Acadia
who lived with the Indians of Nova Scotia in the winter of
1605-06, Brûlé was the first of the *coureurs de bois*, young
Frenchmen who spent their lives in Indian territory, living
like Indians and trading in furs. Brûlé did most of the
exploring and travelling that was later credited, incorrectly,

to Champlain. Despite his importance to New France and his unique place in Canadian history, he received meagre rewards and less honour. He was, in fact, almost erased from the history of his country by Jesuit chroniclers, not because of his lawlessness, but because of his open contempt for Christian religion and Christian sexual taboos.

Brûlé, whom Champlain in his early journals calls "my boy" or "my servant," came from a peasant family in Champigny, France. The date of his birth is unknown, but there is strong circumstantial evidence to suggest that he was no older than fourteen when he arrived with Champlain at Tadoussac, the trading post at the mouth of the Saguenay River on the lower St. Lawrence, on June 3, 1608.

Champlain was agent for a colonizing company that had been given a monopoly on the North American fur trade by the King of France. He had come to found a colony and, if possible, to make money for his employers. But there were other French fur traders, all of them now trading illegally, and Tadoussac was their headquarters. Most of those traders were Basques, a people whose country had been overrun and divided by France and Spain (it still is). They spoke their own language, followed their own customs, and obeyed French law only when forced to do so. Besides, they had been trading in furs on the lower St. Lawrence for many years before Champlain's arrival and had little inclination to give up their livelihood just because of a charter issued by the government in far-off France.

In order to divert the flow of furs from Tadoussac and to enforce his monopoly as far as he could, Champlain decided to move upriver to Quebec, a site discovered many years earlier by his countryman Jacques Cartier. Here he would be closer to the heart of Indian territory, on an easily defended headland where a fort could be most effective, and in a position to receive furs from Indians trading to the north and west. The move was successful to an extent, but not completely because some Indian traders continued to come down from the north by way of Lake St. John and the Saguenay River to Tadoussac and to sell their furs to the "poachers," as Champlain chose to call them.

While Champlain was still building his stockade at Quebec, a group of his colonists led by Jean Duval hatched a plot to murder him and to turn his trading post over to the Basques. Champlain discovered the plot and had Duval strangled in a halter, then beheaded and his head mounted on a pole. He sent three other conspirators back to France, where they were likely chained to the oars of a galley. The rest he pardoned. By this show of force and clemency he established an authority that was never afterwards questioned.

While the colonists were building the fort and the sturdy living quarters that were to become the capital of New France, the boy Étienne Brûlé began consorting with the Montagnais Indians, a branch of the Cree who hunted over all the land between Quebec and Hudson Bay and eastward into Labrador. The young lad proved to have a gift for languages and was soon speaking Cree after a fashion—a most useful language, as it turned out, because slightly varying dialects of Cree are spoken all the way from the Atlantic Ocean across northern Canada to Saskatchewan.

Winter set in and with it, disaster. Champlain's colony was all but wiped out by disease. Cartier and Roberval, both of whom had tried to found colonies on the St. Lawrence in the previous century, had been defeated by scurvy, a fatal illness caused by living on food with no vitamin C content. Champlain had no solution to the problem of scurvy. By spring only eight of his colonists were still alive. One of the survivors was Brûlé, who had spent his time with the Indians and would have been eating what they ate.

In the spring of 1609 Champlain got involved in the Indian war that was, in the end, to prove fatal to his colonizing efforts. The forest-dwelling Montagnais of the north and the Hurons of the west were engaged in sporadic raiding against the powerful Iroquois confederacy whose lands lay south of the St. Lawrence River and Lake Ontario in what is now New York State.

The Iroquois had formed (under the influence of an inspired chief named Hiawatha) a strong political federation of "universal peace," which all Indian tribes were invited to join. In particular, they had tried to gain the accession of their powerful relatives, the Hurons, who spoke a closely related language and occupied a large territory to the north and west of them, but the Hurons had refused and had become rivals of the Iroquois for the flow of furs coming out of the centre of the continent. Both peoples were traders, buying furs from other tribes farther inland, but the Hurons, allied with the Cree, traded to the French and Basques on the St. Lawrence, while the Iroquois traded to the Dutch and English by way of the Hudson and other rivers flowing south.

Champlain made an alliance with the Cree and Hurons and offered to join them in raids against the Iroquois. At that time North American Indian raids still had the character of a dangerous blood sport, rather than of serious warfare as we know it. It was a highly ritualistic procedure with much ceremony, singing, warpaint, and bravado. No Huron, Cree, or Iroquois would be caught dead wearing armour or carrying a shield—indeed, the rules of the game decreed that on the war path they went completely naked, wearing nothing but paint. Unfortunately, the European influence eventually turned this ritual warfare into a true war of attrition.

Champlain took the war path with his Indian allies in June 1609 and caught a party of Iroquois encamped on the shore of Lake Champlain with a small stockade for protection, some eighty kilometres south of the St. Lawrence River.

While the Indians loosed flights of arrows at one another, Champlain and two companions, one of whom may have been young Brûlé, blasted away with their arabesques. Champlain felled three Indians with a single load of powder and shot and quickly put the Iroquois to flight. A dozen prisoners were captured, most of them to be taken back to Quebec, either to become slaves or to die in torture ceremonies as ordered by the Cree and Huron tribal councils. But the war party decided to torture one prisoner that very night on the way home. They tied him to a stake and began applying fire to various parts of his body. But Champlain, who disliked torture except when it was properly prescribed and administered by French authorities (as it often was), remonstrated with the Indians, and so great was his influence that they allowed him to end the man's sufferings with a musket shot.

We know for certain that Brûlé was present at Champlain's next skirmish with the Iroquois. It took place on June 19, 1610, at the mouth of the Richelieu River where it empties into the St. Lawrence. Again the Iroquois were defeated. This time important Montagnais and Huron chiefs were present, and the torture ceremony proceeded without any interference from Champlain. The Indians also cooked and ate one of their fallen foes—perhaps a man who had impressed them with his bravery in battle.

After these ceremonies they held a council, and Champlain told the Huron chief Iroquet that he had a boy who wished to go live with the Huron nation, "to learn the nature of their country, to see the great lake, to observe the rivers and the tribes that lived on them...."

Brûlé must have seemed to Champlain especially well fitted for the mission. He had already lived with the Cree and learned their language. He had survived two winters in Canada, had proven himself brave and trustworthy, and the Indians seemed to like him. The Hurons agreed to take him and insisted that Champlain must take one of their own youths in exchange. So Brûlé, at about the age of sixteen, went off to live with the Hurons, to learn his second Indian

language, and to explore the lands between Quebec and
Lake Huron, while an Indian youth of about the same age,
whom the French called Savignon, sailed for France with
Champlain.

That summer Étienne Brûlé became the first European to
ascend the Ottawa River. From there he crossed Ontario to
Georgian Bay. This journey of some fifteen hundred
kilometres from Quebec was remarkable enough in itself
but was just the beginning of Brûlé's explorations. As he
travelled with his adopted tribe, he observed the nature of
the country, memorized the customs of the people, learned
to do everything like an Indian, to prefer their food, their
dress, their lifestyle, to show at least token respect for their
nature spirits and for their magic rites.

The Indians had no religion in the European sense, so
they made no special demands on the French boy but merely
instructed him, as they would one of their own youths, to
observe the proper taboos and make ritual offerings to the
spirits. (The belief that all Indians worshipped a Great Spirit
named Manitou or Gitchi-Manitou was an error based on a
French Jesuit misunderstanding of their languages.
"Manitou" was the Cree word for "magician," although in
other dialects it could be interpreted as spirit, or god.)

Brûlé grew up with Cree and Huron sexual customs,
which included total permissiveness toward the young and
the unmarried. Visitors, moreover, were offered sexual
hospitality, and the white-skinned youth must have been an
attractive novelty to Huron girls—perhaps to certain Huron
men as well, because the Indians were equally permissive
about homosexuality (many of their shamans were homo-
sexuals), and there were hints from the Jesuits that Brûlé
engaged in "unspeakable acts," although this didn't necess-
arily mean much. To a priest of that period anything not
sanctioned by the Church, especially of a ritual or sexual
nature, was an unspeakable act.

On June 11, 1611, Brûlé and Savignon were reunited with their own people at a trading site near present-day Montreal. Both had been well treated by their hosts. Brûlé, by now speaking Huron fluently, had volumes of information to pass on to Champlain, and the latter faithfully recorded it in his journal. Savignon, too, had much to tell the Hurons about life in France, but, according to Champlain, the Indians regarded these tales as the inventions of an imaginative liar.

The experiment worked well. Mutual adoption of children was an established Indian custom for cementing alliances between tribes. Champlain was glad to discover that after Brûlé's year with the Hurons, they regarded themselves as firmly attached to the French and specifically to the French chieftain himself. Some of the eastern Indians continued to travel to Tadoussac for trade with the French or Basque "poachers," but the great majority dealt with the royal colony at Quebec. So far, the alliance was working well.

After the meeting Brûlé went back to live with the Hurons, and Champlain sent another youth, Nicolas de Vignau, to live with the Algonquins, one of the tribes of the Cree. Unfortunately, de Vignau's mission did not work out very well, and Champlain later dismissed him as "the world's greatest liar," but there was one story brought back and dismissed as a lie which, in retrospect, was probably true. The Indians, he said, had told him that an English ship had been cast away that year in the great salt sea to the north (which de Vignau said he had reached, travelling with a band of Indians). All the castaways, he said, had been killed by the tribe that lived on the shore of the sea, except for a young boy who was adopted into the tribe. That was the year Henry Hudson was cast adrift in a whaleboat in Hudson Bay by his mutinous crew. He and his young son and the sailors who accompanied him were never heard from again, except by this indirect route.

In this period Champlain was spending most of his time in France, and Brûlé was living with the Hurons, but Champlain returned to Canada in the summer of 1613 and again in 1615, in time for renewed warfare with the Iroquois. With Brûlé as guide and interpreter he now made his first and only major expedition into the Canadian wilderness. Before this he had gone only as far as Lake Champlain and had made an unsuccessful attempt to reach Hudson Bay by going up the Ottawa River. This time he travelled all the way to Lake Huron, then known as *la mer douce*. His purpose, however, was not exploration but warfare. He had decided to organize a massive attack on the Iroquois. Instead of the ritualistic skirmishing that had gone on up to now, Champlain visualized battles on the European model with thousands of men in the field, Iroquois towns invested and put to the torch, and the Iroquois confederacy destroyed.

He travelled westward, visiting six or seven Huron villages, finally arriving at Cahiagué (Huron and Cree names of the period have a suspiciously French sound to them), a stockaded town about ten miles west of Lake Couchiching, where the French and the Hurons had agreed upon a council of war before setting out to destroy the principal town of the Onondagas, one of the five Iroquois nations, near present-day Syracuse, New York. After defeating the Onondagas, they would deal with other Iroquois tribes, the Mohawk, Cayuga, Oneida, and Seneca.

Champlain was badly disappointed in the number of warriors who showed up at the council of war. Out of a possible army of five thousand, only about five hundred arrived at Cahiagué—the Hurons were not as ready for large-scale warfare as he had supposed. He had, besides his five hundred Hurons, probably not more than a dozen or so Frenchmen, including Brûlé. Champlain was anxious to get started, but the Indians were in no hurry. They feasted, danced, sang war songs, for days and weeks on end, and while all this was going on messengers arrived from the

Andastes, allies of the Hurons living to the south of the Iroquois in the valley of the Susquehanna River. They were willing to join the war and offered to put a large party into the field (Champlain said five hundred men, but it is doubtful if the Andastes could have voluntered so large a force).

The Hurons decided to send a delegation of twelve men to Carantouan, the principal town of the Andastes, and Brûlé offered to go with them. He would support the Andastes' attack while Champlain and his companions supported the Hurons'. The party of which he was a member set off on September 8 in two canoes. They travelled south by way of Lake Simcoe and the Humber River to Lake Ontario. Brûlé was the first white explorer to see that lake and to visit the site of the future city of Toronto.

In order to outflank the principal Iroquois towns, they travelled westward to the head of the lake, crossed the Niagara River, and then headed south and east toward Carantouan. This was the most dangerous part of their journey; they had to traverse lands occupied by the Senecas, members of the Iroquois confederacy. They proceeded with great caution but nevertheless ran into a Seneca hunting party. In the fight that ensued they killed four of the enemy and captured two others, whom they took to Carantouan for torture. There was a jubilant welcome, a great feast during which the two Iroquois warriors died slowly in the flames, and many days of dances in preparation for the attack on the Onondagas. Brûlé's appeals for haste had no effect. Indians made war when they were ready, after adequate ritual preparations.

Meanwhile Champlain and the Hurons had set out for the eastern end of Lake Ontario. Travelling slowly at first to hunt and to allow stragglers to catch up, they went by way of the Kawartha Lakes and crossed the St. Lawrence River among the Thousand Islands. There they hid their canoes and travelled southward along the shores of Lake Ontario on foot. On October 10 the invaders reached and surrounded the Onondaga settlement, a large village defended by a stout stockade. By this time the Onondagas had been alerted to the invasion and had withdrawn into their town for defence. There was no sign of Brûlé and the Andastes.

For five days Champlain and the Hurons laid siege to the town. They attacked with flights of arrows and with musket fire that had no great effect. They tried to storm the wall and were driven back. Champlain was wounded twice in the leg with arrows and was no longer able to walk. This, perhaps, was the deciding factor in their defeat. In any case, his great war against the Iroquois was a fiasco. He had to retreat in a basket carried on another man's back. The Hurons, demoralized by their failure and perhaps disillusioned by the failure of Champlain's powerful "medicine," refused to make the dangerous journey downriver to Quebec but headed north through their own territory to Huronia. Champlain had no choice but to accompany them. He spent the winter with the Indians, recovered from his wounds, and made a journey along the shore of Georgian Bay before returning to Quebec the next year.

Brûlé and the Andastes arrived at the Onondaga town two days after Champlain had abandoned the siege. The Onondagas were jubilant behind their stockade. They laughed at the attackers and told them their allies had been driven off with many dead. They waved fresh scalps from the ramparts to prove their victory. The Andastes retreated without a fight.

Champlain's war was the turning point in the rivalry between the Hurons and the Iroquois. Until then, the Hurons had been on the offensive. Now they were on the defensive. And they remained on the defensive until they were finally destroyed by the great Iroquois sweep through Huronia thirty-three years later, when the French priests were captured and burned at the stake, and the remnants of the Huron tribes scattered, many of them absorbed into the Iroquois confederation.

Champlain returned to Quebec, then to Tadoussac, and sailed home to France. Two years later he returned to Quebec with the full title of governor and began inserting the aristocratic "de" into his name, becoming Samuel de Champlain, as he is known to most Canadians today. Brûlé was also at Quebec in 1618 and told this astonishing tale of his adventures.

After the failure of the attack on the Onondaga town, the Hurons who had travelled with Brûlé disappeared, and, unwilling to attempt the journey to Quebec or to Huronia alone, Brûlé returned with the Andastes to Carantouan. That winter he explored the valley of the Susquehanna River all the way to its estuary on Chesapeake Bay. He was not the first explorer in the area—the Englishman John Smith had already sailed into this great arm of the sea, hoping it might lead him to China—but Brûlé was the first European to reach it overland.

He returned to Carantouan in the spring, and the Andastes offered a six-man escort to take him to Huronia.

Brûlé headed back by the same route he had come—west of Lake Ontario—and somewhere in Seneca territory his party encountered a band of Iroquois. The Andastes were outnumbered; they scattered to avoid capture. Brûlé escaped but found himself alone and lost in unfamiliar country. He wandered for several days until hunger compelled him to approach an Iroquois fishing party and ask for food. He explained that he was lost, pretending to be English or Dutch, not French. After the Iroquois had shared a pipe of tobacco with him, they took him to their village.

Somewhere about here, Brûlé's story becomes less credible. According to what he told Champlain, the Iroquois refused to believe that he was not French and voted to torture him to death. They plucked out his beard, ripped off his fingernails, and staked him out naked for more extreme torments. One of the chiefs, he said, tried to stop the cruel sport, but with no effect. They brought burning sticks from the fire and began applying them to his body. And then he was saved by a miracle.

Around his neck he wore an Agnus Dei, a Catholic medal that he kept perhaps as an amulet or perhaps just as a souvenir from France. One of the torturers reached for it, and Brûlé cried out, "If you touch that, the God of the French will strike you dead!" Ignoring the threat, the Indian grabbed the medal. At that moment the sky suddenly darkened and great thunderbolts rained down on every side. The Indians scattered, terrified. The friendly chief then released Brûlé and took him to his lodge. Later, when he was well enough to travel, the same man took him to the Niagara River, from which he returned with a party of Neutrals to Huronia. The Neutrals were friendly to both Iroquois and Hurons and occupied a small territory between the two great trading alliances.

At some point Brûlé must really have been tortured to the extent of losing his fingernails, because he would have to be able to show Champlain the scars. Some historians speculate that the Senecas tortured him only enough to make him admit he was French and then released him in the belief that he would act as a peace emissary. There can be no doubt that they did desire peace. They made repeated overtures for a treaty with the French, but all their offers were either refused or, later, accepted and then disregarded as soon as it suited French policy to renew their Indian war.

The story of Brûlé's calling up the thunderstorm was a typical piece of fabrication. He loved to mock Christian beliefs, make fun of the priests, and shock their sensibilities. He once told Brother Gabriel Sagard that he had escaped a moment of great danger by gabbling out the only prayer he knew—the Benedicte, which is a mealtime prayer. He added that he had also made a ritual sacrifice of tobacco to a river spirit and that it had worked just as well, ensuring him a safe journey.

Champlain seems to have believed Brûlé's story, miracle and all. He reported it as fact in his journal and sent the *coureur* on a new mission into Huron country, this time to explore Lake Huron and whatever water might lie westward from it. Champlain still thought this might be a route to China. Brûlé was also to look for the mines from which the Indians had brought nuggets of native copper. He promised Brûlé that he would visit Huronia himself next year, reward the young man for his work, and renew the war with the Iroquois.

These promises were never kept. Champlain was now too busy with his administrative duties and with the struggle to get financial support in France to waste time in journeys of exploration. Brûlé carried out his orders to explore. On this journey he seems to have reached both Lake Erie and Lake Superior and may have crossed the entrance to Lake Michigan as well.

During this period Brûlé's most important mission was to ensure that the largest possible volume of furs reached Quebec rather than Tadoussac or the Hudson River, and in this he seems to have been successful. For this work, the company paid him one hundred pistoles a year. The pistole of that time was the *Louis d'or*, a gold coin with a value nearly equal to an English pound. Brûlé was receiving about ten times the annual wage of a common labourer.

In the years between 1618 and 1628 Brûlé also made the famous Catholic mission to the Hurons possible by acting as guide and interpreter for the first Recollet priests to venture westward from Quebec. He was essential to the work of the missionaries, but they hated him and had nothing but evil to say of him in their "Relations." He lived what they considered a scandalous life, eating meat on Friday, never bothering to confess his sins or attend Mass, bedding down with any willing Indian lass who craved a bit of sexual adventure. They sent reports of his behaviour to Champlain demanding that he be brought to book.

There was a curious irony in this. Champlain, in his forties, had married a twelve-year-old girl, but his marriage was blessed by Church and State, and besides, the girl was French. The priests condemned Brûlé not because his promiscuity was any more shocking than Champlain's paedophilia, but because he ignored the rules laid down by the Church and refused to keep up the pretense of "respectability" with the Indians. But Brûlé's value out-weighed his faults. He remained in good grace with the governor until the final dark phase of his career began in 1629.

In 1627, England and France being now at war, King Charles I issued a commission to David Kirke, a swash-buckling gentleman of fortune, to attack and capture New France. Kirke fitted out a private fleet with each of his brothers as captain of a ship (there were five of them), sailed up the St. Lawrence, received the surrender of Tadoussac, and sent a demand to Champlain for the surrender of Quebec. Champlain, not knowing that Kirke had already sunk or captured all the supply ships heading for Quebec that year, refused. Kirke, overestimating the strength of Quebec, decided not to attack until the following year, when he knew the garrison would be suffering shortages of sup-plies and ammunition, if not actual starvation.

After assisting with the English capture of Port Royal in Acadia, Kirke returned to the St. Lawrence in the spring of 1629 in time to intercept a relief fleet of eighteen ships from France. Only one of the eighteen escaped. Champlain's col-ony was now starving. They had been living on scanty rations of peas and corn when Kirke started his blockade in 1628. By the summer of 1629 they were living on wild roots, acorns, and whatever they could beg from the Indians.

Unaware that Kirke had intercepted the relief squadron from France, Champlain sent Brûlé and three other men downriver to pilot the French ships to Quebec. At Tadoussac Brûlé found the English in control and promptly entered their service. He guided three of Kirke's ships to Quebec. Kirke then sent a message to Champlain calling on him to surrender, "knowing your miserable condition and inability to resist." Champlain really had no choice. He surrendered on condition that he and his colonists be given safe passage to France, and Kirke captured Quebec without having to fire a shot.

Later, on an English ship at Tadoussac, Champlain came face to face with Brûlé for the last time and gave full vent to his anger, denouncing his former servant as a scoundrel, an outlaw, and a traitor. Brûlé, perhaps remembering what had happened to the earlier traitor Duval, said that the English had forced him into their service, but this Champlain refused to believe. He cursed Brûlé and prophesied that he would end his life as a renegade, rejected by his new masters, and "abhorred by both God and man."

Brûlé elected to remain in what had formerly been New France and to continue his work among the Indians, guiding cargoes of furs into Kirke's storehouses as he had formerly guided them into Champlain's. Over the next three years, with David Kirke's younger brother Lewis as governor of Quebec, the Kirke family reaped a fortune in furs. They were the first corporation ever to enjoy a true monopoly in Canada.

In 1632 when the English and French called off the war and negotiated a peace treaty, King Charles decided that Canada was of no real use to him. He gave it back to the King of France and rewarded David Kirke by giving him a knighthood and making him the first royal governor in and over the Island of Newfoundland.

Why Étienne Brûlé did not sail away with Kirke is not clear. He was probably far off in the interior with the Indians when the English agreed to abandon New France to the French. In any case, he was living with the Hurons when

Champlain returned to Quebec in 1633, and within a month of Champlain's arrival Brûlé was dead.

In the Huron village of Toanche on Penetanguishene Bay, Brûlé was taken before a council of the chiefs of the Bear Clan of the Hurons and condemned to death. This time there was no miraculous thunderstorm. He was killed, cooked, and eaten. Some writers say that he endured savage torture before death, but there is no evidence on this point. The fact that he was eaten suggests that the Indians regarded him as having superhuman powers.

About the time Brûlé died, Champlain had an Algonquin Indian executed at Quebec for killing a Frenchman. The Algonquins passed word of this along to the Hurons and suggested that they would likely be punished for Brûlé's death. But Champlain sent a message to the Hurons assuring them that they had done the right thing. Brûlé, he said, was no longer considered a Frenchman but an outlaw.

Nevertheless, the ghost of the *coureur* continued to haunt Huronia, and the chief of the Bear Clan, who had condemned him, was treated by other Huron chiefs as a pariah. Shortly after Brûlé's death a disastrous epidemic of smallpox swept through the Hurons, killing off half the population. As many as fifteen thousand people may have died in the epidemic—far more than were ever killed, before or after, in their wars with the Iroquois.

The people of Toanche, fearing that the ground where Brûlé died was cursed, abandoned their village and built a new one nearby. A story spread from village to village that a pale woman, Brûlé's sister, wandered the forests breathing pestilence upon the people who had killed her brother.

Three years after his death, Brûlé's bones became the object of a dispute that disrupted the great Huron Feast of the Dead, a ceremony held once every twelve years, in which the Hurons gathered all the bones of their dead from temporary graves and gave them common burial at a central grave pit with suitable rites. They wished to include the bones of Brûlé, perhaps in the hope of atoning for his death.

Father Jean de Brébeuf, head of the first Jesuit mission to the Hurons, was to preside at the rites, and he told the Indians that the bones of a Christian, even those of an outlaw like Brûlé, could not be buried in the same grave with those of unbaptized heathens. He agreed, however, to allow Brûlé's remains to be buried in a separate grave adjoining the large pit into which the Indians's bones were to be cast.

This compromise might have worked except that various villages began quarrelling over whose grave pit should have the honour of being beside that of the fabled outlaw. The Bear Clan wanted him because he had died in their midst and they had the most need to make peace with his ghost. Others declared that they deserved no such honour, and he should be laid to rest among his true friends. The dispute was never resolved, and the bones were left in the unmarked grave beside the fire where Brûlé had been eaten. Father Brébeuf expressed his satisfaction at this result. He was pleased not to have to give Christian burial to "that infamous wretch [who] did not deserve to have such honour shown him."

Brûlé was quickly disowned and forgotten by French Canadians, but his spirit lived on in his successors, the *coureurs de bois*, who, for the next hundred years, continued to save New France from bankruptcy, despite the French government which continued to enact laws sentencing them to death. Every *coureur* was officially an outlaw, trading illegally with the Indians and under threat of fines, imprisonment, flogging, or hanging if caught. That's what the law made in France declared. At Quebec, however, the law was rarely enforced. At most a *coureur* might be hauled before a magistrate and sentenced to a small fine. As one historian expressed it, the whole of New France conspired to protect them, because without them there would have been almost no fur trade. Once the Hurons were effectively eliminated by the Iroquois, the flow of furs into Quebec and other towns along the St. Lawrence depended entirely on these outlaws who took their own canoes up the rivers of the north and west, into Lake Superior and even well beyond it, returning with the only product that kept New France solvent.

The taxes went into the treasury; the profits on the furs went to the official traders; the money paid the *coureurs de bois* never left the colony; they spent it on trade goods and liquor and clothes, then headed back to the wilderness for more of their illegal but essential commerce with the Indians. They took Indian wives and fathered numerous halfbreed children to the disgust of the priests who declared that halfbreeds inherited all the worst traits of both races.

Occasionally the laws against the *coureurs de bois* were resurrected. A few *coureurs de bois* were flogged. At least one was hanged, but apparently because he was selling his furs to one of the governor's trade rivals. Occasionally, the French even tried to enforce the law at the very highest level. François Perrot, a governor of Montreal, was sent back to France and thrown into the Bastille for trading with the outlaws.

At last, in 1700, the *coureurs* were given legal status by the French government. They were then sent on missions down the Mississippi and out west as far as the foothills of the Rocky Mountains. They not only survived as a separate subculture in New France but survived even the conquest of New France and finally became the famous *voyageurs* who took Scottish fur traders from Montreal across Canada and beat Lewis and Clark to the Pacific Ocean by twelve years.

Brûlé himself was utterly ignored by both French and Quebec historians of his time. His journeys and discoveries were reported in their books as the journeys and discoveries of Champlain. Ironically, it was only when English-Canadian historians began digging back into the early history of New France that Brûlé began to emerge from the darkness as one of the great free spirits of the early years of the nation.

CHAPTER 4

RADISSON AND GROSEILLIERS

EVERY SCHOOLCHILD in Canada has heard of this pair of backwoods adventurers who added such colour to the early history of New France. What the schoolbooks don't mention is that they were a pair of completely unprincipled scoundrels, outlaws, and pirates who miraculously escaped hanging, although Radisson, for a while, had a price on his head.

Groseilliers, much the elder of the partners, was born in France in July 1618 and christened Médard Chouart. He later became the Sieur des Groseilliers when he inherited a plot of family land where gooseberry bushes (*groseilliers*) grew in great abundance. Tradition says he arrived in Canada in 1641—a year of major immigration, when many French landowners who had fallen upon evil days began developing farms in New France.

He did not, however, begin farming at once but entered the service of missionaries and traders who were trying to establish a new presence among the Indians of the west after the Iroquois had driven the Hurons out of most of the lands they formerly held between Lake Huron and Lake Ontario.

Father Paul Ragueneau, Jesuit superior in Huronia in the late 1640s, described Groseilliers as "a man capable of anything, bold, hardy, stubborn in his undertakings, who knows the country and has been everywhere...."

In 1647 Groseilliers married Hélène Martin, daughter of Abraham Martin for whom the Plains of Abraham were named. Through his marriage he became acquainted with the powerful fur traders of Acadia, the de la Tours, who in turn had connections with important planters in Newfoundland and New England and an interest in "The Great Bay of the North"—Hudson Bay, which they thought might open into the Pacific. But to Groseilliers, who was learning something about the fur trade, the northern frontier was more interesting as an untapped source of furs, revenues for money-starved New France, and a fortune for himself.

Hélène did not long survive her marriage to Groseilliers, and in 1653 he remarried, this time to the half-sister of Pierre Esprit Radisson who, then little more than a boy, was a captive among the Iroquois.

Radisson had arrived in Canada in May 1651 with his family, who settled in Trois Rivières on the north shore of the St. Lawrence, upriver from Quebec. Scarcely a year later he was captured by the Iroquois while duck hunting with some friends. His companions were killed and scalped, but Radisson was spared, according to his own story, because the Indians admired his courage in putting up a fight. But it is much more likely that he was spared because of his youth. He was fourteen, or at most fifteen, at the time.

From the very first hour the Iroquois raiders treated Radisson as an adopted member of their tribe. They stripped him, painted him with warpaint, and gave him an Indian haircut. A man whom he had wounded in the fight was especially kind to him, teaching him to throw a spear and paddle a canoe. When he was unable to eat the mouldy meat that they carried as field rations, they tried to find food suitable to his stomach. Upon arrival at the Iroquois village the boy was formally adopted by a family who had lost their son in war. The adoptive father was a renowned warrior who bore nineteen scars on his thigh, the record of nineteen enemies slain in battle. His adoptive mother was a Huron who doted on her new son. The French youth got along well with the natives, and they soon trusted him as one of their own. He later reported: "I took all the pleasures imaginable, having a small peece [gun] at my command, shooting patriges, squerells, playing most of the day with my companions. The old woman wished that I would make meself more familiar with her 2 daughters, which weare tolerable among such people."

During his year or more of captivity, Radisson learned to enjoy Indian life, but he longed for his family and friends in Trois Rivières, and when an Algonquin captive decided to make a run for it, Radisson agreed to join him. The Algonquin killed and scalped three Iroquois during the escape. They almost made it to Trois Rivières but once again were intercepted, within sight of the town, by Iroquois raiders. The Algonquin was killed, and Radisson, along with other French, Huron, and other Algonquin prisoners, was taken back to the Iroquois village.

Again the Iroquois spared his life, but they made him run the gauntlet, naked, between two lines of men armed with whips cut from the forest. According to Radisson they also punished him in other ways, including prodding him with sharp sticks and scorching the soles of his feet. But in all this he was luckier than the other prisoners who, he reported, all died horrible deaths by mutilation and fire. Once again he was the only survivor.

When he recovered from his ordeal, Radisson tried to regain the Indians' trust. Perhaps they were impressed by his spirit and courage, for they allowed him to join a war party in a raid against a neighbouring tribe. Late in 1653 he escaped for a second time.

He made his way to Fort Orange, a Dutch trading post. The Iroquois went looking for him, but the Dutch hid him and smuggled him to New Amsterdam (now New York) where he got passage on a ship to Holland. The next spring he got passage on a French fishing ship to Percé Rock in Gaspé and from there canoed with a party of Indians upriver to Quebec.

That same year, 1654, Groseilliers made a trading expedition into the far west. He may have gone as far as Green Bay on Lake Michigan; in any case he opened up new trading territory, returning after two years with a flotilla of canoes laden with furs. The expedition was of great importance to New France, then critically short of revenue, and may well have saved the colony from bankruptcy. Radisson later claimed to have been with Groseilliers on this expedition, but it seems unlikely because just about the time of Groseilliers' return, the Jesuits were building their mission to the Iroquois, Fort Onondaga, south of Lake Ontario, and Radisson was with them, perhaps as an interpreter.

The Iroquois had requested the mission, one more of their repeated efforts to get the French to agree to a permanent peace. Fifty-three Frenchmen, priests, lay workers, and soldiers, were at the new fort only a few months when they began to believe that they were prisoners inside their own stockade.

Whether this paranoia was justified or not is now impossible to judge. In any case, they began to hatch a plot to escape, and in the Jesuit "Relation" for 1657 the credit for its success is given to "a young Frenchman who had been adopted by a renouned Iroquois, and had learned their language."

Inside the walls they secretly built boats, then invented an excuse for a feast and invited all the local Indians, whom they stuffed with food in an orgy of gluttony outside their stockade. The kettles brimmed with corn, wild game, pork, poultry, and fish. Etiquette demanded that an Iroquois must eat everything offered by his host, and the hosts saw that everyone ate until he could hardly move. Perhaps the food was also laced with laudanum from the fort's medicine chest. The Indians were invited to dance and sing. The party went on till they dropped, exhausted, and fell into deep sleep. Then the French stole off in their boats and headed for home. The priests had to prevent some of the men from cutting the throats of the sleeping Indians.

Back at Trois Rivières, Radisson and his brother-in-law, Groseilliers, began planning a journey to the west for trade and exploration; they were ready to start by August 1659. The governor forbade them to go unless they took one of his own men, and the Jesuits added that a priest must accompany them. Groseilliers, never noted for his tact, replied that he needed neither priests nor governors. Permission was denied, but Groseilliers, who held the rank of captain, bluffed his way past the town guard.

The two adventurers joined a party of Algonquins, ascended the Ottawa River, fought a skirmish with a band of Iroquois, crossed to Lake Huron, then paddled to Lake Superior and set up a post somewhere on the Wisconsin shore, near the western end of the largest of the world's lakes.

From this headquarters, a rough cabin surrounded by a clever alarm system of strings and bells, Radisson and Groseilliers traded with the Sioux and the western Cree. The two tribes were at war with each other, but both wanted to trade with the French, especially for guns.

Despite periods of hunger, a near-fatal accident when Radisson fell through the ice, and torturing clouds of mosquitoes in summer, they gloried in their freedom and dreamed of an empire in furs. Radisson wrote in his journal, "We were Cesars, being nobody to contradict us."

They explored parts of Wisconsin and Minnesota and some of the Cree country north of the great lake. Radisson claimed that they reached Hudson Bay, but this seems hardly credible. His knowledge of a canoe route from

Superior to Hudson Bay probably came from the Indians. Radisson wrote his journal to raise backing in England for an expedition to Hudson Bay, and his claims were probably exaggerated.

In the summer of 1660, after the longest and most successful canoe journey made by any white explorers up to that time, the two *coureurs de bois* led a parade of Indian canoes down the Ottawa River, through the rapids of the St. Lawrence, and on to Quebec.

Their return should have been a triumph. For the second time, Groseilliers had saved the fur traders from financial ruin. Moreover, he and his young partner brought back a wealth of new information about the lands to the west. They had even learned of the "Stinking Lake" (Lake Winnipeg) that no Frenchman had heard of before. Instead, they were arrested for leaving the post illegally and trading without a licence.

Groseilliers was jailed, both men were fined, and most of their furs were confiscated. The governor, Vicomte d'Argenson, spent some of the money on fortifications, but Radisson bitterly accused him of taking large sums for himself "that he might yet better maintain his coach and horses at Paris."

Groseilliers, furious, sailed for France, hoping to obtain redress and backing for an expedition to Hudson Bay. He failed on both counts and returned, embittered, to New France in 1661. For a year he tried vainly to find a sponsor in the colony. Then, disgusted, he turned to the English.

Pretending that he was off on another exploratory trip up the Ottawa, Groseilliers picked up Radisson and sailed off to St. Peters on Cape Breton Island. There they met Nicolas Denis, a fur trader who had worked for the English and was associated with the de la Tours, whom Groseilliers knew through his first wife. From there they went to New England, carrying letters of introduction to wealthy planters who might be willing to back an expedition to Hudson Bay.

In 1663 a ship sailed out of Boston with Radisson on board bound for "The Great Bay of the North." They reached Hudson Strait before the captain, unnerved by ice, turned back. A second vessel on the same mission was shipwrecked on Sable Island off Nova Scotia.

Disappointed, the New England backers sued Groseilliers and Radisson to recover their losses, but the Boston commissioners of the British government "advises us to come to England and offer our selves to ye King, which wee did. Those of New England in generall made profers unto us of what ship wee would if wee would goe on in our Designs; but wee answered them that a scalded cat fears ye water though it be cold."

In 1665 the two adventurers, accompanied by George Cartwright, King's Commissioner, sailed for London. En route they fell foul of a Dutch privateer and after a two-hour battle were taken prisoner. They were landed in Spain, while the Dutch sailed away with their ship, and from Spain took passage to England. They landed while the Great Plague was raging in the late summer of 1665, and Londoners were dying at the rate of six thousand a month.

Cartwright took the two Frenchmen to Oxford, where King Charles II had fled with his Court to escape the epidemic. There they were taken under the wing of Sir George Carteret, a man who had made a fortune in piracy and was now a member of the King's Privy Council and perhaps the wealthiest man in England. Carteret, who had a great interest in the northwest and still believed Hudson Bay would prove to be the shortest route to China, got them an audience with the King, who commanded them to give an account "of the Manners Languages and Scituacon of the severall parts of that Country [Canada]...."

So Radisson began writing his journal. It was subsequently lost for two hundred years, but turned up in 1885 during a search of the papers of the diarist Samuel Pepys, one of Radisson's contemporaries.

In January 1666 the King sent Radisson and Groseilliers to London and provided them with a generous expense account. There they were entertained by Sir Peter Colleton, head of a cartel of noblemen, merchants, and scientists willing to invest in a voyage to Hudson Bay.

Among the growing cartel interested in the venture were Prince Rupert, the King's venturesome cousin, Sir John Kirke, who had helped his elder brother David capture Quebec from Champlain and whose daughter Mary would later marry Radisson, John Fenn, Admiralty paymaster who borrowed government funds for private investment, and Sir Robert Vyner, London's biggest banker.

The investors were a hard-headed group who smelled profit and power. Some of them were members of the Royal Society, scholars who adapted the findings of science to the world of business. For two years these men, with Radisson and Groseilliers always at the centre, worked toward their great venture.

There were setbacks. In 1666 the Dutch held temporary supremacy at sea, and a voyage to Hudson Bay was considered too dangerous. The next year Cartwright purchased a ketch, the *Discovery,* for the explorers' use, but she proved unseaworthy and had to be laid up.

Meanwhile Holland and France, through their agents in England, learned of what was afoot and began to woo the two Frenchmen from their English backers. A French spy named La Tourette was arrested in London while attempting to recruit Groseilliers for the Dutch. Although they denied having any intention of going over to Holland or France, the two Canadian renegades were placed under strict watch in the belief that they would gladly sell themselves to the highest bidder.

The expedition finally sailed June 3, 1668, Groseilliers on the commercial ketch *Nonesuch,* and Radisson on the larger naval vessel *Eaglet.* The *Eaglet* was dismasted in a violent storm in the Atlantic and had to put back to England, but the *Nonesuch* sailed on through Hudson Strait and southward into James Bay where Groseilliers established Fort Charles, a house surrounded by a log wall, at the mouth of the Rupert River.

A long, cold winter followed. The English mariners huddled indoors around the fire, drinking home brew while "Mr. Gooseberry" carried on trade with the James Bay Cree. He did well. When the *Nonesuch* returned to England in October 1669, she carried over thirteen hundred pounds worth of beaver pelts, purchased with beads, tools, and other trade goods of trifling value. (On later expeditions the Indians sometimes refused to deal with Groseilliers because he drove too hard a bargain.)

The investors were pleased and promptly planned a second voyage. They also drafted a charter which received the Royal Seal on May 2, 1670. It gave the "Governors and Adventurers trading into Hudson's baye" absolute control over all lands whose rivers drained into that bay; large portions of Quebec and Ontario, all of Manitoba, most of Saskatchewan, half of Alberta, and a considerable chunk of the Northwest Territories—more than 1,486,000 square miles. No one knew at the time just how large "Rupert's Land" really was. But so well constructed was their charter that for two hundred years political and commercial rivals tried in vain to find a loophole.

The first governor was Prince Rupert, who held the position until his death in 1682. The first colonial governor appointed to run things in the bay was Charles Bayley, a troublesome Quaker who had been jailed in France, in Rome (where he had tried to convert the Pope), and finally in London. Despite his obnoxious proselytizing, Bayley had connections at Court, which may account for his being released from the Tower to serve the Hudson's Bay Company in the New World in an important position. The advantage was that it got him out of the way.

Two ships, *Prince Rupert* and *Wivenhoe*, sailed for the bay on the last day of May 1670, with Bayley, Radisson, and Groseilliers on board. After passing through Hudson

Strait, the *Prince Rupert* with Groseilliers aboard headed for Fort Charles, while the *Wivenhoe* with Bayley and Radisson aboard headed for the western shore where they hoped to establish Port Nelson at the mouth of the Nelson River. They ran into trouble and the captain of the *Wivenhoe* died of scurvy. The attempt to found the new post was abandoned, and the *Wivenhoe* headed south to Fort Charles, where Groseilliers was already busy trading with the Indians and directing the building of a barracks and a dock.

In July 1671 they sailed for England, arriving in October with two shiploads of furs valued at close to £4,000. They made voyages in 1672 and 1673, when Groseilliers remained over winter in the bay with his ship the *Employ*. Again he tried to set up a post at Port Nelson, and again he failed.

Meanwhile the French grew alarmed at this English invasion of the Canadian fur trade and sent expeditions north from Quebec to encourage the James Bay Cree to send their furs southward by way of the Ottawa and Saguenay rivers. When this failed, they plotted to establish their own posts on the bay and, if possible, to persuade Groseilliers to return to the fold.

In 1674 Father Charles Albanel reached Fort Charles overland with letters from Governor Frontenac of New France addressed to Governor Bayley and to Groseilliers. Bayley was justly suspicious of correspondence between Frontenac and Groseilliers. Though the two countries were at peace, he had Albanel's men arrested, held captive through the winter, and sent to England in 1675.

Radisson was not in Hudson Bay that year, and when Groseilliers returned to England he found his brother-in-law fighting a losing battle with the Company of Adventurers for a large share of the profits from the fur trade. The Company had paid their expenses and allowed them a limited amount of private trade, but Radisson and Groseilliers were far from reaping the fortune they had dreamed of for so long. The Company offered them £100 a year each—a comfortable income—and the King awarded them gold medals, but this was not enough for the ambitious *coureurs de bois.* Late in 1675 they slipped quietly out of England and crossed the channel to France, where the great statesman Charles Colbert secured royal pardons for them from Louis XIV. Colbert then helped them in their efforts to organize a French rival to the Hudson's Bay Company, but the scheme collapsed. French money simply wasn't as venturesome as English at that time.

Groseilliers, discouraged but protected by the King's pardon, returned to his wife and family in New France. He hadn't seen them in fourteen years! Radisson did whatever he could find to do, which included fighting the Dutch at sea on an English ship of war.

By 1681 Radisson was back in London as a spy for a powerful French fur smuggler, Charles de la Chenaye. If the English had no plans for Port Nelson, then Chenaye would send Radisson and Groseilliers in two ships to establish a post and to trade there. The furs would be taken to Percé Rock and transferred to the aptly named *Black Eagle* to be sold in Holland and Spain. Radisson discovered that the Hudson's Bay Company was indeed planning a third attempt to open the Port Nelson post, but instead of backing off as Chenaye expected, he began a frantic scramble to get there before them.

In fact there were three expeditions heading for Port Nelson in 1682. First to arrive were the French Canadians. They built shelters near the mouth of the Hayes River, a few miles south of the Nelson, and Radisson travelled up the river with Jean Baptiste Chouart, Groseilliers' son, to invite the natives to trade at his post.

The second group were also poachers—from New England. Sailing with Benjamin Gillam, son of Zechariah Gillam who happened that year to be captain of the Hudson's Bay Company's ship, they made their headquarters on an island in the Nelson River, a few miles upstream from the site of Port Nelson.

The third group, the only one operating legally, were Hudson's Bay Company men. Each group was ignorant of the other two until September, when Radisson played the most brazen game of deception in his career.

He had just returned from his trip up the Hayes when he heard the sound of distant guns, investigated, and discovered Ben Gillam's ship, the *Bachelor's Delight* (a name borne by a succession of famous pirate vessels), anchored in the Nelson.

Radisson, with a group of Indians and French all dressed as natives, approached the vessel and quickly learned that the New Englanders were trading without licence or commission. Radisson convinced Gillam that the territory had been duly claimed by the French Crown. He exaggerated the strength of the French and promised the New Englanders French protection, provided they stayed close to their ship and engaged in no illicit trade.

Radisson's company had barely left the *Bachelor's Delight* and paddled a few miles down the Nelson when they saw the *Prince Rupert* piloted by Ben Gillam's father, Zechariah, entering the mouth of the river. On board was John Bridgar, commissioned to build a post at Port Nelson and run it as governor. Radisson brazenly went aboard and told them they were trespassing on French territory. The Hudson's Bay Company men retorted that their company had sole right to trade in Hudson Bay, but their argument wilted before Radisson's description of a strong French force even now building a powerful fort a few miles upriver.

Radisson left the *Prince Rupert*, sent the rest of the party home, and spent two days lurking in the woods, spying on the English as they made preparations for winter. Then he went back to Groseilliers to conspire how they might best profit from the situation.

They had two English parties, one legitimate, one poaching, to deal with. The captains were father and son.

Ben Gillam would not want to be caught poaching on Hudson's Bay territory. Zack Gillam would not want to arrest his son. Neither was sure where the French "fort" was, because Radisson had given them false and contradictory information. The wily Canadian arranged a meeting between the two captains, and old Zack never did tell Governor Bridgar about it.

The New Englanders were now well aware of the Hudson's Bay Company post and took care to avoid it. Company scouts sighted the New Englanders but thought they were a patrol from the French fort and took care to avoid them. Things were working out nicely.

October came, and the *Prince Rupert*, running in newly formed ice, cut through her planking at the water line and sank. Zack Gillam and his crew went down with their ship. The survivors of the Hudson's Bay Company expedition, Governor Bridgar with fewer than twenty men, were now at Radisson's mercy, stranded in the sub-Arctic with most of their provisions lost. He visited them frequently that winter, bringing them food, and kept them ignorant of the New Englanders a few miles upriver.

In the spring both the French ships, the *St. Pierre* and the *Ste. Anne*, were badly damaged by ice. While some of the crewmen tried to repair one of them with timber salvaged from the other, Radisson and an armed party descended on the *Bachelor's Delight* and took Ben Gillam's crew prisoners. The seizure of the ship was an act of pure piracy, without any kind of legal authority whatsoever. One of the crewmen escaped to Bridgar's camp, and the English governor finally learned how he had been hoodwinked by Radisson. He complained to the outlaw only to learn that he and his men were also Radisson's prisoners.

The French now burned down the posts built by Bridgar and Gillam, loaded their haul of furs onto the *Bachelor's Delight*, and gave Bridgar the ship they had patched up from the two wrecks to sail to the English post in James Bay. At the last moment Radisson learned that Bridgar planned to return to Port Nelson as soon as he was gone, so he took the governor prisoner on the *Bachelor's Delight* while the other Englishmen sailed the leaky *Ste. Anne* to James Bay.

The *Black Eagle* failed to put in its promised appearance at that smugglers' roost in the Gaspé, Percé Rock, so the *Bachelor's Delight* sailed on to Quebec, arriving in October 1683. There they learned that their patron's smuggling scheme had been discovered. Bridgar was released; so was Gillam and his crew, with their ship. But the load of hijacked furs was impounded and sold for the profit of the government and traders of New France. Radisson and Groseilliers were once again lucky to escape prison or the gallows.

Boldly they went off to France to try to claim some part of the spoils. The French Government refused to listen to them, but the Hudson's Bay Company decided that they needed their services after all. This pair of unprecedented schemers had an unmatched knack for getting furs out of the north.

Letters were exchanged, and Viscount Preston of Haddington, representing the Duke of York, invited them for an interview. The result was that Radisson joined the English once again in 1684. He is believed to have escaped from France with the aid of Frenchmen working at the English Embassy in Paris. Though some French officials were glad to see the last of him on almost any terms, others would have preferred to see him in the Bastille.

At this point in his career Radisson must have had intimations of mortality. Instead of taking the money advanced to him by the Hudson's Bay Company, he left it on deposit in London with instructions that it was to be used to build a monument to himself if he failed to return from his voyage.

Quickly the Company fitted out an expedition, and Radisson sailed from England in May 1684 on the *Happy Return* with the two other vessels, one of them commanded by John Outlaw, Ben Gillam's former mate. The ships ran into bad weather and ice in Hudson Strait and became separated. Radisson was deeply concerned about this because he wanted to be the first to reach Port Nelson and explain his change of loyalties to his nephew, Jean Baptiste Chouart, whom he had left in charge there.

When he reached the mouth of the Hayes River he learned that Chouart had retreated inland on sighting the other English vessels. The Indians also told him that during the winter one of the Cree warriors had been hired by the English to kill Chouart. Young Jean had overpowered the would-be assassin in hand-to-hand combat, thereby gaining great respect among the Indians—he would be a most valuable asset to any trading operation.

So Radisson set off upriver, found the French camp, and persuaded his nephew to join him. Chouart was as fickle in his loyalties as his father and uncle. He loaded his furs aboard the *Happy Return* and sailed for England with Radisson.

Groseilliers' whereabouts at this time are uncertain. He was not with Radisson, and it seems likely that he had retired to his farm in New France. He was now 65, getting a little old for the roustabout life of a soldier of fortune. He may have been on board a ship that sailed to relieve Chouart's party that summer (it arrived too late) as Radisson says he died "in the Baye", but there seems to be other evidence that he died in New France, perhaps as late as 1697.

Radisson arrived in England in the autumn of 1684. The Company men were relieved to see him and happy with his cargo of furs. They had taken a gamble sending him out at all, understandably worried that he would double-cross them once again. For his feat of recapturing Port Nelson without bloodshed, Radisson was rewarded by the Company and entertained by the King and the Duke of York.

Charles II died early in 1665 and his brother, the Duke of York, became King James II. Lord John Churchill succeeded James as governor of the Hudson's Bay Company and on

instructions from the new king continued to treat Radisson
well.

Meanwhile, Jean Baptiste Chouart was having second
thoughts about serving the English. He and the other
Frenchmen from Port Nelson accepted employment from
the Company, but refused to change their citizenship by
taking the oath of loyalty to the English king. He wrote to
his mother in New France telling her that he had been
misled by his uncle. He was hoping for a pardon and an
opportunity to escape to France or Quebec.

That year Governor Jacques Denonville issued an open
warrant for Radisson's arrest, offering a reward of fifty
pistoles to anyone who would bring the outlaw to Quebec,
where he proposed to have him hanged.

In May 1685 the Company sent another expedition to
Hudson Bay. One of their ships, the *Perpetua Merchant*,
was captured by French warships in Hudson Strait. The
Frenchmen were bounty hunters looking for Radisson and
were disappointed to learn that he had passed through the
strait earlier on another vessel.

A few days later the *Success*, another Company ship,
tried to get the French to release the *Perpetua Merchant*.
On board the *Success* was John Bridgar, Radisson's old foe
who had been offered the governorship of Port Nelson but
at Radisson's insistence had been redirected to James Bay
because Radisson refused to serve under a man who had
recently been his prisoner.

Bridgar had a meeting with the French commander,
demanding to know why he had seized an English ship
when the two countries were not at war. The French commander explained that they were out to get Radisson, and
at the sound of the name, Bridgar flew into a rage. He called
Radisson "a traitor and a thief" and "swore he would kill
him whenever he should find him."

Bridgar sailed on to James Bay without the *Perpetua Merchant.*

That year Radisson established Fort York—later called York Factory—at the mouth of the Hayes River, just south of Port Nelson. From this headquarters he supervised trade and sent explorers to probe the hinterland of the northwest. Among his team of pathfinders was Jean Baptiste Chouart who had not yet deserted him. Another was young Henry Kelsey who would later earn fame as an explorer.

Radisson also took part in the in-fighting that was a constant pastime of Hudson's Bay Company employees. Governors and officers of the various trading posts wrote frequent letters to London complaining of each other's illegal trading and other abuse of authority. As a result of these exchanges, Radisson, understandably regarded as untrustworthy, returned to England in 1687 as a prisoner on a Company ship.

His luck had held. He was taken out of the bay just in time to escape the clutches of Pierre Lemoyne d'Iberville who had led a series of French raids into Hudson Bay, captured the English posts including Fort York, and managed to keep the northern trade in a state of turmoil for a decade until the English regained control. Had Radisson fallen into French hands he would certainly have been hauled off to Quebec to end his life on the gallows.

As it was, he was acquitted of the charges against him, only to spend his last years in restless retirement and poverty in England. After the fall of James II (which ended the Stuart dynasty and brought a foreign king, William of Orange, to the throne) he had no support at Court, and his pension from the Hudson's Bay Company was whittled away to almost nothing.

Some time in the 1690s, Radisson married his third wife, Elizabeth, with whom he had three children. He was probably nearing the age of sixty at the time of this marriage, and his prospects were poor. He applied in 1700 for a job as warehouse keeper with the Hudson's Bay Company, but his application was unsuccessful. He tried to collect the money the Company owed him, with equal lack of success.

In June or July 1710 Radisson died. In his will he bequeathed to his wife and children the eighteen hundred pounds which, according to his calculations, he was owed by the Hudson's Bay Company. But all Elizabeth ever received from the Company was £16, which they took care to designate as "charity." She died in extreme poverty in 1732.

The gravesites of Pierre Esprit Radisson and Médard Chouart, Sieur des Groseilliers, are not known. Although they had been world shakers, they died in complete obscurity and neglect. Ambition and greed had driven them to open the door to a vast new Canadian frontier where they made magnificent fortunes for smaller men who lacked their daring and their willingness to risk death in battle or on the gallows, but who knew much more than they about the art of lining one's pockets with other men's gold.

CHAPTER 5

JOHN PHILLIPS

A TYPICAL EIGHTEENTH-CENTURY desperado, John Phillips began his pirate career in Newfoundland and ended it less than a year later off the coast of Massachusetts with an axe through the middle of his skull. But his short career was violent, bloody, and well-documented because, although he didn't live to be hanged, some of his companions did, and the full story came out at their trial. The complete transcript is preserved in the public archives of the State of Massachusetts, and various related documents are in the maritime museum at Boston.

The greatest days of piracy in eastern Canada were between 1610 and the French military occupation of 1662, when the great port of Placentia was fortified and garrisoned. Those were the days of the pirate admirals when gentlemen of good family (and some not so good) commanded whole fleets and dealt with kings on almost equal terms.

A full century later, after the French power had been shattered by the War of the Spanish Succession, there was another great upsurge of piracy in the western and eastern Atlantic—this time by a new breed of brigands. No longer commanders of private navies like those of Ango, Rawleigh, Easton, and Mainwarring, they were mostly men of low birth and little education, who learned to sail ships by rule of thumb and to capture unarmed merchant vessels while avoiding encounters with warships, which in those days were heavily gunned but rarely built for speed or for pursuit among islands in shallow waters.

This second period of piracy is often called the "Golden Age," not because there were more pirates or more successful ones than in earlier times, but because Daniel Defoe, the author of *Robinson Crusoe*, was on hand to document and romanticize their careers. Defoe wrote a book on the pirates of his times, undoubtedly compiled from interviews with men who had sailed on the ships of the major pirate captains. It became a best seller and ran through many editions, making household words of such names as Blackbeard, Anne Bonny, and Edward Low, and giving the false impression that these were among the most successful pirates in history. There was no Defoe on hand to popularize the lives of such vastly more successful pirates as Easton and Mainwarring.

Phillips arrived in Canada when the Golden Age was all aglitter with doubloons and pieces of eight. He started life as an honest enough lad. Born into a family of English shipwrights, he decided in 1720 to emigrate to Newfoundland where there were opportunities in his trade because the English had taken over the shipyards at Placentia from the French under the treaty of 1713 and were operating a flourishing shipbuilding industry in their oldest colony.

The vessel on which John Phillips was travelling to Newfoundland was captured by a pirate as it came in over the Banks, and the young man was impressed into the pirate crew as ship's carpenter. As it happened, Phillips had fallen foul of one of the most blackhearted villains in the history of the sea, a sadistic cutthroat named Anstis who committed all the crimes of which pirates are usually accused.

Anstis fought without quarter, tortured any prisoners who fell alive into his hands, then flung them to the sharks.

Captured women were gang-raped and murdered. The Anstis gang seemed really to be at war with the human race.

After some months of this, the company of thieves and butchers among whom Phillips had fallen decided to call it quits and seek a pardon, signing a round-robin petition for this purpose. Pirates of the Golden Age often retired in this way with a modest share of loot—a few hundred pounds a man, perhaps. Pardons were often freely granted in an effort to secure experienced seamen for the merchant fleets—if you couldn't get a pardon from one government, you could often get it from another, along with a change of citizenship.

The pardon was granted by Great Britain, and Phillips found honest work on a trading ship bound for England. There he transferred to another ship outward bound to Newfoundland and finally arrived at Placentia in the spring of 1723, three years after he had first set out for the colonies.

He failed to find work as a shipwright and went on to St. Pierre (then called St. Peter's Harbour because it was in English hands and not to be confused with St. Peters in Cape Breton Island which was still in the hands of the French). Here again no men of his trade were needed, and he was forced to sign on as servant in a fishing crew. He found this work so irksome and unrewarding that he began enquiring whether any of his fellow fishing servants would be interested in going on the account with him.

In those days many fisherman signed on for a season at almost no wages, while others served under indenture as virtual slaves. Even free men like Phillips were expected to work eighteen hours a day for little more than room, board, and a ration of rum. Food and rum were charged against their annual wages so that at the end of the fishing season they might get less than the cost of their passage home. In the circumstances he had little trouble finding sixteen men who agreed to join him in a pirate voyage—a very small crew for such a venture, but they expected to recruit others from captured vessels.

They conspired to seize a fine ship then lying in harbour at St. Pierre—a trading schooner belonging to William Minot of Boston. Apparently something went wrong with the plan, for on the night of August 29 only five of the conspirators actually showed up. Nevertheless, with courage worthy of a nobler cause, they decided to continue with their plan.

Luring the watchman from the deck, they bound and gagged him and left him on shore while they quietly slipped the cable, hoisted sail, and by dawn were hull down on the horizon. Once out of sight of land they held a meeting and signed a set of pirate articles.

The actual document that these five men signed on their first morning at sea is preserved in the Massachusetts archives—one of the few such documents in existence. It seems to prove that Phillips was a fairly literate man, although the fetish on which they took the oath, the blade of an axe since they lacked a Bible, does not argue a strong case for their religious training.

The articles they signed provided that deserters would be marooned—stranded on an uninhabited island—that thieves who stole from the company's communal loot would be marooned or shot, that anyone who endangered the ship or started a fight with a shipmate would be flogged, and that there would be compensation from the common store for those who lost limbs in battle. Rape or molestation of a woman was to be punished by death.

In some respects the pirates were ahead of their age. There was no compensation for injury in any other employment at the time.

The commonest punishment in Phillips's articles was "Moses's law on the bare back"—thirty-nine lashes pre-scribed for such crimes as carrying an uncovered candle or smoking an uncovered pipe below decks. It may seem to us hardly credible that men would vote such punishment for themselves, but it was hardly severe by the standards of the time, and when the pirates gave a shipmate a whipping they probably used something a good deal less deadly than the notorious cat-o'-nine-tails favoured by English naval captains and the magistrates on shore.

The names affixed to the pirate articles were John Phillips, John Nutt, Thomas Fern, James Sparkes, and William White. They renamed the ship the *Revenge* and proceeded to raid the fishing fleets on the Banks. In the following eight months they ran down and captured at least thirty-three ships, some of them armed and one that was actually fitted out for war, mounting twelve guns.

The original five were quickly joined by a full crew from captured ships—most of them volunteers, but some impressed to fill jobs that the volunteers were not qualified for. One of the new recruits turned out to be an already famous pirate named John Rose Archer, former lieutenant of the notorious Blackbeard who had been killed five years earlier in a frightful hand-to-hand conflict on the deck of a British sloop-of-war. Another early recruit was John Fillmore who not only escaped the gallows, but after his trial for piracy in Boston, founded an important family. John Fillmore's great-grandson, Millard Fillmore, became thirteenth President of the United States.

From an English ship captured a few days later the pirates received another enthusiastic recruit, a man named William Taylor, an English tradesman who had fallen into debt and was being sold into bondage on a Virginia plantation. Like Fillmore, he later became founder of an important family. Among the ships they took in the early days was the brigantine *Mary* under Captain Moore inward bound to Carbonear with a cargo valued at £500. They also took a French ship carrying more than a thousand gallons of wine.

With a full crew and plenty of provisions, they next sailed for the West Indies. But among the islands they had much worse luck than on the banks. Piracy had almost stopped the West Indian trade at this point, and pickings had become lean. Their supplies were running low when they captured a French sloop-of-war and sailed it into Tobago for a refit. The cove where they careened their ship was a small, sheltered bay with a sand beach, plenty of fresh water, and dense jungle coming down to the sea on either side. At Tobago they captured another small vessel and began to fit her out for piracy.

There was now trouble in the ranks. Thomas Fern, one of the original company of five, conspired with four of the crew to take the small ship and head for the high seas on their own account. They almost got away, but Phillips pursued and captured them, brought them back, and held a trial. The four lesser pirates were pardoned and allowed to rejoin the crew, but they condemned Thomas Fern to death, tied him to a palm tree, and shot him through the heart, as the articles he had signed prescribed.

Fern had been ship's carpenter. To replace him Phillips chose Edward Cheeseman, the carpenter from a captured ship, the *Dolphin*, that they had taken on the Banks of Newfoundland. Cheeseman (impressed into the crew) had been conspiring from the start for Phillips's overthrow. Within a few weeks Cheeseman had a powerful confederate, a New England fishing skipper named Andrew Haradan.

It was April 1724 when Phillips seized Haradan's ship on the Banks. She was so new that parts of her topsides were actually unfinished, and men were still working on her decks with carpenter's tools while she pursued her fishing voyage. Since she was a better vessel than the one they were then using, the pirates transferred all their stores and loot to the captured ship and allowed the fishing crew to sail away empty-handed in the *Revenge*. But, perhaps because of his experience in seamanship and navigation, Haradan was forced to remain on board. It took him and Cheeseman less than three days to bring their plot for a mutiny to violent fruition.

First they moved all the carpenter's tools up on deck—a thing they could do without arousing suspicion because the decks were still not quite completed. Broadaxes, adzes, mallets, and hammers were left lying about where the conspirators could reach them in a hurry. Then they pretended to be busy under Cheeseman's direction while awaiting the signal from Haradan to attack the pirates at the most auspicious moment.

It came at noon on April 17, 1724. Phillips was below in his cabin. The conspirators seized John Nutt, the first mate, and flung him over the side. A moment later James Sparkes, the chief gunner and another of the original band of five, was stunned by a blow and dumped overboard. Hearing the commotion, Phillips rushed on deck. Cheeseman was waiting for him at the companionway with a large shipwright's caulking hammer. With this he delivered a blow to the head that broke Phillips's jaw. Nevertheless, the pirate grabbed a weapon and lunged for Cheeseman, but at that moment Haradan came up behind him and clove his skull with an axe. What was left of Phillips's head was then cut off as a trophy, and his body thrown overboard. Cheeseman next went below, laid out John Rose Archer with his trusty hammer, and herded the other pirates on deck. There the conspirators butchered ten of them and flung their bodies overboard, the remainder being bound and locked up to face trial ashore.

Andrew Haradan now resumed command of his own vessel and sailed her back to Massachusetts Bay in triumph, with Phillips's head hanging from a yardarm. He tied up at his home dock, sent seven chained pirates ashore to face trial, and had Phillips's head cured in a barrel of pickle which he forwarded to Boston.

Cheeseman and Fillmore were tried for piracy and promptly acquitted. Fillmore, who had been in Newfoundland when the *Revenge* was first captured, then testified against the only survivor of the original five, William White. John Rose Archer, who had started life as a Newfoundland fisherman, served with Blackbeard, and finally as second officer under Phillips, was convicted on his record. He had been on the public "wanted" list for years.

Thirteen of the pirates had been killed on board ship. Most of the survivors were either acquitted or reprieved. Even William Taylor, who had turned pirate voluntarily to escape the life of a plantation slave, was first convicted and then pardoned. He subsequently settled in Newfoundland, where his family became honest planters and seamen.

John Rose Archer and William White were publicly hanged with all due ceremony, including a long oration from the Reverend Cotton Mather, the famous hanging parson of Boston whose greatest delight was to officiate at executions, whether of pirates or witches. The body of White was buried in the ordinary way, but Archer was hanged in chains on a small island in Boston Bay with the black flag of the *Revenge* bearing its white skeleton fluttering above him. Phillips's pickled head, hanging from a pole, was also exhibited on the Boston waterfront as a warning to visiting sailors.

CHAPTER 6

BARTHOLOMEW ROBERTS

IT WAS EARLY June in the year 1720, and the little village of Trepassey on Newfoundland's south coast lay quiet in the light mist of predawn. Houses and stages and fishing stores crowded the shoreline. Here and there a merchant's premises stood out somewhat larger and better built than the small wooden houses of the fishermen. More than twelve hundred men and a few women lay in exhausted sleep, having worked from dawn the day before until midnight or even later splitting and cleaning and packing fish into salt, working under the reddish light of cod-oil lamps after daylight had failed.

It was the time of the "caplin scull" when billions of small silver fish, a species of sea smelt, crowded toward shore to spawn on the beaches, and the great schools of codfish crowded after them, feeding voraciously. Most the season's catch of cod would be taken in the next few weeks in nets and on baited lines, and everyone worked to exhaustion, sometimes twenty hours at a stretch, to start the lengthy process of "shore cure" by which the fish were converted to the best grade of salted fillets that commanded the highest price in all the major ports of Europe.

There were just a few "planter" families at Trepassey, all of them recent arrivals, for the port had passed into English hands only seven years earlier when the French had finally given up their settlements in southern Newfoundland under the Treaty of Utrecht that ended the War of the Spanish Succession. The fishing crews were composed mainly of transients, men from western England and Ireland, but included a few women as cooks (but they worked at the fish, too, when they weren't cooking), and many young apprentices to the fish-curing trade, some 1,200 people altogether.

In the harbour about 150 fishing smacks and shallops lay at anchor. In another hour they would be crowded with men and boys hurrying off to the fishing grounds just beyond the headlands. There were also twenty-two ships at anchor, mostly fishing and merchant vessels from Bristol, their crews on shore with the other fishermen, only their watchmen left in charge.

It was around 4:00 A.M., and the first light was staining the sky above the hills toward Biscay Bay when the peace of the sleeping village was shattered by a hellish uproar of gunfire and trumpets, a continuous cannonade accompanied by the blaring of brass horns. Up the long, narrow reach from the south, fire belching from every port, came a ship under full sail, a huge black flag with a white skeleton drinking a toast to death fluttering from her masthead.

The flag identified the pirate at once. This was none other than "Black Bart," the pirate who had spread fire and death along the coasts of Africa and North and South America, the most feared man of his time. His ship, the *Royal Rover*, had never been defeated in a sea fight. His most recent exploit was still the talk of the North Atlantic ports.

A few months earlier, while he was still supposed to be plundering the slave ships along the coast of the Gulf of

Guinea in Africa, he had appeared off the coast of Brazil where a fleet of forty-two Portuguese merchant ships were at anchor guarded by two warships, preparing to sail for home. The *Royal Rover* had sailed straight into the middle of this fleet, selected the most prosperous-looking prizes, raked them with gunfire, boarded them, and carried off loot rumoured to be worth some ten thousand pounds. The helpless merchantmen had signalled frantically for the protection of the two warships, but by the time they had their anchors hoisted and their sails aloft, the *Royal Rover* was off and away before a fresh breeze, her trumpeters and fiddlers playing a merry tune, and her crewmen dancing on the decks.

News of this incredibly brazen raid had reached Newfoundland with the fishing schooners from New England more than a month before, but no one suspected that the *Royal Rover* was heading for Newfoundland. She had appeared off Canso a few days before and picked over the fishing fleet at her leisure, but no ship from Nova Scotia had since put in at Trepassey. The wealthy Bristol merchants who traded there, the stolid masters of fishing rooms, seamen, women, young boys on their first voyage away from home, all huddled on the foreshore like a flock of frightened fowl while the pirate ship bore down on the largest of the anchored merchant vessels, and the watchmen from the ships' decks fled in rowboats for the safety of the shore.

"Black Bart," perhaps the most flamboyant pirate who ever lived, was formerly the respectable Bartholomew Roberts, one of the most brilliant navigators of his time. Of Welsh parentage and working-class background, he had risen from a common sailor to first mate (sailing master) of a sloop trading to the West Indies. But no matter how great his ability, he would never make captain of a ship unless he was also its owner. Captains, in those days, did not rise from the ranks. He was a mere third mate of the *Princess*, taking slaves on the coast of Africa in June 1719, when she was captured by pirates and he was impressed into the crew.

The leader of the gang that captured Roberts was a famous Welsh pirate named Howell Davis. Six weeks after the capture Davis was dead, slain in an ambush by Portuguese slave traders, still on the Coast of Guinea. The pirates escaped in their ship and in a conference at sea decided to offer Roberts the leadership. He proved his worth at once by leading them back to the Portuguese slaving station where Davis had been killed. In a furious surprise assault he sacked the small settlement and put it to the torch. Then off they went, capturing prizes along the coast of Africa. Tiring of this after a few weeks, they headed for the coast of Brazil and the great *coup* that made Roberts and the *Royal Rover* famous on both sides of the Atlantic.

Roberts kept an entire orchestra on his ship—trumpeters, drummers, and fiddlers who were required to play when going into battle and also to amuse the crew on any day except Sunday. As he headed for the centre of the fleet at Trepassey, the orchestra blared out a din of military music while the ship's thirty-two cannons and twenty-seven swivel guns roared away. Because they were meeting no resistance, the pirates didn't waste shot. They just stuffed the guns with as much powder as they would safely hold and set them off in a continuous cannonade designed to intimidate everyone within earshot.

There were no shore batteries at Trepassey to dispute the *Royal Rover*'s command of the harbour. If anyone dared to put off from shore in a boat, it could be sunk with ease. Roberts looted the anchored ships at his leisure. He sank a few fishing smacks and set fire to some of the ships, perhaps as a means of spreading more terror among the watchers or perhaps just from the love of arson.

As the day wore on, fishing and trading vessels began arriving from the Banks. One by one they sailed up the long, narrow bay leading into Trepassey Harbour. One by one Roberts bore down on them and took them prisoner, four ships in all, making a total of twenty-six that he captured in Trepassey. The crews he disarmed and sent ashore. The ships he looted of whatever valuables they contained.

One of the ships at anchor was a fine Bristol galley, probably well known to Roberts since she came from his home port. He decided to make her his flagship. He transferred to her the best of his armament and the most valuable bales of his loot and renamed her the *Royal Fortune*. Before he departed, he had three well-armed ships, for among the other loot he had captured from the anchored merchantmen were forty cannons and numerous swivel guns, with powder and shot for them.

The new flagship was a square-rigged three-master, flying about 3,000 square yards of canvas, and perhaps capable of a speed of fourteen knots under full sail with a strong wind. She was also provided with oars and oar ports so that she could be rowed if becalmed or if she found herself in narrow waters where sailing was impossible.

Before leaving Trepassey, Roberts decided to loot the shore stations of whatever useful goods they might possess. He began a bombardment of the merchants' premises, and sure enough, everyone fled to the woods and hills. The pirates landed almost unopposed. A few shots were fired at them from the shelter of nearby trees, and a few of the pirates may have been hit by musket balls. After looting the merchants' stores of everything they considered of value, they set fire to the stages and stores and rowed back to their ships, leaving Trepassey in flames.

The *Royal Fortune* then sailed off into Trepassey Bay, rounded Mistaken Point and Cape Race, and headed north

along the shore past Renews, Ferryland, and Cape Broyle.
The pirates on board were having a high old time with the
puncheons of rum they had captured at Trepassey, but they
found time to intercept and loot the cabins of all the fishing
ships they met between Cape Race and Cape Spear.

A ship's most valuable cargo, including whatever money
she carried, was usually stored in her "great cabin." Thus
she could be fleeced rather easily. A brief inspection of the
hold soon revealed whether she carried valuable cargo. If
there was nothing but fish or salt, Roberts would depart
with the captain's chest, leaving the ship and crew free to
pursue their lawful occasions.

Here and there he took a recruit. Only rarely did he
"enforce" anybody, and then only if the man was a
tradesman whose talents he might need. From the *Blessing*
of Lymington he received one of his most interesting
volunteers, a 22-year-old able seaman named John Walden.

This young pirate had many remarkable qualities. He
was fearless, an excellent fighter, an expert seaman, and a
good-looking man who soon became Robert's mate and
bedfellow. The crew called him "Miss Nanny" behind his
back, "Nanny" being eighteenth-century slang for a passive
homosexual.

The term "mate" did not mean, as it would today, that
Walden was second in command. It only meant that he was
the captain's confidant and transmitted his orders. Other
men, elected by the crew or appointed by Roberts, held
more responsible positions such as sailing master, quarter-
master (in charge of the common store of loot), and boat-
swain (in charge of the deck).

The pirates usually elected all their officers and might
change them at will, but Roberts, once in charge, was much
more an authority figure than most pirate captains. Not
only was he a renowned navigator, but he issued a standing
invitation to any crewman who disagreed with him to go
ashore and settle the issue in a duel. No one ever took him

Peter Easton's ship the *Happy Adventure* at Harbour Grace, October 7, 1612. John Guy's colonists from nearby Cupids are landing fisheries salt to be placed under protection of the pirates' fort. (Painting by J. W. Hayward, 1909, in the Conception Bay Museum; the artist's conception is based on record entries of the Cupids Colony for 1612.)

Fanciful portrayal of a "slight brush" between His Majesty's Ship *Resistance* and the pirates' fort and ships at Harbour Grace, June 4, 1614. The Jolly Roger flying over the fort is not historically accurate. Pirates of the seventeenth century flew flags of solid black or solid red; the skeleton, or skull and crossbones, were added by pirates about a hundred years later. (Painting by J. W. Hayward, 1909, in the Conception Bay Museum.)

PETER EASTON

PETER EASTON "THE PIRATE ADMIRAL" FORTIFIED THIS SITE IN 1610 AND MADE NEWFOUNDLAND HIS BASE UNTIL 1614. HE DEFEATED A FRENCH SQUADRON AT HARBOUR GRACE IN 1611, RECRUITED 5,000 FISHERMEN FROM THIS COLONY INTO HIS CREWS, AND RAIDED FOREIGN SHIPPING AS FAR AS THE CARIBBEAN. IN 1614 HE INTERCEPTED THE SPANISH PLATE FLEET AT THE AZORES, CAPTURED THREE TREASURE SHIPS, AND DIVIDED AN IMMENSE FORTUNE AMONG HIS CREWS. HE WAS TWICE PARDONED AND INVITED HOME BY JAMES I, BUT RETIRED INSTEAD TO SOUTHERN FRANCE WHERE HE BECAME MARQUIS OF SAVOY AND LIVED IN GREAT SPLENDOR.

ERECTED BY THEIR FRIENDS IN MEMORY OF
JEROME C.* & PAMELA E. BARTON LEE
* FIRST CURATOR CONCEPTION BAY MUSEUM 1974

Inscription on bronze plaque on the exterior wall of the Conception Bay Museum, Harbour Grace. The museum is built on the site of the pirate fort first occupied by Easton and later by Mainwarring. This is believed to be the only public memorial to a pirate in Canada.

Harbour Grace schoolboys at the opening of the Conception Bay Museum re-enact the landing of Peter Easton and the establishment of the pirates' fort in 1610. Contemporary documents show Easton at Harbour Grace in 1611, 1612, and 1614.

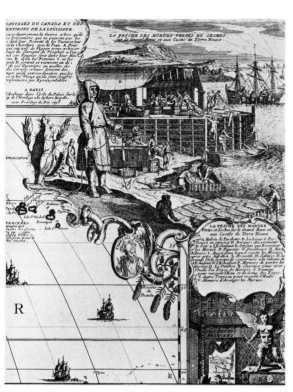

A Newfoundland fishing outport in the early eighteenth century. The harsh conditions drove many fishermen into piracy. Later in the century a handful of fishery workers and naval deserters fled inland to become the outlawed Masterless Men. (Library of Congress)

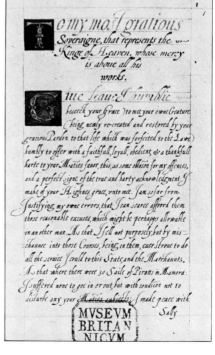

Sir Henry Mainwarring's *Discourse of the Beginnings, Practice and Suppression of Pirates,* written for King James I of England after Mainwarring had made a fortune in piracy and obtained a Royal pardon. (British Library)

affin de nôtre pas surpris par aucun mauvais
battiment ;

6. Il aura aussy attention de n'embarquer à bord
de ladite goalette que huit personnes ainsy qu'il
est Expliqué dans la permission qu'il a de
nos superieurs ;

7. Suposé que ledit Sieur Simonin fasse quelque
prise il l'Expediera pour Louisbourg, en
observant de donner ordre au chef de prise
de Relacher au premier havre de Cette isle
s'il est Contrarié par les vents ou chassé par
quelque mauvais navire, et s'il Relache dans
quelque havre donner aussy ordre de n'en
sortir sans nous en avoir donné par un exprés
avis, s'il est dans le Cas de le pouvoir faire,
Et si ledit Sieur Simonin Etoit obligé de
Convoyer la prise et que la goalette qu'il
Commande ne fut pas chargée de sel ou
en partie, il tachera de Relacher dans le
premier havre & nous en donner aussy
avis, s'il va à Sainte Anne il pourra
laisser la prise a Mr Courthiau dudit
lieu, et Ensuite il pourra prendre le
monde nécessaire pour aller chercher le
sel, ou faire quelqu'autre prise, Enfin
faire le tout pour le mieux, ne pou-
vant prevoir les Inconveniants, Mais
surtout il fera ses efforts pour avoir du
sel, Ledit Sieur Simonin Consent de même
que son Equipage de navoir pour tout
Salaires que la part des prises qu'ils pour-
ront faire suivant les uz et Coutumes
de Cette Collonie, n'exigeant autre chose
desdits Sieurs Imbert & Lamelongue pour

Often the only distinction between a pirate and a privateer was that the latter carried a *letter of marque:* permission from his government to attack enemy shipping. Documents such as the two represented here outlined the rules privateers had to follow.

The French sample originated from Louisbourg, Cape Breton, in 1756. (PAC#C-120408)

George R

Instructions for the Commanders
of such Merchant-Ships, or Vessels,
(L.S.) who shall have Letters of Marque
and Reprizals for private Men
of War against the States General
of the United Provinces, or their
Subjects, or others inhabiting
within any of the Territories of
the aforesaid States General,
by virtue of Our Commission,
granted under Our Great Seal
of Great Britain, bearing Date
the Twentieth Day of this Instant
December. Given at Our Court at
Saint James's, the Twenty-first
Day of December, One thousand
seven hundred and eighty, in
the Twenty-first Year of Our Reign.

Article I.

That it shall be lawful for the Commanders
of Ships, authorized by Letters of Marque and
Reprizal for private Men of War, to set upon
by Force of Arms, and subdue and take the
Men of War, Ships and Vessels, Goods, Wares and
Merchandizes of the States General of the United
Provinces, and their Subjects, and others inhabiting
within any of the Territories of the aforesaid
States General: But so as that no Hostility be
committed, nor Prize attacked, seized, or taken

within

The English letter, dated 1780, was issued by the Court of St. James in London.
(PAC#C-120409)

In a drawing by C. W. Jefferys, Étienne Brûlé becomes the first European explorer to visit the future site of Toronto. (PAC#C-73635)

In a painting by Rex Woods, Samuel Champlain and Étienne Brûlé part company near the Huron town of Cahiague in 1615. Brûlé's mission was to recruit Andastes warriors to support Champlain's attack on an Iroquois town near present-day Syracuse, New York. (Confederation Life Collection)

Betrayed by Brûlé, Champlain is a prisoner on David Kirke's ship in this drawing by C. W. Jefferys. (PAC#C-70267)

Bartholomew Roberts, the "Puritan Pirate," as he appeared in Daniel Defoe's book on piracy. (Library of Congress)

In defiance of the laws of New France, Radisson (standing) and Groseilliers explore uncharted wilderness in their quest for furs. (Painting by Frederick Remington, Remington Art Museum, Ogdensburg, New York)

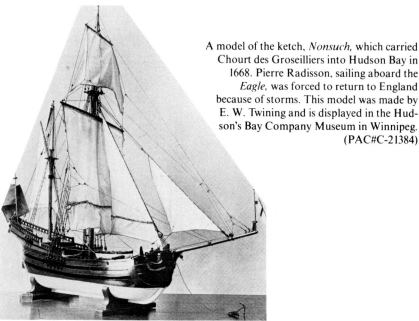

A model of the ketch, *Nonsuch,* which carried Chourt des Groseilliers into Hudson Bay in 1668. Pierre Radisson, sailing aboard the *Eagle,* was forced to return to England because of storms. This model was made by E. W. Twining and is displayed in the Hudson's Bay Company Museum in Winnipeg. (PAC#C-21384)

up on this, even though he once shot a defiant crewman dead on the deck.

He also dressed and acted like a gentleman, a man who expected to be obeyed. Instead of carousing on deck around the rum barrel with his fellow pirates, he sat alone in his cabin drinking tea. When going into action or receiving the surrender of a ship, he stood on his quarterdeck dressed in all the finery of a courtier: scarlet damask waistcoat and breeches, a hat with white plumes, pistols hung from silk sashes, and a diamond-studded gold cross with a gold chain. Even in battle he paced his deck in this conspicuous uniform, as though defying fate to strike him dead.

Some of his enemies called him a puritan—which he clearly was not—but he did seem to believe in the sobering effect of religion on the rough and superstitious gang over which he held sway. All hands were called together nightly to say prayers. The sabbath was strictly observed as a day of rest. Even for swearing, a man was liable to be whipped.

These and other rules, their articles of war, were drawn up and agreed to democratically. Every man had an equal vote.

Among their articles were these:

No fighting on board ship. Quarrels to be settled ashore by duelling with pistols or cutlasses.

All to have equal shares, but clothing in addition if a man needed it.

Any who should defraud the company even of a single dollar should be marooned.

Any who should rob a shipmate should have his nose and ears split and be put ashore where he would be sure to suffer hardship.

No lights or candles after eight at night. Drinking at night only on deck and without lights.

No smoking of uncovered pipes or carrying of lighted candles below deck.

No gaming for money, either with dice or cards.

No boy or woman to be allowed among the crew. Any man seducing a woman and carrying her to sea in disguise should suffer death.

Most of these articles had nothing to do with morals, but were designed for the safety of the ship. Boys and women were not excluded because Roberts or anyone else on board objected to buggery and fornication—they revelled in such activities whey there were ashore—but because they could easily become centres of jealousy and fighting.

Despite crimes that should have condemned him to the lowest level of hell, Roberts may well have considered himself religious. The cross he wore was probably a religious talisman. One of the ships he captured had a Protestant parson on board. He made every effort to persuade the clergyman to become chaplain to his crew. When the man steadfastly refused, Roberts had him released.

After scouting the Newfoundland coast and replenishing munitions, provisions, and crewmen, Roberts headed back to Nova Scotia. At that time Cape Breton Island and Quebec were still French. Cape Breton was the principal rendezvous of the French overseas fishing fleet, and here Roberts captured six large French vessels. One of them was an even finer ship than the recently acquired *Royal Fortune*, and she became the second ship of that name. Once again, the best cannons were transferred, together with Roberts's favourite furnishings. He now had crews sufficient for three ships (perhaps as many as four hundred men) and more loot than a single ship could carry, so Roberts fitted out two others—the *Great Ranger* and the *Little Ranger*. If a single sail of moderate size came into view, the *Great Ranger* would be ordered off alone to capture it, while the *Royal Fortune*, accompanied by the *Little Ranger*, was reserved for major exploits.

A few of the Frenchmen captured on the coast of Cape Breton Island were impressed into Roberts's crew since they were lucky enough to possess skills that he needed. They were not made sharemen with the pirates but were treated as slaves. The other captured Frenchmen were mostly slaughtered with vengeful ferocity. The Governor of Bermuda, reporting to Great Britain, said that some Frenchmen "were whipped nigh unto death," others had their ears docked, still others were hung by the hands from a yardarm and used for target practice. English prisoners, on the other hand, were usually released unharmed except for being stripped of anything that the pirates wanted. The most dreadful incident of Roberts's career occurred when they captured a ship containing eighty negro slaves. The white crewmen escaped but the pirates burned the ship and roasted the negroes alive, still in their chains below decks.

Roberts could also be personally vengeful. Before arriving in Canada he had operated for a while in the Caribbean. There the governor of Martinique (the most important of the French islands) made strenuous efforts to get naval ships to pursue him, and Roberts announced that sooner or later he would hang this man from a yardarm. He now headed south to the West Indies, paid a surprise visit to Fort-de-France, the capital of Martinique, sent a raiding party on shore, kidnapped the governor, and sailed away with his body dangling from his main-top yard.

The *Royal Fortune* lingered among the West Indian Islands as long as there was any loot to collect. Shipping came to a halt. No one dared send a valuable cargo to sea so long as the pirate squadron ranged the waters. They sailed where they willed, exchanged stolen goods for money and services, and spent their time in wild orgies with booze and women in Caribbean ports where pirates were regularly entertained by the local rabble of blackmarket merchants and whores. Most of their loot they took with them to be exchanged for gold in West Africa which was to be their last landfall.

Early in the summer of 1721 the pirate fleet arrived on the coast of Senegal, the westernmost tip of Africa. Then they sailed southward to Sierra Leone, where they exchanged most of their captured goods for gold and enjoyed the hospitality of the English blackmarket merchants and freelance slave traders who flourished there in a competition with the Royal Africa Company which was supposed to enjoy a monopoly of English trade in West Africa.

Refreshed and refitted, the fleet then headed southward and eastward along the Guinea coast, where they captured a whole fleet of slave ships belonging to the Royal Africa Company and held them for ransom. The company paid up, but the two warships that they had secured from Britain to police the Guinea Coast were soon on Roberts's trail.

The *Royal Fortune* by now mounted forty cannons, like a regular battleship, and Roberts was so used to defying governments and winning every skirmish that he shrugged off the presence of the two powerful British cruisers and remained on the slave coast collecting loot and carousing ashore long after he knew about them and could easily have escaped. By this time he had captured some four hundred merchant ships—the exact tally would never be accurately computed.

The warship that caught him was the *Swallow* under Captain Chaloner Ogle. He sighted Roberts's flotilla at anchor on the coast of Ghana and cleverly turned away, as though wishing to avoid them. Roberts, thinking the *Swallow* a merchant ship and an easy prize, sent the *Great Ranger* off in pursuit. Ogle drew the pirate far offshore, out of sight and sound of the other ships, then turned on her and battered her into submission without a single casualty among his crew. He sent her off to Cape Coast Castle, the headquarters of the Royal Africa Company, with a prize crew on board and the pirates in leg irons. Then he headed back to the place where he had sighted the *Royal Fortune*.

Five days after luring the *Great Ranger* out of her sight, Ogle caught up with the pirate flagship for the second time. He happened to meet her at the most opportune moment when her crew were helplessly drunk and hung-over following an all-night debauch. Roberts, a teetotaller, was eating breakfast, and most of his crew were comatose on deck when he realized a warship was bearing down on him.

He changed into his scarlet, gold, and plumes, then rushed about the deck rousing as many pirates as possible to a state of semi-consciousness. Those who failed to respond he beat into wakefulness with the flat of his sword. By this means he managed to get the sails hoisted and the ship under steerage. Then, in an act of pure madness, instead of fleeing for his life he headed straight for the warship to do battle.

The two ships passed within point-blank range of each other and exchanged broadsides. The ragged fire of the drunken pirates did little damage to the *Swallow*, but the rigging and spars of the *Royal Fortune* were so torn and shattered that flight became impossible. The *Swallow* followed up this first exchange of fire by raking the decks of the *Royal Fortune* with grapeshot. Roberts was killed by the first rounds, and the crew utterly demoralized. Too late, they tried to flee. The *Swallow* came about hard on their heels, overtook them, and raked their decks with more grapeshot.

John Walden, Roberts's "mate," lost a leg in the battle, but lived to be hanged. However, he managed to carry out Roberts's last wishes by throwing the captain's body, scarlet damask, white plumes, and all, over the side so it could not be hanged in chains from a gibbet on shore. Then the surviving pirates, many of them already dying, hauled down their flag and asked for quarter.

Besides those killed in action, the *Swallow* took 254 prisoners from the three ships and landed them at Cape Coast Castle in Ghana for trial and execution. They were housed in the "slave hole," a dungeon under one of the Royal Africa Company's forts, where nineteen of them died of wounds before the trial began.

Seventy-four prisoners, believed to be conscripts, were

acquitted. Fifty-four others were sentenced to death, but two of those were later reprieved. Fifty-two were actually hanged, in batches, over a period of several days.

Twenty pirates were sentenced to a far worse death than hanging. They were sent into the Royal Africa Company's gold mines, where every one of them died under the overseers' whips. Seventeen were sentenced to prison and were shackled like slaves in the hold of a ship bound for England. Only four of them survived the voyage.

Captain Ogle stole the hoard of gold dust that he found in the cabin of the *Royal Fortune*. The rest of her cargo he turned over to the authorities. He returned to England both wealthy and famous and was given a knighthood for ending Roberts's rampage—the only English officer who was ever knighted for suppressing piracy. He eventually rose in the ranks to become an admiral.

CHAPTER 7

SEA WOLVES
OF THE GOLDEN AGE

IN THE SEVENTEENTH and eighteenth centuries—and even to a lesser extent in the nineteenth century—war was the great prelude to piracy. Since no nation maintained a truly powerful navy, governments had a habit, the moment war broke out, of licensing privateers to prey on enemy commerce, allowing them to keep most of the loot they could capture. So profitable was this frightful trade that corporations were organized for no other purpose than fitting out fleets of privateers, and many private warships were built specifically to go commerce-hunting among the shipping lanes.

With the coming of peace, these private navies had no legal employment. So, between wars, the seas swarmed with pirates.

From 1704 to 1713 approximately one hundred privateers flying the Cross of St. George and licensed by Good Queen Anne of Great Britain captured some two thousand French and Spanish ships, to the great profit of their captains and their owners. When this easy flow of wealth was cut off by the Treaty of Utrecht, the Golden Age of piracy followed.

One of the most colourful characters of this Golden Age was Captain Charles Bellamy. He has been called "the socialist pirate." But the name does not stand up to scrutiny. There seem to have been two Captain Bellamys sharing the Atlantic between them in 1717 or thereabouts. Neither of them was a socialist, but Samuel Bellamy may be said to have had some socialist leanings. He was not much of a pirate—his career lasted only a few months before he ran himself aground and drowned almost everyone on board his ship.

Charles Bellamy is first reported on the coast of New England and then in the Bay of Fundy in the early summer of 1717. His three ships scouted the north shore of the bay, what is now the coast of New Brunswick but was then regarded as part of the colony of Nova Scotia. Here they chose a safe, easily defended cove and made it their headquarters.

The location is uncertain, but such description as we have suggests St. Andrew's, a harbour well protected by reefs and islands with a river flowing into it, good pine timber for building and for the repair of ships, and well off the shipping routes between the New England and the Newfoundland colonies. Here the pirates built not only a careenage on which to clean and repair their ships but also a fort with a breastwork and gun emplacements. Well separated from the rest, a powder magazine was constructed, where their stores of shot and their barrels of black powder would be safe from accident or attack.

Bellamy was a good organizer and was able to undertake this ambitious project because he had plenty of slave labour at his command. He had captured the crews of several ships farther south, and the pirates stripped the prisoners naked and drove them with whips "after the same manner as the negroes are used by the West Indian Planters" (Defoe).

While the chain gangs toiled in the sun, Bellamy and his lieutenants lay about sipping rum and discussing plans for founding a new nation with Bellamy as its president and his associate pirates as chief ministers. This romantic nonsense must have seemed vaguely possible at the time and place, hundreds of miles from any of the established colonies but in the same region where the French had successfully founded Acadia more than a hundred years before.

With everything shipshape once more, Bellamy's fleet next crossed the great bay to Yarmouth, then headed out around Cape Sable and northward and eastward over the western fishing banks to a temporary anchorage in Fortune Bay on Newfoundland's south coast. Here they captured and sank a number of fishing and trading ships and enlisted some of the crews as pirates. Then they scattered, looking for prey.

Bellamy's ship headed into the Gulf of St. Lawrence where he sighted the sail of a large vessel heading westward and gave chase. He came up with the ship in late afternoon, a Frenchman by her colours, probably carrying both money and supplies for the trading posts at Tadoussac or Quebec.

The ship came about, hoisted her ports, and ran out a formidable array of cannons. She was, in fact, a warship mounting thirty-six guns, carrying soldiers to the fortress at Quebec. Bellamy immediately realized that he was in mortal danger and tried to escape, but the French ship was a good sailer and could run both on and off the wind fully as well as the pirate. Grapeshot and canister shot ripped through Bellamy's rigging. Heavy balls came tearing across the deck, carrying everything before them. He replied with his own guns in a battle that lasted for three or four hours. Fortunately for Bellamy, darkness was falling and a rainstorm was coming on. He escaped being captured or sunk, but his ship was badly mauled, and thirty-six of his men were killed.

He limped back to Newfoundland waters, found sanctuary on the west side of Placentia Bay, and set up a new careenage where his fleet reassembled and the ships were repaired. Again, the exact location of this pirate fort is unknown. It was certainly not at Placentia, as some writers have said (confusing the former French fortress, by that time in the hands of an English garrison, with the bay of the same name), but may well have been at Oderin, a beautiful haven among islands on the opposite shore where the sunken remains of ancient marine works can still be seen—slipways and the like—that cannot be accounted for by any marine works known to history.

According to the pirate historian Philip Gosse, Charles Bellamy continued to prowl the western Atlantic for nine years and assembled a fleet in Newfoundland as late as 1726. This, however, may be an error, for Gosse, like Daniel Defoe before him, attributes the short-lived career of Captain Samuel Bellamy to the apparently much more successful Charles.

Unlike Charles who simply disappears (and probably retired, like many other pirates, with a comfortable nest egg), Samuel can be neatly fitted into the months between February 1716, when he was a legitimate salvage operator in the West Indies, and April 1717, when his ship foundered near Cape Cod and he and nearly all his crewmen were drowned. Because a few of them lived to be hanged, the crewmen who sailed with Samuel Bellamy left a detailed record in the court proceedings of Massachusetts, and because of these documents we can eliminate many of the stories that have gathered around Bellamy's name.

If the speeches published by Daniel Defoe were ever made at all, then they were made by Samuel Bellamy, not by Charles. These speeches, often reprinted, were undoubtedly written by Defoe, but there is some slight background for them in the evidence produced at the trials. "They rob the poor under cover of law. We plunder the rich under the protection of our own courage," thunders Defoe's Bellamy at the captain of a captured ship whom he is trying to convert to piracy. Nothing quite like this was quoted in court, but the Bellamy who emerges there from the tangled evidence is at least the kind of man who might have said something of the sort.

The story that he was intentionally led ashore by the captain of a captured whaler is not true either. His ship ran aground because of his own lack of navigational skill and was soon buried under many thousands of tons of sand. But not before she was stripped by local wreckers, some of whom were hailed before court in an unsuccessful attempt by the Government of Massachusetts to recover a share of the loot.

In 1982 an American salvage company, one of whose members was the son of the late President John Kennedy, reported that they had located Samuel Bellamy's ship and were preparing to recover the vast treasure that they were sure it contained. Whether, in fact, the wreckers of 1717 left such a treasure in her cabins or holds or wherever it was supposed to be would seem, at best, to be doubtful.

In any case, Charles Bellamy never grounded on the Nantucket Shoals, never had any of his crewmen tried for piracy in Boston, and was not, so far as any contemporary records reveal, stranded on the coast of Massachusetts in 1726 or at any other time.

During Bellamy's reputedly long career there were a number of minor pirate captains, some of them associated with him, also operating in the waters of Eastern Canada.

George Lowther was captain of one such ship and took a number of fishing and trading vessels as prizes, most of them along the coast of Newfoundland. In 1723 he sailed to the West Indies and put his ship on careenage there. With her guns dismounted and the ship hove down for cleaning, Lowther had the bad luck to be caught by the South Sea Company's armed merchant vessel *Eagle*.

Most of the pirates were taken prisoner and condemned to lifelong slavery, some in the galleys, others on the West Indian plantations. Lowther himself escaped with three other men and a small boy, but a few days later he was found dead with his pistol beside him. The handgun was said to have misfired and exploded. So perhaps he died accidentally. Others said he deliberately shot himself. But there was never any investigation of his death. He may well have been killed by one of the other escaped pirates.

Another notorious ruffian of the period was Thomas Anstis who captured the ship on which John Phillips was a passenger in 1721 as she headed in over the Banks of Newfoundland.

Anstis (the archetypal fiend who tortured, raped, and murdered his prisoners) was master of the *Good Fortune*, a name borne by many pirate vessels. When he captured the larger and faster *Morning Star*, a ship out of Bristol in the Newfoundland trade, he gave command of the *Good Fortune* to his mate, Brigstock Weaver, and headed south for the West Indies in the larger ship.

The two ships met again at Tobago where Anstis put the *Morning Star* on careenage and, like Lowther, was caught by a warship. Forty of the pirates were captured, but Weaver and Phillips were among those who escaped into the woods, barefooted and empty-handed, while all their loot and personal possessions were confiscated. The marines from the warship found Anstis dead in his hammock, apparently murdered by one of his own crew.

Phillips later got work on a merchant ship, and Weaver also managed to return to England where he was seen two years later, a barefoot beggar seeking alms in Bristol. He was recognized by a merchant captain whose ship had been seized by Anstis and denounced to the authorities. Arrested and taken to London, he was tried, convicted, and hanged at Execution Dock.

The longest career of any pirate of the Golden Age was that of Captain Lewis (first name unrecorded). Although many pirates of the seventeenth and eighteenth centuries carried young boys in their ships, Lewis was the first such waif to achieve notoriety and the distinction of becoming a pirate leader.

Lewis was only about ten years of age when he was on Captain Bannister's ship which was raiding merchant ships off Jamaica in 1687. When the vessel was run down and captured by an English warship commanded by Captain Spragge, Bannister and the other pirates were hanged from the yardarm, presumably after a brief courtmartial. But Spragge, rather surprisingly at a time when children were often hanged for very minor crimes, took pity on Lewis and another young boy, and instead of hanging them by the neck like their older shipmates, he hanged them by their middles from his mizzen topmast, took them into Port Royal, and released them, thoroughly terrified but physically unharmed.

Apparently well-chastened by this treatment, Lewis worked on ships sailing out of Port Royal as a ship's boy and ordinary seaman "till he was a lusty lad." Then a ship on which he was sailing was captured by Spanish raiders and taken to Havana.

Lewis remained in Cuba as a Spanish slave for a number of years, but eventually he and six other captives managed to escape in a canoe to a wild part of the Cuban coast where they joined other escaped captives and set up as small-time outlaws, stealing from the Cuban plantations, raiding ships whenever they could, gradually building up a store of arms and ammunition until they were strong enough to attack and capture a sloop mounting twelve guns. With this ship they set themselves up as regular pirates, elected Lewis as their leader, and sailed northward.

By now Lewis was in his late 30s, a man of experience and talents. As a sailor out of Jamaica he had learned navigation and seamanship. His adventures had made him fluent in both English and Spanish, and somewhere he had learned to speak French and one or more of the dialects then current among West Indian natives.

He and his crew went pirating off the coast of Florida, which was at that time still Spanish, and then off the Carolinas which had flourishing English colonies. At last they arrived in Newfoundland, where they put their heavily armed sloop on careenage for cleaning and repair and finally sailed boldly into Trinity in Bonavista Bay, a splendid harbour and a centre of the fishery where Sir Richard Whitbourne, a century earlier, had convened the first Vice-Admiralty Court outside the realm of England.

When Lewis sailed into Trinity the fishing fleet was at anchor and very lightly manned, most of the crews being at work on the fishing stations ashore. The pirates went through the fleet at leisure, taking whatever they wanted from the ships and replacing their twelve-gun sloop with the finest English ship in the fleet—the twenty-four-gun *Herman*.

But among those on the shore stations was a Bristol captain named Woodes Rogers, father of the Woodes Rogers who became governor of the Bahamas and the greatest scourge of pirates in his time. Rogers got his fellow captains together and laid a plan to trap Lewis and his crew.

Trinity is a closed harbour with a narrow run into the sea and a point of land from which the entrance can be covered by shore batteries. There was already a rudimentary fort on this point, probably neglected and certainly without guns, but some of the guns from the fleet had been dismounted and taken ashore. There was also a magazine with plenty of shot and powder. Rogers and the other captains managed to move the guns to the fort, mount them, and cover the entrance. Since Lewis felt quite secure and was in no hurry, they probably had three or four days in which to accomplish their task. They now thought they had the pirates trapped.

The manoeuvre would likely have succeeded had Lewis not been favoured with a dark and moonless night. Quietly his crew hoisted sail and made a run for it. The ships' crews at the fort were expecting just this and had their guns primed and ready. They fired round after round at the pirate ship as she slipped quickly past on the ebb tide. They could hear the shot strike. But the *Herman* kept on, and vanished into the darkness, although somewhat disabled with "many shot into her hull," according to the report they sent to St. John's.

With daylight they sent off a fast packet to St. John's, where Captain Tudor Trevor was at anchor in the British warship *Sheerness*. It took the packet two days to make port, and the warship a few more hours to make sail and clear the harbour. Meanwhile, lookouts on Signal Hill reported that the pirate ship had sailed past, well out to sea, heading southward. The warship set off in pursuit, some four hours after the *Herman* was out of sight, but meanwhile the *Herman* had vanished into one of the numerous hidden coves along the coast.

There is one such mooring place about five or six hours' sail south of St. John's at a harbour named Cape Broyle—a safe mooring completely invisible from the sea where rings were formerly fastened into the solid stone cliffs, and a ship could lie in deep water moored fore and aft as though in dry dock.

When the warship had called off the chase, Lewis slipped out to sea once more, rounded Cape Race, and sailed along the south coast of Newfoundland. He hovered off the coast for two weeks until he was able to surprise and capture in harbour a large French ship that had been used as a privateer in the recent War of the Spanish Succession.

This ship, like the *Herman*, mounted twenty-four guns, but was a faster sailer and capable of mounting even more armament. Lewis transferred his best armament to her, enlisted some of her crew, and set off for the coast of Africa, where some of the best pirate pickings were to be found, provided you had a strong, well-armed ship.

He made the ocean passage without incident and prowled along the coast of Guinea, where he "captured a great many ships, English, Dutch and Portuguese."

By now Lewis was chief of an unwieldy organization, a robber band consisting of English and French crews working three or four ships at a time. They soon split into factions and began to quarrel. After a while, the English and the French crewmen divided, took separate ships, and agreed to go their separate ways. But they were unable to resist raiding each other. In one such raid Lewis was killed by the French faction, and his crews eventually disappeared.

Despite research by several historians of piracy, not much is known about Lewis's early life. He was probably of English descent, although this is by no means certain, and he was between 38 and 40 years old at the time of his death. Beyond that, nothing is known except for a few incidents from his childhood, his captivity and escape from Cuba, and the massive pirate raid that he carried out in Newfoundland.

Among the many pirates who swarmed over the Canadian seas in the so-called Golden Age, none was more vicious than Eric Cobham, unless it was his wife and partner in piracy, Maria Lindsey. It seems that they killed for sport, followed a policy of leaving no survivors to bear evidence, and, according to Cobham's own account, managed to get away with piracies spread over a period of twenty years.

The Cobhams' favourite base was in the Gulf of St. Lawrence, although they occasionally raided farther south. According to tradition, their fort and careenage was in Bay St. George, at a place called Sandy Point. There, early in the eighteenth century, they were safe from detection except by occasional French or Basque crews of fishermen and a few Indians and French colonists who had strayed northward from the colony of Acadia.

Eric Cobham was born in Poole, one of the Channel ports of England, and went to sea as a boy. He may well have been engaged in the Newfoundland fisheries at the age of fourteen or fifteen, but by his late teens he was a member of a smuggling gang running brandy from France to England. One operation that he took part in was reported to have landed ten thousand gallons of spirits successfully.

At about the age of nineteen or twenty he was caught, flogged, and sent to Newgate prison, where he spent some two years. On his release he got a job working at an inn in Oxford. There he succeeded in robbing one of the wealthy transients of a bag of gold coins. The innocent innkeeper was hanged for the theft, while Cobham moved south to Plymouth and bought a small ship.

Like many ships of her time, the vessel was armed. Cobham recruited a crew of desperadoes from the docks, probably many of them his former associates in the smuggling trade, and set off on a career of piracy.

Rounding The Lizard and heading northward to see what pickings might be found in the Irish Sea, they ran into a great stroke of luck—an East Indiaman heading up the channel toward Bristol, carrying cargo worth forty thousand pounds, some of it in gold. Most pirates would have retired on the spot. Not Cobham. He scuttled the ship and drowned the crew, showing already the ruthlessness that marked his later career. Then he headed for the French Mediterranean ports to establish contacts with pirate brokers. There he sold his stolen goods and returned to Plymouth as a successful soldier of fortune.

In Plymouth he met Maria Lindsey and formed with her a partnership that lasted the rest of their lives. There is no record of their ever being churched, but they were certainly wedded. Shortly after they met, they enlisted a fresh crew of renegades and sailed for the New World.

They made landfall at Nantucket and captured their first trans-Atlantic prize there. Then they cruised northward until they found their way past the tip of Cape Breton Island and discovered the supply route to Quebec where money going upriver and furs coming downriver provided a rich killing ground virtually untouched by other pirates.

The harbour that they chose for their careenage was far enough north of the shipping lanes to be safe from accidental discovery. The great walrus hunts that had reddened the waters of the Gulf of St. Lawrence a hundred and two hundred years before were now over. South of the Straits of Belle Isle the walrus was almost extinct, and except for the trade route that ran past the island of Cape Breton and the Percé Rock to Tadoussac and Quebec, the Gulf lay quiet. No one was likely to follow them into Sandy Point, or if he did, to find his way safely past the mass of shoals that guarded it from the sea. The long sand spit that curves around Flat Bay just south of St. George's great closed barachois would later become the "capital" of western Newfoundland, an important naval base and a centre for the Gulf and Labrador fisheries, but all this was far in the future.

From St. George's Bay the pirates could reach their favourite theatre of operations around Cape Breton and Prince Edward Island (then called the Isle of St. John or Isle St. Jean) in two days' sail. They were within striking distance of all the traffic going to what are now the Maritime Provinces of Canada and all the St. Lawrence traffic in and out of New France, most of which now moved through Cabot Strait, although some still moved by way of the Straits of Belle Isle.

At that time the Canadian fur trade was immensely valuable, and the price of the individual furs was rising. Certain varieties, then or a little later, were literally worth their weight in gold. The trade had been subject, from its inception more than two centuries before, to hijacking.

The Cobhams merely refined this art and added their own brand of ruthlessness. Everything that they captured, they sold in the Mediterranean ports, but rather than risking frequent Atlantic crossing themselves, they probably shipped their loot second-hand by way of traders who picked up cargoes at Percé. It was said that at Percé, in season, you could buy or sell anything from beaver pelts to crown jewels.

Cobham later boasted that he had operated for twenty years without ever being caught, but this probably included the later years of respectability up to his last *coup* in the English Channel. He attributed this good fortune to his policy of leaving no survivors. "Dead cats don't mew," the pirates used to say, but few pirates of the eighteenth century could bring themselves to operate with the Cobhams' thoroughness. Not until a hundred years later did piracy usually include massacre. The Cobhams murdered all hands and sank the ships which were then listed as missing, without survivors, and presumed lost at sea.

The stories of Maria Lindsey's behaviour as a pirate strongly suggest homicidal insanity. She poisoned one ship's crew, had others sewn into sacks and thrown overboard alive, still others tied up and used for pistol practice. Such are the stories later told by her husband, uncorroborated by witnesses, but quite possibly true.

When the Cobhams judged that their wealth had grown sufficiently, they sailed for France, disposed of their final ships and cargoes, and bought a fine estate near Le Havre from the Duc de Chartres. They also bought a yacht in which they sailed on the Baie de la Seine and along the French shore of the English Channel.

They now had a private harbour, servants, and a respectable place among the landed gentry. But even then Cobham could not resist temptation when it fell his way. On one cruise he found a brig becalmed in the channel, inward bound from the West Indies to England, and apparently defenceless. Stealing on board, he and his servants took the crew by surprise, overpowered them, murdered them, and dumped them in the sea. He then sent both ship and cargo to Bordeaux to be sold.

Cobham, wealthy squire and landowner, pillar of respectability, was appointed magistrate, a judge in the French county courts, a position that he held for twelve years. But he and Maria gradually became estranged. He took to almost public wenching. She took to alcohol often laced with laudanum. While he made a reputation for himself as a lover, she became more withdrawn and solitary.

Then, one day, she was missing. Her husband reported it and instigated a search, and after two days her body was found in the sea below a cliff. A doctor certified that she had taken enough laudanum to kill herself, and she was assumed to have leaped over the cliff as insurance against failure in suicide. This seems probable because Cobham, when he later confessed to everything else, did not include Maria's murder among his many crimes.

He died a natural death. When his end was near, he called a priest and made a lengthy confession, had the story of his life committed to writing, and asked that it be published.

His wishes were carried out, and the priest saw that the little book dictated by the ex-pirate was published, but Cobham's heirs, by now a respectable family, tried to suppress it, buying and burning every available copy. One somewhat defective copy found its way into the French archives, and this is the only primary source on Cobham. But he also had his biographer, who supplied other details, presumably from people who knew the pirate in his early or late career and possibly from some who served under him in the days when he hovered, a veritable angel of death, beside the supply line that ran between France and Canada.

CHAPTER 8

SIMON GIRTY

IN THE AUTUMN of 1813, when American invaders seemed about to succeed in their war of conquest against Canada, a 72-year-old refugee joined the troops evacuating Fort Malden on the Canadian side of the Detroit River. The old man was fleeing for his life, with a bounty on his head. If caught by the Yankees he probably wouldn't even live to face a trial—he'd be hanged, shot, or hacked to pieces by the first Americans to lay hands on him.

This was Simon Girty, the Great Renegade, who had fought on both sides of the American War of Independence, on both sides of the Indian Wars, who knew no law except his personal code of honour which he had learned from Indians whom he admired and emulated—Dirty Girty who, the Yankees declared, whooped and sang around the torture stake while their revolutionary hero, Colonel Crawford, died in the flames.

Girty was born near Harrisburg, Pennsylvania, in 1741, the second of four sons of Simon Girty, an Irish immigrant, and his English wife, Mary. The Girtys were poor pioneers, used to hard work, loneliness, the threat of Indian attacks, and the danger of thieves and outlaws. When Simon was ten years old his father was killed. The stories of how it happened vary. One says he was killed by a thief. Another

says he died in a brawl with a neighbour. The one most
accepted by tradition (but one which was probably a later
fabrication) has him tomahawked by an Indian named The
Fish during a drunken quarrel at the Girty cabin while
young Simon looked on in horror.

Mary Girty married a man named John Turner and
had another son, John Turner Jr. Legend has it that Turner
killed The Fish to avenge his wife's former husband. In any
case, an Indian war party captured the family and burned
Turner at the stake. Thomas, the oldest of the five boys,
escaped, but Mary and her other four sons were scattered
among various tribes—Simon to the Senecas, James to the
Shawnees, George to the Delawares.

Simon was probably twelve or thirteen at the time of his
capture, and like many Indian captives he soon learned to
prefer the Indian way of life. He became an expert hunter,
woodsman, and interpreter of Indian dialects. He was such
a favourite with the Indians that one of them, a Delaware
chief named Katepaconen, honoured him by exchanging
names with him.

In 1759, when Simon was seventeen or eighteen, the
government arranged an exchange of prisoners. Simon, his
mother, and his brothers were all sent to Fort Pitt. John
Turner Jr. was too young to have "gone Indian," as the
saying went, but all the Girty boys gave up Indian life much
against their wishes. Torn from their families and sent among
strangers, they tried running away to rejoin the Indians but
discovered that the Indians had to honour the treaty and
send them back again.

Fort Pitt was a hostile place to "Injun lovers" like the
Girtys. To most of the settlers the Indians were dangerous
beasts, best dealt with over the barrel of a gun. White men
who sympathized with them were regarded as traitors to
their race and fair game for the town bullies.

Simon Kenton, a noted frontiersman who would later
play an important role in Girty's life, reported that the first

time he met the young man he had to rescue him from a mob of rowdies who were beating him up. Kenton had to threaten them with a cocked rifle to scare them off.

Girty managed to survive in the vicinity of Fort Pitt for about ten years, working from time to time as a scout and interpreter. Then, in the early 1770s, at about the age of thirty, he entered the employment of Lord Dunmore, the last British governor of Virginia, at a time when Virginia and Pennsylvania were quarrelling violently over their boundaries. In these intercolonial battles, Girty proved himself an able street-fighter, and he soon became one of Lord Dunmore's trusted lieutenants.

While his quarrel with Pennsylvania was still going on, Dunmore also had to mobilize his militia to meet an Indian uprising led by the Mingo Chief Logan and the Shawanese chief Cornstalk, who had taken to the warpath because settlers from Virginia had seized large parts of their land and murdered Logan's family. In Dunmore's War, as it came to be called, Girty acted as scout and interpreter for the governor. He was probably not involved in any actual fighting, but he was still at war against his former friends — perhaps out of loyalty to Dunmore, perhaps to prove his "whiteness," perhaps for reasons known only to himself.

After the Battle of Point Pleasant in which Cornstalk was defeated (October 1774), Chief Logan alone among Indian leaders refused to make peace with the whites. Dunmore, knowing that any meaningful peace must include the Mingos and their leader, entrusted Girty with the delicate mission of approaching Logan and making peace. Girty took his life in his hands and walked boldly into Logan's camp on a chilly November day, knowing full well that the slightest breach of protocol could send him to the stake. He must have been persuasive because he returned to Dunmore's camp having memorized a speech in which Chief Logan set out his reasons for going to war and announced his willingness to cease hostilities.

Girty never learned to read or write, so he had to memorize the speech word for word. Then, in Dunmore's camp, he dictated it to John Gibson who wrote it down. The Logan speech became famous for its eloquence, and generations of American school children were required to read it and even learn it by heart. It is one of the many distortions of history in America that Simon Girty was deliberately written out of the story and the negotiations with Chief Logan attributed to Gibson who had merely acted as a stenographer.

Peace was temporarily restored to the western frontier, and Dunmore rewarded Girty by giving him a lieutenant's commision in the Fort Pitt militia. At about the same time he renamed the post Fort Dunmore.

Trouble between the colonies and Great Britain had been brewing for years and was now so serious that Dunmore began compiling a list of those whom he considered trustworthy and loyal to the Crown. On the list he included Girty's name. A few months later the American Revolution broke into open war and Dunmore went east to fight for the king. His militia was disbanded and the post became Fort Pitt once more. Simon Girty now found himself unemployed in a rebel community, and, with the same easy switch of loyalties that he had shown toward the Indians, he promptly joined the Patriots, as the rebels liked to call themselves, acting as guide, interpreter, and recruiter.

In May 1776 Girty had a job as interpreter with George Morgan, the American Indian agent. Three months later he was fired for what Morgan called "ill behaviour." He then went to work as a recruiting agent for the rebel militia, expecting that once a company was raised he would receive a commission as captain. But another man received the honour and Girty became a second lieutenant. He resigned after a few months, sought compensation for his work and expenses as a guide and interpreter, and was turned down. He was said to have sworn on the spot that the quarters of the officers who denied him his money would soon be "awash in blood," but this story has all the marks of a later invention.

In the summer of 1777 there was a widespread report of a conspiracy to seize Fort Pitt and hand it over to the British. Alexander McKee, an outspoken Loyalist, was rumoured to be leader of the conspiracy. Simon Girty, friend of McKee and former protégé of Lord Dunmore, was also suspected. He was arrested and imprisoned in the guardhouse, broke out and escaped, but then returned and gave himself up, explaining that he simply didn't like jails. He was tried and acquitted.

Meanwhile Indian allies of the British were devastating the American western settlements. The year 1777 was known as the "Year of the Bloody Sevens" because of the frequent Indian raids. In February 1778 General Edward Hand launched an offensive against the Indians, using Fort Pitt as his headquarters. Girty may have accompanied the expedition as a scout. It was a dismal failure. Hand succeeded only in killing one man, several women, and an Indian child. His men dubbed it the "Squaw Campaign."

A few weeks after the Squaw Campaign ended, three men fled from Fort Pitt and headed for the British fort at Detroit. They were Simon Girty, Alexander McKee, and an Irish adventurer named Matthew Elliot. Detroit was commanded by a British governor, Sir Henry Hamilton, known among the rebels as the "Hairbuyer" because he was said to pay bounties to the Indians for American scalps.

The flight of Girty and his friends threw Fort Pitt into a state of panic. No trio could be better equipped to organize an Indian war, and indeed the frontiers of Kentucky and the Ohio Valley were on the verge of what the rebels would later regard as the most nightmarish period of their history.

Fear touched off a rash of desertions from the American militia regiments. The officers responded with a reign of terror. Those deserters whom they caught were shot, hanged, or flogged half to death. The most dangerous of the deserters was Simon Girty. He was tried *in absentia* by a Pennsylvania court and declared an outlaw, and a bounty of $800 was put on his head.

Girty, McKee, and Elliot spent two months travelling through Indian lands, reputedly talking up a war against the Yankees, or the Long Knives as the Indians called them. In June they reached Detroit where they reported to Governor Hamilton, and Girty was promptly hired as an interpreter. Officially, that is the only rank or post he ever held with the British army.

Simon liked to style himself "Captain Girty," and sometimes he did, indeed, perform the duties of an officer, but he never held a commission. Unofficially, his duties were to encourage the Indians to wage war against the rebels and to accompany them on their raids. He was also to give them advice, gather information for the British, and so far as he could, prevent the Indians from torturing prisoners or killing women and children. Despite the charge of being a "hair-buyer," Henry Hamilton repeatedly instructed the Indians to bring him prisoners, not scalps.

Girty was quite unable to enforce the British rules among the Indians who regarded themselves as allies, not subjects of the King. He used his considerable powers of persuasion but had no powers of command.

The Americans regarded the British alliance with the Indians as inhuman—"the unleashing of savages against the innocent!" They had tried to do the same thing themselves without success; George Washington had proposed scalp bounties; they had managed to drive a small wedge into the Iroquois confederacy, but on the whole had been unlucky in their attempts to convert Indians into rebels. In the circumstances, self-righteousness was easy.

Simon Girty's defection to the British was followed by that of two of his brothers, James and George, who also became interpreters and raiders for Governor Hamilton. Thomas Girty and John Turner remained with the rebels and became American citizens. It is said that Simon visited them on occasion and hid in the barn if there were American militiamen about.

Girty was an excellent raider. He struck deep into Yankee territory, leading raid after raid with complete disregard for his personal safety, risking not only death in combat but certain death if captured. He not only took part in raids and in several major frontier battles, but he also disguised himself as an Indian and went on spy missions into hostile territory.

In October 1779, with his brother George and a party of Indians, Girty ambushed the command of Colonel David Rogers and captured several boats loaded with war supplies. From the body of the American officer he took a pair of silver-plated pistols.

In June 1780 two Kentucky forts, Ruddles' Station and Martin's Station, fell to the British and the Indians. On both occasions prisoners were slaughtered before the British commander, Captain Henry Bird, could stop it. Girty was Bird's guide and interpreter and was held responsible by the Americans for the war crimes.

Early in his career as a British agent, Girty encountered his friend Simon Kenton who was working as a scout for the rebels. Kenton was captured trying to steal Indian horses and was subjected to beatings and made to run the gauntlet. When an Indian woman tried to humiliate him further by sitting on his face, he sank his teeth into her rump, to the amusement of the Indian men. He was condemned to die, and his face was painted black.

While the Indians were preparing to torture Kenton at the stake, Girty rode into their village, fresh from a raid into Kentucky. To their great surprise Girty embraced the prisoner, explaining that he was his friend, and begged them to spare his life. The Indians turned Kenton over to Girty who took him to his lodge and nursed him back to health. Thus Girty repaid Kenton's action of rescuing him from the Fort Pitt rowdies so many years before.

For several weeks they hunted together, and Kenton later reported that Girty told him he might have acted "too hastily" in joining up with the British. Unfortunately, Kenton's reprieve was short-lived. The Indians, after having a war party mauled by the Yankees, once more decided they needed to burn one of the Long Knives at the stake. Since none other was available they again selected Kenton for torture.

This time Girty's eloquence and persuasiveness could not sway them, so he took the supreme risk of tricking them instead. Pretending to agree with the decision of the council, he suggested that Kenton was too important a prisoner to be burned in a small village and should, instead, be taken to a big Sandusky village where he could be burned before a large crowd. This was an attitude the Indians could understand. The Long Knife was, after all, an important man on the frontier and deserved the most spectacular death they could provide.

Sandusky was a major trading centre for British and Canadian merchants, and Girty hoped they might be able to offer a big enough ransom to save the prisoner's life. The plan worked. Kenton was taken off to Sandusky for burning, and there he was ransomed by a Canadian trader named Druyer, who paid the Indians a hundred dollars' worth of rum and tobacco, then turned Kenton over to the British army at Detroit. Kenton never met Girty again, but eventually returned to the United States and ever afterward defended the reputation of the man who had saved his life twice.

There were many other occasions when Girty intervened on behalf of American prisoners. He also showed kindness to captives, especially to children, who were not always ill-treated by the Indians but were often neglected and left in terror and misery. "You be a good boy," he told one lad, "and some day you'll get home again."

Saviour that he was to many, Girty went down in American history books as a monster because of the death by torture of one American officer. American histories, legend, and literature all present Simon Girty as a sadistic fiend who whooped with joy while his Indian allies tortured to death their helpless American prisoners. So far as these stories have any basis at all, they stem from the death of Colonel Crawford, an event over which Girty had no control. Before it he was just one more outlawed Tory. After it he was the "White Savage."

Thirty-five years before the outbreak of the American War of Independence, Moravian missionaries went to the Ohio Valley to try to convert the Indians to their brand of Christianity. By the time of the war they had several mission stockades, the largest being Gnadenhutten, "The Houses of Grace," in western Pennsylvania.

Most of the Moravian converts were Delawares, a harmless group who wanted no part of the war that was raging around them, but their villages were in the war zone, and each of the warring factions considered them either a nuisance or a threat.

The Senecas regarded the Delawares as a subject tribe and the Christian Delawares as the cowardly lackeys of foreigners. Even the unconverted Delawares, such as those who fought with the chief Captain Pipe for the British, despised the converts as traitors.

The British, for their part, suspected the Moravian ministers of being spies for the rebels (which in fact they were), while the Americans, for their part, regarded Indians, Christian or not, as vermin and the missionaries as wasting their time with such degenerate heathen.

To make matters worse, the Christian Delawares acted like real Christians and fed their enemies between raids, even if these enemies were fighting against the Patriots.

Simon Girty visited the missions on several occasions during the war, and it is certain that he was not there to listen to sermons. Gnadenhutten was a good place to eat, rest, and pick up information.

In 1781 Major DePeyster, the British officer commanding at Detroit after Hamilton was captured by the rebels, sent a band of Indians and Loyalist Rangers (led by Matthew Elliot) to Gnadenhutten with orders to evacuate the missionaries and their followers to Sandusky, said to be a place of safety and also a place where the British authorities could keep an eye on the pro-rebel Moravians. In the course of the evacuation much of the Christians' personal property was stolen by Elliot.

At Sandusky the Moravian community was reduced to near starvation. Even firewood was in short supply. Canadian hunters sometimes supplied the missionaries with gifts of meat, but in general the missionaries led a less than hand-to-mouth existence. Girty went out of his way to make life there more difficult. He had no love for Christians and delighted in tormenting the ministers. One of them wrote:

"He appeared like a host of evil spirits. He would sometimes come up to the bolted door between us and him, threatening to chop it in pieces to get at us. No Indian we had ever seen drunk would have been a match for him. How we should escape the clutches of this white beast in human form no one could foresee."

Starvation at Sandusky became so bad in the early months of 1782 that the Christian Delawares decided to send foraging parties back to Gnadenhutten to glean the remains of the frozen corn still standing in their fields. By March over a hundred people were there trying to salvage whatever the frost, the crows, and the racoons had left intact. While they laboured in the frozen fields, a band of American militia led by Colonel David Williamson arrived.

The colonel told the unsuspecting Christian Indians that he had come in friendship and could provide both food and shelter for them—something the British hadn't done at Sandusky. To prove their trust they must surrender their knives, hatchets, and hunting guns. They did this and were herded into the village, where Williamson had them locked into two large buildings, men in one, women and children in another.

The women and girls were then dragged out of the prison in small groups and raped. Realizing that they were to be killed, the Indians began a loud wailing of mixed Christian prayers and traditional Delaware death songs. Their sexual appetites sated, the militiamen then began the orgy of murder, wading into the shrieking masses with knives and hammers. One man, after bashing in the skulls of fourteen people with a cooper's mallet, handed the tool to another. "My arm fails me," he said, "but I think I have done pretty well."

None of the victims fought back. Some tried to escape and were shot. Two boys, only, managed to get away and carry word of the massacre to the Indians at nearby mission towns. Ninety-six men, women, and children were butchered in the Moravian massacre. When the killing was done and all the bodies scalped, Colonel Williamson went home and reported his "victory."

He was hailed throughout the American frontier as a hero. He had taught the untrustworthy savages a lesson they would not soon forget! But in the cities on the American seaboard as well as in Canada and Great Britain, the massacre was condemned as an inhuman atrocity. Civilized Americans were shocked that their countrymen could be capable of such cowardly mass murder. Nevertheless, nothing was done to make Williamson or his butcher boys answer for their crime. The British used the incident to incite the Indians to greater efforts against the Americans, and the Indians responded enthusiastically. Most of the bands that had formerly remained neutral now took the warpath against the Long Knives.

In this atmosphere the Americans launched their offensive against the Indians under Colonel William Crawford, a friend and business partner of George Washington who had served before the war with Simon Girty under Lord Dunmore. Scarcely three months after the Gnadenhutten atrocity, Crawford rode against Sandusky at the head of an army.

The offensive went badly from the start. Crawford had little control over his militia units, many of whom preferred Williamson as commander. Crawford had won the command by a narrow margin in an election, and Williamson reluctantly served as second in command. They had hoped for a surprise attack but suffered so many delays en route that the Indians had several days' warning of their approach and were well prepared. Their defence was assisted by Simon Girty, Matthew Elliot, and Captain William Caldwell's Canadian Rangers.

Fighting began on June 4 and continued through June 5. It ended in a disaster for the Americans, with the army fleeing in a disorderly rout. Crawford, while searching for his missing son-in-law, was separated from his troops and became lost in the woods. There he met another straggler, an army surgeon named John Knight, and after two days of wandering the two men were captured by a band of Delawares. Meanwhile, Williamson, when he saw the tide of battle turning against him, was among the first to dash for the safety of Fort Pitt.

The Indians took Crawford and Knight to the Wyandot village of the chief Half King. On the way there they were joined by Simon Girty. Crawford spoke to Girty and, according to Knight, reminded him that they had been comrades under Dunmore. Girty allegedly promised to do whatever he could to save the American officer. But he knew the Indians were in no mood for clemency. The Moravian massacre was too fresh in their minds. Crawford could be neither released to Girty nor ransomed by some trader

The identity of the man in this portrait is not certain, but some historians believe it to be a likeness of Simon Girty. It does fit verbal descriptions of the "White Savage." (M. Malott)

Simon Girty's monument near Amherstberg, Ontario. His unmarked grave is somewhere in the background. (H. I. Johnson)

Bill Johnston, the Pirate of the Thousand Islands and self-styled "Patriot Admiral" in the 1837 Rebellion. (PAC#C-329)

Fort Whoop Up, most notorious of the whiskey posts American outlaws established on Canadian soil. Note the cannon, the loopholed walls of the bastion, and John Healy's personal banner. (PAC#C-17492)

Jerry Poetts, the tough, laconic plainsman who guided the NWMP to Fort Whoop Up in 1875. (PAC#C-1792C)

James MacLeod

James Macleod and Sam
Steele, members of the original
force that chased the whiskey
traders out of western Canada.
(PAC#C-17494B, #PA-28146)

Sam Steele

Allan

Charlie

The murderous McLean Gang—Allan, Charlie, Archie, and their pal Alex Hare at the New Westminster Penitentiary. (Provincial Archives of British Columbia, #3387, #3389, #3390, #3386)

The cabin near Douglas Lake where, after a shootout, the McLean Gang finally was taken into custody. (Provincial Archives of British Columbia, #3388)

Archie

Alex

This photograph, circa 1894, is alleged to be Almighty Voice, the Cree Indian whose career in outlawry was launched when he killed a cow. (Saskatchewan Archives Board, #RB-4512)

The North West Mounted Police guarding the bluff where they finally caught up with Almighty Voice in May 1897. (Saskatchewan Archives Board, #RB-4522)

Bill Miner, the "Gentleman Bandit," at the time of his capture in 1906. (Provincial Archives of British Columbia, #B-3597)

Bill Miner, with his accomplices and captors, before the Kamloops Provincial Jail. (Provincial Archives of British Columbia, #B-3244)

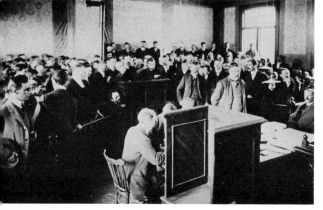

The train robbers on trial in Kamloops. Bill Miner and Lewis Colquin occupy the prisoners' box. Shorty Dunn is leaning on the railing to the left. (Provincial Archives of British Columbia, #B-2860)

The Mad Trapper's cabin on Rat River after it was blown up by the Mounties. (Glenbow Archives, Calgary)

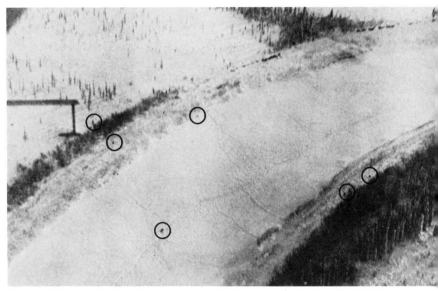

Aerial photograph, taken by Wop May, of the final shoot-out between the Mounties and the Mad Trapper. The outlaw is in the centre of the river, caught in a three-way crossfire. (Glenbow Archives, Calgary)

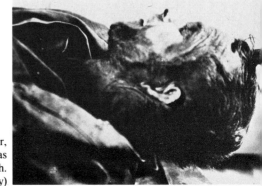

The Mad Trapper of Rat River, known but never confirmed as Albert Johnson, in death. (Glenbow Archives, Calgary)

for tobacco and rum. A council which included the Delaware Chief Captain Pipe condemned both Crawford and Knight to the stake. Another Delaware chief, Wingenund, who had been a friend of Crawford's before the war, told the officer, "If Williamson had been taken, you might have been saved, but as it is, no one would dare to interfere on your behalf. The King of England, if he were to come in person, could not save you."

Dr. Knight, who witnessed the torture and later escaped, gives an account of Crawford's death and of Girty's involvement:

> The Colonel was stripped naked, ordered to sit down by the fire, and then they beat him with sticks and with their fists.... The Colonel then called to Girty and asked if they intended to burn him. Girty answered yes. The Colonel said he would take it all patiently.... The Indian men then took up their guns and shot powder into the Colonel's body, from his feet as far up as his neck. I think not less than seventy loads were discharged upon his naked body. They then crowded about him and to the best of my observation cut off his ears.... Three or four Indians would take up individually burning pieces of wood and apply it to his naked body already burned black with the powder. These tormentors presented themselves on every side of him, so that whichever way he ran around the post they met him with burning faggots and poles. Some of the squaws took broad boards upon which they would put a quantity of burning embers and hot coals and throw on him, so that in a short time he had nothing but coals of fire and hot ashes to walk upon.... In the midst of these extreme tortures he called upon Simon Girty and begged of him to shoot him. But Girty making no answer he called to him again. Girty then by way of derision told the Colonel he had no gun, at the

same time turning to an Indian who was behind him,
laughed heartily, and by all his gestures seemed delighted at the horrid scene. Girty then came up to me and
bade me prepare for death....

Crawford proved a rather poor subject for the death
ritual, and after about two hours one of the Indians bashed
out his brains with a tomahawk.

Simon Girty's reputation as a monster rests almost
entirely on Knight's story. Singled out as a sadistic beast, he
became one of the most hated men in American history.
Little attention was paid to witnesses in the Indian camp,
including one anonymous American woman prisoner who
reported that both Girty and Elliot tried to save Crawford
and that Girty argued to the point where his own life was
threatened. Both men, in later years, insisted they had
pleaded for Crawford's life, offering the Indians everything
they had, including Girty's prized white horse. Apart from
any question of humanity, an officer of Crawford's importance would have been a valuable prisoner for the British.
Moreover, he had told Girty and Elliot that he would
"communicate something of importance" if he could be
spared.

Once Crawford was dead, the Indians slapped Knight
across the face with the colonel's bloody scalp and told him
he would be next. Then, for some reason, they decided to
send him to another town. Knight was accompanied by
only a single Indian, and on the way there, he bashed the
man on the head with a piece of wood and escaped. At
least, that was his story. After many days of wandering in
the forest he arrived at an American fort and reported all he
had been through.

There is no evidence that Knight's escape was engineered
by Girty. But the doctor's almost miraculous deliverance
bears a striking resemblance to that of Simon Kenton.

In August of 1782, two months after Crawford's defeat,
Indians and Rangers led by Girty and Caldwell laid siege to

Bryan's Station in Kentucky. They had hoped to catch the Americans by surprise and were unaware their approach had been reported to the defenders. What followed, if the story is true, was one of the truly heroic acts of the war.

The station had no water supply of its own, depending on water from a nearby stream. Without water, it could not withstand a siege of more than two or three days. A party of women volunteered to go out unarmed, knowing that the woods were filled with hostile Indians, and to bring back water in buckets. They reasoned that this action would lead the attackers to believe the station was wholly unprepared for an assault.

It did, indeed, achieve its purpose. The Indians and Canadians believed that the stockade had not been alerted and that they could rush the gates at any time. Instead, the moment that the water bearers were back inside, the gate was slammed shut, and the stockade bristled with armed men.

Failing to take the fort by assault or guile, the attackers decided to starve it into submission. For several days they sniped across the stumpfields surrounding the stockade. Once an arrow flew through a cabin window and lodged in the framework of a cradle in which the infant Richard Johnson, future Vice-President of the United States, was sleeping. When Girty tried to talk the defenders into surrender, a brazen young rebel named Aaron Reynolds called him "a good-for-nothing dog."

Indian patience was wearing thin and the squalor inside the fort was growing unbearable when scouts brought word to Girty and Caldwell that a relief force led by Daniel Boone was approaching. The attackers withdrew, taking care to leave a visible trail, and at a crossing of the Licking River known as "Blue Licks" they laid a carefully prepared ambush.

The men from the fort joined Boone's company and went in pursuit of the Great Renegade. Ignoring Boone's advice to be cautious, the Kentucky militia rode right into the trap at Blue Licks. Within five minutes they were shot to pieces. Boone was able to organize a rearguard to defend the retreat and in so doing prevented the militia from being entirely wiped out. One of those killed was Boone's son Israel. Blue Licks was one of the worst defeats the Kentucky militia, famous among revolutionary armies, ever suffered and was Girty's greatest moment of triumph. It was one of the last battles of the American War of Independence. Shortly afterward word reached the frontier that Cornwallis had surrendered to the French and the Americans at Yorktown, thus ending the war.

The Indians were stunned by the British surrender and resentful of the double-dealing by which their allies signed Indian lands over to the Americans, just as though they owned them (which they didn't). Some followed Mohawk Chief Joseph Brant to a new home in Upper Canada. Others were determined to save what they could from the Americans, by peaceful treaty if possible, by war if necessary.

Thousands of Loyalist refugees sailed to the British Isles or to British lands in the Caribbean, but the greatest number moved to Britain's Canadian colonies. Among those granted land in Canada were Simon, James, and George Girty. Simon had been raiding in the vicinity of Fort Pitt when he was told of the surrender and at first refused to believe it. The truth did not register until he returned to Detroit and was ordered to release his prisoners. He now had good reason for moving to Canada. He was an outlaw with a price on his head and had a young wife to protect.

Catharine Mallot, a native of Maryland, was eighteen or nineteen years old and a captive in a Delaware camp near the end of the war when Girty, over forty, saw her and was instantly smitten by her. She had been a prisoner for four years. He arranged her release and married her. They settled on a grant of land near Amherstburg, just south of Windsor and Detroit. There they began to farm, but the domestic life of farmer and husband could not hold Girty's interest for long.

Indians to the south were still resisting American conquest, and British garrisons had refused to abandon their posts in Indian lands. British traders in the ceded territory continued to benefit from the fur trade. The army even built a new post and named it Fort Miami.

For several years Girty engaged in this illegal warfare against the Americans, dividing his time between Canada and the Ohio Valley where he continued to act as intermediary between the fur traders and the Indians. Again he arranged the release of several prisoners, including one American woman who had been bought from the Indians as a slave and was being mistreated by her white owner. Girty's sympathy for the Indians had in no way diminished. He encouraged them to drive a hard bargain over the surrender of their territory, and American officials reporting on the treaty talks complained of his "insolence" toward them.

The inevitable war came in 1790 when General Josiah Harmar led an American army against the Indians and was driven back by skillful and determined defence. Simon Girty, Matthew Elliot, and Alexander McKee were probably responsible for Harmar's defeat. A year later General Arthur St. Clair led another army against the tribes of the northwest and again was defeated. Among those in the council of victors this time were Simon Girty and a rising young Shawnee chief named Tecumseh. For the next three years the frontier was a "dark and bloody ground" as Indians raided at will and Dirty Girty was again the scourge of the American frontier. According to the stories brought back to the eastern American cities, he was everywhere, including several places at the same time. Whenever an American saw a white face among Indian raiders, it was reported as a sighting of the White Savage.

By this time the middle-aged Girty must have been an unnerving sight to any American frontiersman. He was not only a long-standing object of almost superstitious terror, but he *looked* the part. Although of only medium height, he was heavy set and muscular. He had a wild mop of black hair and wore a red bandanna like a pirate to hide an ugly scar that he had received in a drunken brawl with Joseph Brant. He was always armed to the teeth, with knife, tomahawk, brace of silver-plated pistols, as well as his rifle— looking every inch the wild man of legend.

But his days as a freedom-fighter were running out. What he was now doing could only be a desperate rearguard fight. In June 1794 Girty joined the Indian attack on Fort Recovery. It failed. In August General Anthony Wayne (called Mad Anthony because of his reckless style of fighting) routed the Indians at the Battle of Fallen Timbers. British prestige reached a new low with the tribes of the northwest when Fort Miami refused to open its gates to the fleeing Indians.

Wayne's victory ended Indian hopes for an independent nation in the northwest. They were forced to cede vast tracts of land. The British agreed to hand over all posts south of the Great Lakes, including Detroit. Loyalists still living in the northwest pulled up stakes and headed for Canada. Many of them set fire to their farms before they left and filled their wells with stones.

Simon Girty was one of the last to leave. When American troops came to take possession of Detroit in 1796, he was in the town, roaring drunk, declaring that he wouldn't move except at gunpoint. But when he saw boatloads of American soldiers bearing down on him, he leaped on his horse, plunged into the river, and swam the animal across, gaining the Canadian shore far downstream. Looking back at the land where he had been branded a traitor and outlaw, he unleashed volleys of oaths at the American soldiers who had come so close to capturing him.

The only time Girty crossed the river after that was during the War of 1812 when Detroit surrendered to General Brock. Canada would be Girty's refuge for the rest of his life. But his life was by no means tame, for all that. He was wild, demonstrative, and violent. Indeed, he seems to have grown more violent as he grew older. He used to ride through the town of Amherstburg roaring drunk, brandishing weapons, shouting Indian war whoops. He bullied and beat his wife, and she finally left him after bearing four of his children.

During the War of 1812 Girty was too old for active fighting, but he probably did some interpreting for the Canadian forces who were once again enlisting Indian allies. Girty's eldest son, Thomas, died trying to help a wounded officer off the field during a battle. With an American invasion imminent in 1813, Girty fled to Burlington Heights to live with the Indians. The people there were a generation younger than the stout warriors who had fought at his side twenty and thirty years before. They regarded him as a drunken, cranky old man who had to be fed and tolerated. He had no place in the councils. He tried to hunt with Indian parties, but his eyesight was failing.

In 1816 he returned to Malden and lived with his son Prideaux. Catherine moved back to take care of him as he was now almost totally blind, crippled by rheumatism, and lamed by a broken ankle that had never healed properly. Most of his time was spent in an Amherstburg tavern owned by his daughter Ann and her husband, Peter Govereaux— he had no trouble travelling between the tavern and his farm because his horse knew the way and would carry him back and forth even when he was dead drunk. He would sway and fall asleep in the saddle, but he never fell off, even if he passed out.

In the United States a story was circulating that the White Savage had been killed at the Battle of the Thames in 1813, fighting beside Tecumseh. The Americans needed *something* to brag about. Their repeated invasions of Canada had all been defeated, and from the Detroit River to Lake Ontario not a single American soldier remained on Canadian soil when the war ended. A pity, perhaps, that Girty could not have died in battle, as rumour had it. His end was sadder and anything but heroic. He caught a chill while riding home drunk from the tavern one cold winter night and died in bed on February 18, 1818, at the age of seventy-seven.

Although he had never been a British soldier, the garrison at Fort Malden decided to give him the honour of a military burial. They lowered him into frozen ground through deep snow, fired a volley over his grave, then left him to become the White Savage of American legend. Although his grave is unmarked today, a small monument near his old homestead commemorates his long service to the British Indian Department.

CHAPTER 9

MASTERLESS MEN

DURING THE YEARS that Simon Girty was aiding the Indians around Lake Erie in their last stand against the Americans, a band of outlaws of a very different sort was ranging the far-off forests of Newfoundland. Visitors to the Southern Shore—that picturesque strip of coastline that runs almost due south from St. John's to Cape Race—will see as they drive from Ferryland to Cappahayden a prominent spur of rock rising to a height of almost one thousand feet some five or six miles inland. This is the Southern Butter Pot, formerly the lookout point and eastern boundary of the territory ruled by the Masterless Men.

Various prominent hills in Newfoundland are called the Butter Pot, the best known of which is in Butter Pot Provincial Park, overlooking the town of Holyrood and the waters of Conception Bay. The *southern* Butter Pot overlooks a wild stretch of Atlantic Ocean and the coastline where such pirates as Peter Easton, Captain Jacob Everson, the man known only as Lewis, and heaven only knows how many others, found haven.

Behind the Butter Pot lies a stretch of caribou barrens, woodlands, and bogs running southward and westward to St. Mary's Bay and Placentia Bay. A herd of between one and two thousand woodland caribou is found there today.

As many as five or six thousand of the same animals may have roamed those barrens in the closing years of the eighteenth century when the Masterless Men lived there under the leadership of an Irish deserter from the Royal Navy named Peter Kerrivan.

The term "masterless men" goes back at least to the reign of King Henry VIII of England who signed into law Acts of Parliament dealing with beggars and vagrants. One such act decreed that any person "having no land, master, nor using any lawful merchandise, craft or mystery" should be taken to the nearest market town and there be tied naked to the end of a cart and beaten with whips throughout the same market town till his body be bloody by reason of such whipping. Masterless Men were vagrants and potential outlaws who, after being suitably scourged, were sent back to the town where they were born or where they had last spent three successive years, there to be hired out to labour "as decent men ought."

In Newfoundland a "masterless man" was a fishing apprentice or seasonal labourer who had run away from a planter or English fishing master or else a deserter from the Royal Navy who had escaped from the floggings, starvation, and scurvy that were still the lot of men serving before the mast—"scum of the ports" as their officers called them, swept up by press gangs, shanghaied, and working as slaves in all but name on His Majesty's ships of war.

At the end of the eighteenth century when Napoleon was ravaging Europe, Ferryland was a fortified town and a major centre of the fishery. A century and a half earlier it had been the seat of the first royal governor of Newfoundland, Sir David Kirke. In Kerrivan's time, the 1790s and the early 1800s, it had magistrates, a court house of some kind, and, in addition to its shore batteries on the cliffs and on the fortified Isle aux Bois, its harbour usually held a British warship.

Those who had sinned by deed or by neglect against the harsh laws of the time were brought to Ferryland to be tried and punished. The flogging of naked men at the cart tail had been replaced in the reign of Elizabeth by less scandalous if no less brutal forms of punishment at the whipping post and the pillory. The little town of Ferryland had three whipping posts set up along its waterfront, one at either end of the harbour and one at the centre. A servant who had wronged his master or committed some other minor crime such as stealing a gallon of rum would be taken to each place in turn to receive a dozen or more lashes with the cat-o'-nine-tails. More serious crimes were punishel ùith hanging or deportation, that is to say, with temporary or permanent enslavement to a plantation owner in Virginia or, later, in Australia.

There were strict laws regarding servants in the fishery. Every fishing master was responsible for the men he employed and had the power to dock their wages, pay debts on their behalf, hire them out to others, and work them up to twenty hours a day. Every shipowner or captain who brought men from England or Ireland to serve in the fishery was responsible to see that he took the same number of men when he returned in the autumn. If not, he was liable to a fine of ten pounds for each missing head that he could not account for. The object of this law was to prevent "masterless men" from running loose in the colony. But the law was not very effective and was probably not often enforced. Ten pounds was still a lot of money in those times, equal to a man's seasonal earnings in the fishery provided he was industrious, prudent, and lucky. Most fishing servants ended the summer with far less than ten pounds. After the cost of their food and their daily ration of rum was deducted, they might have a few shillings coming, or they might not—the chance that any of them could buy his independence with as much as ten pounds was rather remote. If they simply left their stations to seek their fortunes in the colonies, they would be in debt to the captain who brought them out—and debt was a serious offence in those times. Small wonder that some of them ran off to live by their wits or by petty crime.

It was against this background that the Masterless Men of the Butter Pot Barrens emerged. We know very little about Peter Kerrivan, the leader and organizer of the band, except that he was from Ireland originally, that he was young, and that he was a wily outlaw who managed to evade the best efforts of the British authorities to capture him. He was probably a born leader with a gift for organization because, in a colony where the same conditions prevailed along many hundreds of miles of coastline, this was the only place where the Masterless Men formed a community and left some mark on history.

Near the Butter Pot they built an inland settlement of sorts—a shacktown—from which they ranged inland and up and down the coast, living partly by hunting and partly by plunder.

The Oral History of Ferryland, recorded by Howard Morry of that town and by John Hawkins of nearby Cape Broyle in the 1950s, has much to say about the Masterless Men. They were, according to Morry and Hawkins, "country men" who had learned to live and hunt like Indians. The caribou herd was their staff of life. They lived mainly on meat and learned to dress deerskins and used them for clothing almost exclusively. They were semi-nomadic, following the deer, but this would not involve long journeys, for the Avalon herd had little space in which to "migrate." Its seasonal wanderings would cover no more than fifty miles or so.

One or two Micmac Indians may have been associated with the Masterless Men. By their time the native Beothuk Indians of Newfoundland were nearly extinct, and the few remaining were hiding out in the most remote parts of the island where they would soon be sought out by white men and murdered. They had been replaced by Micmacs from Nova Scotia, an Indian tribe that was better able to deal with Europeans. The Micmacs lived mainly in the central and south part of the island, but some of them ranged over all parts of the 42,000 square miles of Newfoundland, including the Avalon Peninsula. According to the *Oral History of Ferryland*, Robert Carter, the most prominent landowner of the Ferryland settlement, shot and killed an Indian in the hills above Ferryland, and it would seem that the Indian in question must have been Micmac because by that date there were no Beothuks anywhere in eastern Newfoundland.

The Masterless Men traded surreptitiously with settlers in out-of-the-way fishing villages, exchanging meat and hides, and probably furs as well, for such supposed essentials as flour, molasses, and rum. If they couldn't get these "essentials" in any other way, they stole them from the fishing rooms where they also took nets, cordage, guns, and ammunition—things that they found difficult to obtain by trade.

Naturally, this set the merchants and fishing masters against them, and these pillars of respectability complained to the colonial authorities, who in turn complained to the Navy, the only effective law-enforcement agency in Newfoundland at the time. Since the Masterless Men included deserters from the Royal Navy, the navy itself had a stake in bringing them to "justice"—that is to say, in capturing them and stringing them up to a yardarm as an example to any others who might be tempted to choose a life of hardship and freedom rather than a life of hardship and slavery.

Kerrivan's Masterless Men were, in a sense, Newfoundland's first road builders. They were the first Europeans to live in the interior where coastal waters could not provide them with transport, and they had chosen a place where no rivers of any size provided canoe routes. So they cut and improved trails paralleling the coastline far enough inland to be on high, relatively dry ground. They also cut trails right across the interior of the Avalon Peninsula to St. Mary's Bay and Placentia Bay, throwing rough bridges across streams and building corduroy duckwalks over peat bogs. Kerrivan, however, was nobody's fool. He knew that even the roughest road could lead the British Navy straight to his door. So some of the most promising-looking roads built by the Masterless Men were false trails leading into a morass of bogland and there petering out to nothing.

It was a wise precaution. The navy sent at least three expeditions into the interior to try to round up the Masterless Men and bring them to Ferryland for hanging. These expeditions accomplished little. They found and burned at least some of the shacks at the Butter Pot, not once, but repeatedly. The shacks, however, were empty of men and chattels when they arrived. Everything that could be moved had disappeared into the woods, for the Butter Pot was an excellent lookout from which to see a troop of marines marching inland from the coast.

The shacks were easy to rebuild. The expeditions got lost in the bogs. At least twice they returned empty handed. But once they returned with two (some accounts say four) prisoners—most likely young recruits to the band recently run off from the ships or the fishing stations and not yet wise to the ways of the woods. The marines never did catch up with their principal quarry, Kerrivan himself, or the main body of his followers. They had to be content with hanging the two (or four) outlaws who had fallen into their hands.

Howard Morry reported that his grandmother, then a child of perhaps five, was taken by her mother from their home in the village of Aquaforte to Ferryland to see the outlaws hanging from the yardarm of the naval frigate where, presumably, their bodies were left for some time "as an example to evil doers." Such examples were expected to impress small children with the wages of sin, and the sight must, indeed, have impressed the child in question because she remembered it and described it to her grandchildren some seventy years later. The date of the hanging seems to have been 1810 or thereabouts.

After that, so far as we know, the Masterless Men were left in peace by the British authorities, and perhaps they also became more cautious, but in any case they continued to live in the backwoods and to trade with (or prey upon) the plantations until the War of 1812 gave anyone who wanted it all the employment, adventure, and opportunity for quick riches he could desire. Those who shrank from serving in the regiments of "fencibles," who went from Newfoundland and Nova Scotia to do battle with the Yankees, could always get berths on the privateers—licensed pirates who were authorized to prey on American merchant shipping and to keep the loot they captured. During the war whole fleets of them from both sides ranged up and down the Atlantic seaboard, north and south through the Gulf of St. Lawrence, and even to the coast of Labrador.

Some of the Masterless Men were certainly absorbed by the War of 1812 in which Newfoundland took a very active part, while others became respectable settlers. By 1818 or 1820 they had disappeared. As social conditions began to improve, as settlement was encouraged rather than discouraged as it had been formerly, it became possible for the Masterless Men to move quietly back to the coast—not to St. John's or Ferryland or Placentia or any other centre of law and order, perhaps, but to little outports where there were no resident magistrates or police. There they took up the occupation, just then becoming respectable, of independent fishermen.

By the 1820s or 1830s it was possible for a poor man without property to live as an independent settler, no longer needing to be bound to a fishing master to prove his legitimacy but owning his own small house and boat and making his living with his own hands. By that date a "squatter" could even build a house on crown land if it was otherwise unoccupied and after a generation or so could legally claim it as his own simply by virtue of long occupation. This was doubtless what happened to most of the Masterless Men. As social conditions changed, they simply melted into the population of the more remote fishing outports where their descendants are still living today.

Their roads remained behind them and continued in use. When the Newfoundland government instituted regular postal service in the reign of Victoria, the mail was taken on foot from St. John's by postal carriers who travelled routes of approximately fifty miles out and back, their mail sacks on their backs, handing over the sacks at designated points to other carriers and receiving return mail to be delivered on their route. The carriers who operated from St. John's to Cape Race along the Southern Shore, delivering mail to such places as Bay Bulls, Cape Broyle, Ferryland, and Cappahayden, travelled over roads cut out of the bush by the Masterless Men. Their roads overland to the western bays disappeared, but the roads they opened parallel to the shore remained in use until they were replaced by a branch railway line early in the twentieth century and, later, by a modern highway.

Between the two American wars, the War of Independence and the War of 1812, the British North American colonies were in a state of great turmoil and sharply divided loyalty. Much of their trade with America was illegal. Many of the merchants had business connections along the American seaboard and depended on three-way trade between Canada, the United States, and the West Indies—trade that, according to British law, was the monopoly of British firms. It was all very confusing and adding to the confusion was the feeling among at least half the population of English Canada that their eventual destiny lay with republican America rather than with far-off monarchist England.

Out of this turmoil emerged two of the later pirate captains of the east coast, one of them the most successful native-born Canadian pirate of all time, the other a pirate of no real distinction except the negative distinction of being the last man hanged for piracy in Canada.

Samuel Nelson was a Prince Edward Islander, born somewhere around the time of the American War of Independence. His father, John Nelson, was a prosperous landowner
who received his first grant of crown land "for cultivation
and for pasture" near Charlottetown on September 5, 1796.
By 1805, when Samuel Nelson married, the family had
become so well-to-do that his father was able to give him a
farm as a wedding present. He also received a commission
in the militia, but neither farming nor soldiering particularly
appealed to him. He had a taste for trade and for the sea.
He bought a brig and set up as a small merchant trading to
Halifax.

The Nova Scotia capital was at that time an important
military fortress, the strongest and best-garrisoned British
post in the world outside Great Britain, and a major con-
sumer of agricultural products. Nelson flourished for a time
as a merchant trading between Prince Edward Island and
Halifax. Then he fell into some kind of disgrace, said to be a
scandalous sexual adventure, and lost his commission. He
left his wife, now the mother of several children, at home in
Prince Edward Island and went off to live in Halifax, where
he received a new commission as a lieutenant in the Nova
Scotia Fencibles.

In Halifax he met a retired privateer named Morrison
who believed that there might be opportunities to exploit
the trade with the former American colonies, especially
because of their willingness to accept cargoes from British
colonial possessions without demanding strict accounting as
to their origin. Morrison had the knowledge and the experience of the privateering trade. Nelson had the money to
finance a voyage. They formed a partnership and bought an
American sloop mounting ten guns.

From the Nova Scotia fishing fleet they recruited a crew
of some ninety men willing to risk their necks for a fast buck
and began their piracies by capturing a trading brig inward
bound with a cargo from Europe. They then sailed the brig
to New York, posing as shipowners and traders, and sold
both ship and cargo at a fair price.

With this comfortable start and a good supply of powder and shot, they next sailed to the West Indies, where they began raiding both the shipping and the plantations. In the West Indies Nelson and his crew acted with great ruthlessness and barbarity. They are reported to have tortured and killed the officers of captured ships and to have murdered both planters and slaves during their raids on the smaller, undefended islands.

Fortunately, although the islands were not defended by forts, there were British sloops-of-war cruising among them. Nelson soon had these pirate-hunters hot on his heels. He fled northward along the Gulf Stream and escaped to the American ports, again paying a visit to New York to dispose of his loot.

After that Nelson and Morrison made a division of the spoils and paid off many of their crewmen, but their piracies were by no means at an end. Sailing northward with a small crew in their ten-gun sloop, they raised the south coast of Newfoundland where they captured ten fishing ships, recruited more crewmen, and replenished their supplies. Some of the captured ships they released. Others they sent to New York for sale.

Wealthy, and perhaps thinking of retiring while they had the chance, Nelson and Morrison sailed to Prince Edward Island, where Nelson was reunited with his estranged wife. But while coasting the shore of his native island, he ran his ship aground in foul weather. Morrison and some of the crewmen were drowned, but Nelson got safely ashore and rejoined his family.

At that point, if not before, he decided to retire from piracy. He now had a fortune estimated at 150,000 pounds (several million dollars in today's funds). He sold his farm and took his family to New York, where he set up as a legitimate merchant trader.

That was the end of Captain Nelson's connection with Prince Edward Island, but other members of his family remained prominent there. Another Samuel Nelson, possibly the son of the retired pirate, bought land there in 1817, apparently from an older member of the family named John (possibly his grandfather), and remained prominent in land transactions until 1851.

A second John Nelson, probably a younger brother of the pirate, married there in 1815 and had three sons and five daughters whose descendants are living today both in Prince Edward Island and in the United States. There is a tradition in the family that this John Nelson became a sea captain engaged in trade to the Far East, and that he was eventually lost at sea in a passage around Cape Horn.

Edward Jordan, the pirate from Gaspé, had been an Irish rebel before immigrating to Canada. In 1797 he was among the leaders who were secretly training volunteers for the "rebellion of '98." He was caught drilling a company of pikemen at night, tried for treason, and sentenced to death by the English.

Before the execution could be carried out, he escaped and rejoined the rebels. After the failure of the rebellion the following year, the government of Great Britain offered an amnesty to those who would surrender their arms. Jordan took advantage of this and later went to eastern Canada by way of New York and Montreal, acquiring a wife, Margaret, on the way. The family settled at Gaspé, where Edward Jordan served as a fishing shareman with a merchant from St. John's, Newfoundland. After five years' service he had accumulated enough money to begin building his own ship.

In June of 1808 Jordan began trading with the Halifax firm of J. and J. Tremain, and in September of that year they extended him sufficient credit to permit him to complete and outfit the schooner which he then had on the stocks at Gaspé. As security, they took a mortgage on the ship.

In July of 1809 he was in Halifax again, with his schooner, the *Three Sisters* (named for his three younger children). There he was arrested for debt, but his merchant suppliers paid off what was owing and sent him back to Gaspé to collect a cargo of fish. No longer trusting him, however, they sent Captain John Stairs to supervise the transaction and to take possession of the vessel if Jordan should prove unable to pay off the mortgage.

According to Stairs, Jordan had promised the merchants one thousand quintals (approximately 51,000 kilos) of dried fish but was able to deliver only a hundred or so—not nearly enough to clear his debt. Stairs took possession of the ship in the name of J. and J. Tremain and collected from the surrounding fishing rooms a cargo of some 600 quintals. Then he sailed for Halifax with Jordan and his family as passengers.

The *Three Sisters* was a 45-foot schooner with a very high stern and a very wide beam. Jordan must have been very fond of his ship and very proud of her. He had painted her in striking colours of black, white, and yellow. Losing her to the merchants must have been a crushing blow.

Besides Captain John Stairs, there were four crewmen on the voyage from Gaspé to Halifax. The mate was an Irishman named John Kelly. The seamen were Benjamin Matthews and Thomas Heath. With Edward and Margaret Jordan were their nine-year-old son and their three younger daughters.

Shortly before noon on September 13, 1809, the *Three Sisters* was about four miles off shore between Cape Canso and White Head, on course for Halifax. The whole Jordan family was on deck and the mate, John Kelly, was at the tiller. Captain Stairs went below with crewman Thomas Heath and was consulting a book or a chart when he saw a shadow cross the skylight. Looking up he saw Jordan pointing a pistol at him. He jumped as the pistol fired. The bullet grazed his cheek and lodged in Heath's chest.

"My God, I'm killed!" Heath cried, falling to the floor. Stairs rushed to his sea chest where he kept a brace of pistols but found the lock broken and the pistols gone. Overhead he heard several more shots. It was Jordan killing Matthews, the other sailor.

Stairs rushed up the companionway and met Jordan on the top step brandishing a pistol in one hand an an axe in the other. Stairs's rush carried the two of them out on deck, and as Stairs was trying to wrestle the weapons away from Jordan, the pistol snapped without going off. It was a misfire. Stairs wrenched the gun from Jordan's hand and threw it over the side. Almost incredibly, the unarmed captain managed to get the axe away from Jordan as well. But just then Margaret Jordan rushed up with a boathook and joined the fray. Captain Stairs rushed forward, followed by the two Jordans, Margaret with the boathook and Edward with another axe. Seeing a loose hatch cover, he threw it overboard and dived after it, caught it, and hung on.

There was a strong wind and the ship was making fast time. Captain Stairs was quickly left in her wake, and Jordan rushed aft, planning to take the second pistol from Kelly, who was still at the tiller, and finish the captain off. But Kelly persuaded him that Stairs was sure to drown anyway, so they kept on course until they could trim the sails, then bore away eastward.

At about 3:30 that afternoon an American fishing schooner, the *Eliza* under Captain Levi Stoddard, fished Captain Stairs out of the water "almost lifeless" and took him to Hingham, Massachusetts, the *Eliza*'s home port. From there Stairs went to Boston, saw the British consul, and had an alarm sent out for Jordan's arrest. The governor at Halifax offered a reward of one hundred pounds for the pirate's capture.

Meanwhile, Jordan, assisted by his wife and Kelly, sailed the *Three Sisters* into Fortune Bay on Newfoundland's south coast and dropped anchor at Little Bay West, a tiny fishing hamlet in a well-hidden cove a few miles from the important fishing settlement of Harbour Breton.

Here they attempted to enlist two fishermen, William Crew and John Pigot, but the men were suspicious of the odd-looking schooner carrying as crew only two men, a woman, and four small children. They also noted the missing hatch cover and the cargo of fish which was not stowed as it should be for a foreign voyage. They refused to sign on.

At this point John Kelly went ashore, located a magistrate (presumably at Harbour Breton), and told him of his pressing need for seamen. The magistrate called in Pigot who was unemployed and threatened to have him tied up and flogged if he refused to join the ship—all this according to Pigot's sworn testimony given later at the trial.

Under duress Pigot joined the ship. They then rounded the Burin Peninsula, crossed Placentia Bay, and ran into St. Mary's, where they attempted to recruit more seamen, without success. They then rounded Cape Race and began calling at ports along the Southern Shore between Cape Race and St. John's, looking for a qualified deep-sea navigator and giving out the information that they were preparing to make a voyage to Ireland.

They found a qualified man named John Power and signed him on for eleven pounds a month—a high wage indeed for a navigator in 1809, at least twice the going rate. Along the Southern Shore they also signed on four sailors, making a total of six crewmen recruited in Newfoundland.

Meanwhile, Mrs. Jordan had been sharing her favours between her husband and the mate, Kelly, and this led to a fight in which Kelly tried to shoot Jordan but was prevented by the navigator, Power. Kelly then stole a boat and rowed ashore where he disappeared.

Finally the *Three Sisters* sailed for Ireland, but she was only about one hour offshore when she was challenged by the Canadian coastguard ship *Cuttle* which had been sent along the Newfoundland coast with the specific mission of finding her and arresting the three pirates, Edward and Margaret Jordan and John Kelly.

Believing Stairs to be dead, Jordan tried to bluff it out, saying he was blown off course while bound for Halifax, but the *Cuttle* took everyone on board the *Three Sisters* to Halifax as prisoners and sailed the ship into port with a prize crew.

The Newfoundlanders were quickly cleared of blame and released, but the two Jordans, man and wife, were put on trial for piracy. It was a full-dress Vice-Admiralty trial presided over by the Governor, with the captains of naval vessels at the Halifax station as judges.

Margaret Jordan was pardoned, but Edward Jordan was hanged in chains on the Halifax waterfront. Finally, in a storm his skeleton blew to pieces and was washed into the sea. Many years later his skull was picked up at the tide line and was preserved in the Halifax museum.

John Kelly was arrested in Newfoundland, tried, convicted, and sentenced to death, but afterwards pardoned — perhaps because he'd had no actual hand in the murders, although he had certainly aided and abetted Jordan's piracy.

A charitable fund was started in Halifax for Margaret Jordan and her four small children, and eventually they took passage for Ireland.

Although Jordan was the last Canadian hanged for piracy, four other men, all guilty of piracy, were hanged for murder at Halifax thirty-five years later. The series of events began in October 1843 when Captain George Fielding and his fourteen-year-old son George Jr. sailed from Liverpool, Nova Scotia, in the *Vitula* for ports in South America. Fielding's ship was seized and sold for smuggling by the government of Peru, and he and his son got passage on the *Saladin*, bound for London.

With several members of the *Saladin*'s crew, Fielding hatched a plot to kill the captain and take over the ship. They carried out the plan, murdering six men altogether, and Fielding took command of the vessel. But he and his son were murdered in their turn by the conspirators.

The six surviving crewmen knew nothing about navigation and, after beating about the Atlantic for some weeks, they ran the ship ashore, with all sails set, on an island off the coast of Nova Scotia. They were arrested and taken to Halifax for trial. The whole story of the *Saladin* murders was that of a sordid, drunken brawl, scarcely deserving to be called piracy. In fact, the survivors were not accused of piracy, but of murder. Nevertheless, the press made a great issue of the "Saladin Pirates." Two of them turned Queen's evidence and were reprieved. Four of them were convicted and were hanged together on Halifax Commons, creating a great sensation. The date of the hanging was July 30, 1844.

CHAPTER 10

THE PIRATE OF THE THOUSAND ISLANDS

THE NIGHT OF MAY 29, 1838, was rainy and cold as the Canadian steamer *Sir Robert Peel* bound from Brockville to Kingston stopped for firewood at Wells Island in the St. Lawrence River. The Thousand Islands, now a great summer resort filling the upper course of the river where it empties out of Lake Ontario, were then the haunt of bands of brigands whose numbers had been increased by refugees from the recent rebellions in Upper and Lower Canada. When the rebels were crushed by the army, hundreds of them had fled, some with a price on their heads, all of them liable, if caught, to be hanged or transported to the penal colonies in Van Diemen's Land, as the island of Tasmania was then called.

As the *Sir. Robert Peel* dropped anchor at Wells Island, a man named Ripley approached the captain and told him he had seen a longboat full of men prowling the narrow waterway as they had approached. Moreover, he had heard a shout, "Here she comes!" The captain laughed at him. He was not afraid, he said, of any gang of ruffians in a boat unless they numbered more than a hundred men.

That was a grave mistake. At two o'clock in the morning, while most of the crew were still ashore and the sixty-five passengers were soundly asleep in their cabins, a band of twenty to twenty-five armed men dressed as Indians with painted faces stole out of the woods, boarded the *Sir Robert Peel*, and captured the ship with hardly a show of resistance.

The "Indians" went whooping about the decks with cries of "revenge for the *Caroline*." The captain well understood the import of this war cry. The Canadians had burned the American steamer *Caroline* a few months earlier while she was attempting to land supplies at the rebel base on Navy Island in the Niagara River—one of the centres of the short-lived rebellion led by William Lyon Mackenzie.

The attackers, armed with rifles, pistols, bayonets, swords, and pikes, placed a guard at the gangway to prevent the shore party from coming on board the ship. Then they smashed the cabin doors, hauled the lightly clad men and women out of their berths, and prodded them onto the deck with gun butts and bayonets. The pirates beat several of the men and were about to kill one of them who was wearing the coat of a British officer when the frightened man convinced them that the coat was not his own, so they spared his life and let him off with a beating.

The passengers, terrified, cold, and half-naked, were herded ashore where they took shelter in a log shed along with the stranded crew while the pirates put off in the *Sir Robert Peel* and quickly ran her onto a reef, whether by accident or design is unknown. There they looted the ship at leisure, getting away with the immense haul of $100,000 in cash, the army payroll destined for the troops in Upper Canada, and valuables, including silver plate, money, and jewellery from the cabins valued at another $75,000. As they left, they set the ship on fire. Next morning, by good luck, the stranded passengers and crew were rescued by an American steamer.

The man behind this attack was Bill Johnston, the most notorious of the St. Lawrence River pirates, a self-proclaimed "patriot" of the Canadian rebels who announced that his capture of the ship was an act of war in the struggle to "liberate" Canada. But in fact it was an act of pure brigandage by a man with little interest in politics but a very deep interest in loot. Johnston was a pirate by choice, a rebel only by chance.

He was born at Trois Rivières, Quebec, on February 1, 1782. In 1784 his family settled at Bath, near Kingston, where, as a young man, he was a farmer and merchant. Then like many others living along the border, he extended his merchant interests into the smuggling trade.

Shortly after the outbreak of the War of 1812, the Canadians suspected Johnston of smuggling and of consorting with the enemy. Among other things, he had married an American woman and had many friends and in-laws on the American side of the river. At the same time, he was charged with desertion from the Canadian militia. He was thrown into jail at Kingston, and all his property was confiscated.

Determined not to sit out the war in prison, Johnston escaped and hid in the woods, where he fell in with a band of American fugitives. Six of them stole a large canoe and headed out across Lake Ontario for the American shore. They were picked up by an American ship and landed at Sackett's Harbour, New York.

To their subsequent grief, the Canadians refused to reimburse Johnston for his confiscated property, valued at some fifteen hundred pounds. Burning with hatred for his country and vowing revenge, he offered his services to the Americans.

For the duration of the war Johnston was an enemy spy and raider. Big, strong, fearless, and ruthless, he led a gang

of irregulars in a swift six-oared boat, prowling the water-
ways of the Thousand Islands which he knew so well from
his years as a smuggler. With this small party of raiders he
terrorized outlying Canadian farms and hamlets and
attacked small craft on the river.

Once his gang robbed a mail coach running between
Kingston and Gananoque, leaving the coachman tied to a
tree and passengers robbed of their clothing. Another time
he ambushed a despatch rider carrying military papers and
shot the man's horse, leaving him to complete his journey
on foot.

As cunning as he was bold, Johnston eluded all attempts
to apprehend him. On one occasion his boat was cast away
on the Canadian shore during a gale. All of the gang were
captured except Johnston who remained in hiding for two
weeks and again managed to make his escape across the
lake in a stolen canoe.

At war's end Johnston settled in French Creek (now
Clayton), New York, as a merchant. As a traitor he could
not, of course, return to Canada without the risk of being
hanged. But he spent almost as much time in his former
country as in the country of his adoption. French Creek was
a notorious smugglers' roost, and Johnston soon became
one of the most successful outlaws in the business, using
various hideouts among the Thousand Islands on both sides
of the border. He swaggered about with six pistols and a
Bowie knife tucked in his belt, ready, as he boasted, to take
on all comers.

He had various boats at his command, but his favourite
vessel was twenty-eight feet long, propelled by twelve oars,
and could easily accommodate a band of twenty armed
men. Johnston had some of the tastes that marked more
famous pirates of an earlier day: he had the hull of his little
ship painted black, the sides white with a yellow stripe, and

the interior a brilliant red. It was so light that two men could pull it up a slipway and move it overland.

By the mid 1830s Johnston's gang included his sons, John, Decater, James, and Napoleon, and his daughter, Kate. Known to romantics as "The Queen of the Thousand Islands," Kate Johnston was a young woman who could handle a boat as skillfully as any of her brothers. From the Johnstons' base in French Creek she acted as spy and informant for her father and kept him supplied with provisions on those occasions when he had to go into hiding.

In 1838 Upper and Lower Canada (now Ontario and Quebec) were mired in the turmoil that followed the rebellions of 1837. Rebels who had fled across the border to the United States began organizing loosely knit "patriot" groups whose common purpose was the invasion and "liberation" of their homeland. They hoped for aid from the Americans; actually thousands of Americans joined them. Some were truly sympathetic, believing that America had a mission to liberate the world and that Canada was ripe for revolution. Others were merely drifters and adventurers looking for any booty they might lay their hands on by raiding across the border. Johnston was one of those.

He became a "patriot" when "General" Van Rensselaer created him "Commodore of the Navy in the East" at Navy Island. The "patriots" made attempts to invade Canada along the Niagara River, but these were all thwarted by the incompetence of the invaders as well as by the presence of regular troops and Canadian militia. After the burning of the *Caroline*, the "patriots" were forced to abandon Navy Island.

At that time neither Canada nor the United States had forces stationed along the St. Lawrence River which were capable of flushing the outlaws from their lairs among the Thousand Islands, but American attempts to co-operate in clearing out those robbers' roosts were half-hearted at best. The situation along the Niagara River was much firmer. The situation along the St. Lawrence was chaotic.

In February 1838 Johnston and Van Rensselaer laid plans to attack Kingston and to capture formidable Fort Henry which had been built by the British and designed to withstand a full-scale attack by an American army. They had a few hundred men armed with rifles and three cannons stolen from American arsenals, but they hoped to accomplish their purpose with the aid of fifth columnists planted inside the town and the fort.

An American schoolteacher named Elizabeth Barnett heard some of the conspirators discussing the plan in French Creek. The courageous woman crossed the frozen St. Lawrence on foot, then travelled up the Canadian shore to Kingston to warn the garrison.

While the alarmed citizens of Kingston carried their valuables to the fort for safekeeping, the militia was called up, soldiers were stationed at vital posts along the river and in the town, and the garrison at the fort prepared for battle.

Meanwhile, the "patriots" assembled on Hickory Island, but their invasion never materialized. Van Rensselaer, a notorious drunkard, chose this time to go on an extended bender, and as the days passed his cold, hungry followers deserted in twos and threes, drifting back to American settlements for food and shelter. By the time a patrol from the army base at Kingston was ready to investigate Hickory Island, there remained only a handful of shivering stragglers and some sacks of scrap iron, ammunition for the cannons.

Johnston, disgusted with Van Rensselaer, now decided to wage his own kind of guerrilla war against Canada. His first (and only major) undertaking in this "war" was the capture of the *Sir Robert Peel*, an act that drew cries of outrage from all sides. It was so obviously an act of piracy that even some "patriot" leaders were shocked, although they still hoped it might help to spark a new war. Perhaps their greatest outrage was caused by the size of the loot Johnston and his confederates shared out. Nothing else like it fell to the lot of any band of raiders in the "patriot" war.

The government advised angry Canadians not to take reprisals against their American neighbours. Lord Durham, newly arrived from England to straighten out the colonial mess, offered a reward of $1,000 for Johnston's capture. The Governor of New York posted another $500 and smaller amounts for known henchmen of Johnston. But many Americans, including some of the militiamen on the border, sympathized with the "patriots" so that no genuine attempt was made to arrest any of the pirates. A few were apprehended and then released. Johnston, full of bravado after his sensational exploit, issued his own proclamation:

To all whom it may concern:
I, William Johnston, a native born citizen of Upper Canada, certify that I hold a commission in the Patriot service of Upper Canada as commander-in-chief of the naval forces and flotilla. I commanded the expedition that captured and destroyed the steamer "Sir Robert Peel". The men under my command in that expedition were nearly all natural-born English subjects; the exceptions were volunteers for the expedition. My head-quarters was on an island in the St. Lawrence, without the jurisdiction of the United States, at a place named by me Fort Wallace. I am well acquainted with the boundary line, and know which of the islands do and do not belong to the United States; and in the selection of the island I wished to be positive, and not locate within the jurisdiction of the United States, and had reference to the decision of the Commissioners under the sixth article of the Treaty of Ghent, done at Utica, in the State of New York, 13th June, 1822. I

know the number of the island, and by that decision it was British territory. I yet hold possession of that station, and we also occupy a station some twenty or more miles from the boundary line of the United States, in what was Her Majesty's dominions until it was occupied by us. I act under orders. The object of my movements is the independence of Canada. I am not at war with the commerce or property of the people of the United States.

Signed, this tenth day of June, in the year of our Lord one thousand eight hundred and thirty eight.

WILLIAM JOHNSTON

Following this bold statement, Johnston continued to terrorize the Canadian riverfront, attacking vessels and raiding farms. In two separate raids on Amherst Island he shot and cut fingers from the hands of farmers who tried to defend their homes, and in one of his attacks a farm boy was killed.

With a small flotilla of pirate craft following, Johnston would man the tiller of his own boat, sitting on a bag that contained the captured flags of the *Sir Robert Peel*. In one of his bragging statements issued from time to time from French Creek, he advised any potential attackers to "bring their own coffins, as he had no time for cabinet making."

Johnston's name inspired fear all along the Canadian shore. On July 8 Colonel Charles Grey, en route to take command of a regiment in Upper Canada, wrote to his father in England, "There was considerable doubt for some time how far it would be prudent to take the Ladies up for fear of attack from Bill Johnston."

Lady Durham, also travelling up the St. Lawrence that month, wrote in a letter to Countess Grey, "Our voyage by the Thousand Islands has been most prosperous, no appearance of Pirates or ill-disposed persons, but we heard afterwards that Bill Johnston, the most dreaded of these robbers, had been very near us."

While Johnston was holding a Fourth of July celebration at one of his island strongholds, eighty men from the Canadian and American forces tried to surround his lair. Because the two detachments did not act simultaneously under combined command, Johnston and all but two of his men escaped, leaving behind their famous longboat. The Canadians blamed the failure on the tardiness of the Americans. The Americans accused the Canadians of moving in too soon.

By November 1838 Johnston was involved with a "patriot" lodge called the Hunters, whose members identified each other with secret signs and symbols and swore oaths to "promote republican institutions throughout the world." This band attempted an invasion of Canada by way of Prescott and nearby Fort Wellington. In command were "Major General" John Ward Birge and "Admiral" Bill Johnston.

Thanks to Captain Van Cleve of the American steamer *United States*, the Canadians had advance warning of the invasion. The Hunters had used the *United States* to transport men and munitions to the Thousand Islands. Van Cleve informed the American authorities, and they, in turn, informed the Canadians.

On November 12 two schooners, the *Charlotte of Toronto* and the *Charlotte of Oswego*, headed for Prescott with a force of several hundred armed men. But the invaders were having problems. The two leaders could not agree on a plan of action. Then Birge complained of sickness, which his companions attributed to cowardice, and withdrew from the campaign. Two hundred others subsequently deserted. After Birge withdrew, a Polish revolutionary named Nils Von Schoultz took command of the *Charlotte of Toronto* with about 170 men on board.

Von Schoultz succeeded in docking the ship at Prescott, but while the invaders argued about what to do next, the mooring rope broke and the ship drifted downriver a mile and a half to Windmill Point. The Hunters under Von Schoultz quickly took over the windmill, a six-storey building with thick walls.

Meanwhile Johnston had run his ship aground. The *United States,* seized by the Hunters, steamed out of Ogdensburg to tow the *Charlotte of Oswego* off the mud bank where she was stranded. Later, another steamer, the *Paul Pry,* joined in the effort to float the stranded vessel.

Meanwhile the Canadians, well aware of what was happening, sent troops to surround the windmill and a small warship, the *Experiment,* to bombard the invasion forces from the river. The action that followed, known in the history books as "the Battle of Windmill Point," would have been pure comic opera except for the fact that a few people actually got killed.

The *Experiment* went into action, lobbing shots from her two cannons at the windmill, the *United States,* the *Paul Pry,* and the *Charlotte of Oswego.* An eighteen-pound ball smashed through the wheelhouse of the *United States* and beheaded her pilot. The two steamers then withdrew, and Johnston used a boat to transfer two of the three cannons to Von Schoultz.

At some point Johnston must have been on board the *United States* as her captain later reported that Johnston had wanted to use her to ram "that damn little boat," meaning the *Experiment.*

A few Hunters from Johnston's ship managed to join those who were digging in on Windmill Point, raising their number to 192. But by next morning all of the vessels used by the invaders had been seized by either the Canadians or the Americans. Some time during the night Johnston, probably realizing the futility of the operation, decamped with thirty of his followers and all the munitions he could lay his hands on.

The stranded invaders in the windmill held out for four days, then surrendered, and eventually Von Schoultz was hanged.

The Americans, accused by the British of aiding piracy, sent Federal troops after Bill Johnston and the others who had been involved in the attempt to capture Prescott. A few days after the battle a search party caught one of Johnston's sons trying to get a boat to his father. Then they tracked the old pirate to a spot near Ogdensburg and cornered him.

Johnston surrendered on condition that he be allowed to give his weapons—six pistols, a twelve-shot rifle, and the ever-present Bowie knife—to his son.

The soldiers took Johnston to Auburn, New York, where "General" John Birge was already in jail. At a preliminary hearing he was acquitted of all charges stemming from the Prescott raid, but United States Marshall N. Garrow insisted that he be held to stand trial for earlier crimes. Before the second trial could be held, however, Johnston escaped, taking Birge with him.

The Americans offered a reward of $200 for his arrest, and within a few days he was caught again. This time he was sent to Albany for trial, where, despite the fact that he was guilty of murder and piracy, he received the astonishing sentence of one year in jail and a fine of $250.

Jail was no great ordeal for Johnston. His daughter, Kate, was allowed to share his quarters and take care of him. He was given day leave to visit his friends in town. He even attended a performance of a play entitled *Bill Johnston, The Hero of the Lakes.*

Comfortable as prison life was, Johnston made another break after serving only six months. He vanished into the Thousand Islands and next appeared in Washington with a petition for his unconditional pardon signed by a host of friends and sympathizers. President Martin Van Buren refused to have anything to do with it, but his successor, William Henry Harrison, a veteran of the War of 1812, cheerfully signed the document giving the river pirate his freedom.

Johnston returned to French Creek where he was employed at various times as lighthouse keeper, tavern owner, and smuggler. He owned several islands, three of which he named Ball, Shot, and Powder. It was rumoured that on festive occasions the Johnston family would bedeck their persons and their table with the jewellery and the silverware stolen from the *Sir Robert Peel*, but there is no eye-witness testimony to this.

In 1843, at age sixty-one, Johnston boasted that he could row or sail against the best boatmen on the St. Lawrence. When asked if he thought the rebellions of 1837 and his subsequent private war against Canada had accomplished anything, he replied, "Do you call the expenditure of four millions of British cash nothing?" Canada had, indeed, paid heavily for the fifteen hundred pounds taken from Johnston in 1812.

The retired pirate continued to live, unrepentant, at French Creek until he reached the age of eighty-eight. He died there on February 17, 1870.

CHAPTER 11

THE GREY GHOST OF FUNDY

THE LAST PIRATE of note to operate in Canadian waters was Mogul Mackenzie, commander of the *Kanawha*, a Confederate privateer that preyed on Union shipping during the War Between the States, then disappeared when the war came to an end and was reported as a ghost ship in the Bay of Fundy for several months thereafter. Mackenzie, a wild man with the instincts of a buccaneer born more than a century too late, was feared not only because of his ferocity in battle, but also because he had the reputation of a fiend who would torture or mutilate a prisoner at the slightest provocation.

When innocent merchantmen began reporting, in the early months of 1865, that they had been chased by a pirate ship, sober authorities on shore generally dismissed their reports as mere nervousness. Piracy was supposed to be a thing of the past, surviving only in the Indian Ocean and the China Sea, stamped out in all Christian lands by the power of the State and especially by Britain's Royal Navy which had run down and captured not only the last of the Atlantic pirates, but also the last of the slave traders a generation earlier. Or so it was believed. It was true that Mackenzie had gone missing, and his ship along with him, but the ship might easily have sunk with all hands after her last battle or, like so many other ships, have simply vanished in a storm.

The reports persisted. And then in May of that year, an American gunboat sighted a sleek grey ship, remarkably like the missing *Kanawha*, off the southern coast of Nova Scotia. The gunboat chased the ship and ordered her to heave-to for identification. She did not heave-to and she hoisted no identifying signals. Instead, she made off at top speed toward the Canadian shore. The waters where the encounter took place were treacherous. Perhaps the American captain was unsure of the coastline. In any case, the ship supposed to be commanded by the former privateer escaped among the channels near Cape Sable, a region of inside passages and long, winding bays where whole fleets might lie undetected.

Later, off the island of Campobello in New Brunswick, a ship that looked like the missing privateer came in sight of a Nova Scotia schooner, altered course, and began to overtake her. A stiff wind was blowing, and the schooner had shortened sail. Risking damage to his sails or rigging, the captain of the schooner ordered the reefs to be shaken out and the course altered two points to windward, his ship's best sailing position. The schooner was a good sailer and especially fast when sailing on the wind. The pursuing ship also altered course, but now no longer seemed to be gaining, and the trading schooner managed to stay ahead until she reached Portland, Maine, where she put in for protection while the suspected pirate veered off to sea. Again the schooner's captain met mostly incredulity. Perhaps he was a nervous commander? Was he sure the pursuing ship was actually trying to overtake him?

Skepticism vanished a few days later when a whaler put into port with the news that she had found the trading vessel *St. Clare* abandoned in the Bay of Fundy but *still under sail*. The ship's strongbox was missing. There was no sign of her crew. Because she was too short-handed to put a salvage crew on board, the whaler brought the abandoned ship to port under tow, along with a small boat that had been tied to the ship's stern with the name *Kanawha* painted on her planking.

There could be little doubt what had happened. The pirates had departed in the *St. Clare's* longboat, either taking the crew as their prisoners or throwing them overboard. Why they had left the ship under sail was never explained. Perhaps they had departed in great haste when another sail hove in sight.

Shortly after this a trading vessel from Boston arrived at Yarmouth, Nova Scotia, with the news that she had sighted the *Kanawha* heading up the Bay of Fundy in the direction of Saint John. The trader's captain had been close enough to read the name of the pirate ship through his spy glass. This seemed to clinch the matter. The harbour master at Yarmouth took a full statement from the American captain and sent off a report to Halifax which was then a major British naval station as well as a fortified town.

From Halifax a small warship H.M.S. *Buzzard* sailed to Yarmouth and began a hunt for the pirate. After several days of fruitless cruising in Fundy waters, the *Buzzard* arrived in St. Mary's Bay, chased into harbour at Meteghan by one of the violent storms for which Fundy waters are famous. St. Mary's, a bay that opens southward to the Atlantic, is separated from the Bay of Fundy by the long, narrow point of Digby Neck and the islands that lie to the south of it. It seems that the *Kanawha* with the sinister Mogul Mackenzie had been in and out of St. Mary's Bay just ahead of the *Buzzard*.

The night before the arrival of the warship an Acadian homesteader at Meteghan, a fishing port about ten miles from Cape St. Mary and thirty miles north of Yarmouth, was awakened by an eerie wailing from his beach. Gun in hand, he crept down to the shore to investigate, and there he found a naked man, exhausted and almost dead, with his tongue cut out. The man had been mutilated and thrown overboard by the pirates. Whether he had been one of the *Kanawha*'s crew or a prisoner was never explained.

The night after the *Buzzard* arrived at Meteghan the wind rose to near hurricane force, and the small warship lay at anchor in the shelter of a long, rocky point, waiting for the storm to blow itself out. Meanwhile the pirate ship had vanished once more into the inner reaches of the Bay of Fundy, a body of water with no natural port along its southern shore from Digby in the southwest all the way to Minas Basin, a distance of nearly a hundred miles.

At the northern end of the Bay of Fundy, near the entrance to Minas Basin, lies Haut Isle, about ten miles from the nearest fishing villages of Ogilvie and Harbourville. It is about the same distance from the tightly enclosed Advocate Basin lying between the entrance to Minas and the north channel of Fundy stretching toward Chinecto.

In earlier times Haut Isle was named by the Acadian French settlers "Ile aux Morts," the Island of the Dead, because it was a trap for ships trying to enter either the north or south channels of the bay and a place from which wrecked sailors had little chance of escape. The tides there have a range of almost fifty feet, and the tide race runs like the current of a great river. The island rises at one point to a height of 300 feet and is surrounded by cliffs ranging from 80 to 200 feet in height. There is only one landing place, at the extreme eastern tip and then only at low tide.

The same night that the *Buzzard* was sheltering at Meteghan, the fishermen along the Nova Scotia shore from Ogilvie to Harbourville saw rockets exploding in the midst of the storm and by the glare of sheet lightning could see a distant ship apparently being swept toward Haut Isle under bare poles, her sails either furled or blown away. She was driven by mountainous seas and sucked toward shore in the tide race. No boat could be launched from the fishing villages, and even if it could, it would be unable to cross the ten miles of chaos that lay between Haut Isle and the watchers. The rockets blossomed and died uselessly, and the watchers saw no more of the ship.

Next day, when the storm died down to a tremendous ocean swell and fishing boats put out from Harbourville to search for wreckage or bodies, they could find no trace of the distressed ship. Every spar, every plank, every drowned body and scrap of clothing had been swept far out to sea by the retreating tide.

No trace of the *Kanawha* or of Mogul Mackenzie was ever found. H.M.S. *Buzzard* called off the search and returned to her station, and it gradually came to be accepted that the sea lanes around southern Nova Scotia were safe once more.

Perhaps not surprisingly, Haut Isle is reputed to be a treasure site. The treasure supposed to have been buried there was not Mackenzie's—his treasure, if he had any, doubtless went down with his ship—but that of an earlier American captain, Samuel Hall, who held American letters of marque back in the eighteenth century and specialized in raiding the Nova Scotia settlements during the American War of Independence. Hall's Harbour, named for this privateer, is a small cove near Haut Isle where Hall moored his armed sloop during his final raid on the Cornwallis Valley in 1778. When Hall's sloop, the *Mary Jane*, was captured by the British, the captain's strongbox was missing. There can be no doubt that Hall had treasure of a sort, valuables collected during his raids on the colony. It was widely assumed that he had concealed his strongbox ashore in the vicinity of Hall's Harbour, with a cache of such things as money and silverplate, and perhaps some rings and other jewellery.

Just after the Second World War some old documents relating to Hall's life were discovered in the United States, and a party of American treasure hunters believed they had reason to hope his treasure might be found on Haut Isle. They fitted out a small expedition and visited the difficult little island in the early 1950s. They reported later in the American press that they had found very little for their trouble—no treasure, but part of a human skeleton and one ancient coin which (they reported) was clutched in the skeleton's fingers. They sold their story and pictures of their find to *Life* magazine.

There was nothing whatever to connect this "headless skeleton" with Samuel Hall or his supposed treasure or, for that matter, with Mogul Mackenzie and the loss of his pirate vessel some seventy-seven years later. From that wreck or from another wreck at some other time, a single sailor had been washed into the cleft of the cliffs or had managed to clamber up the rocks, only to die there, and had left his bones to bleach in sun and rain, the single coin that he carried in his pocket remaining with his skeleton, while his clothing, along with his flesh and his skull, disappeared into the sea.

CHAPTER 12

THE CAMPBELL GANG

BECAUSE ONTARIO REMAINED unsettled for two centuries after the early colonies were founded in Newfoundland, Nova Scotia, and Quebec, and because, by that time, the country was strongly garrisoned with British troops, the outlaw never really flourished in Upper Canada. Sporadic gang raids in Ontario's "wild west," the country bordering Lake Huron, home of the Campbell gang and the Black Donnellys, were minor incidents compared to what happened later, hundreds of miles to the northwest on the shore of Lake Superior. Jesse James allegedly hid out in the Ontario bush, and Windsor was for a time a favourite refuge for American desperadoes on the lam. But even this paled before the mass invasion of American outlaws into western Canada, the so-called whiskey traders who forced the country to organize the North-West Mounted Police to end their reign of terror.

Throughout much of the nineteenth century young Canadians with the urge to become gentlemen of fortune regularly migrated to the United States where the west was still wild enough to suit the most barbaric tastes, and there were plentiful opportunities to earn a living with a gun.

On July 11, 1859, Rattlesnake Dick Barter was gunned down by deputies in California. He had plundered the gold rush country for three years, eluding sheriffs and posses and jeering at the posters proclaiming him "wanted dead or alive." One of California's most daring and colourful bandits, Rattlesnake Dick was from Quebec City, son of one of the many English-French marriages of the period.

Rocky Mountain Jim Nugent was just such another, son of an English soldier who had been stationed in Montreal. Rocky Mountain Jim, a border ruffian of the War Between the States, was such a fearful outlaw that mothers frightened their children into obedience with threats that he might come and get them. Unlike most men in the outlaw business, Nugent survived for more than twenty years and occasionally accepted legitimate work as a guide. In 1873 he took the English journalist Isabella Bird through the Rockies. She seems to have fallen in love with him. He would have been as handsome as Adonis, she reported, had it not been for the claw marks of a grizzly bear on the left side of his face.

A few months after Rocky Mountain Jim left her to continue her journey across the continent, Isabella Bird began to have visits from his ghost (or so she reported). He had in fact been shot dead in a gunfight while she was away.

In the autumn of 1877 the Union Pacific train was stopped by the infamous Sam Bass gang at Big Springs, Nebraska, and robbed of $60,000 in gold. The only bandit to escape with his share of the loot was Tom Nixon, a Canadian about whom nothing is known except that he was the only gang member not killed or captured. Other members of the gang reported that Nixon had returned to Canada and disappeared.

That same year saw the death of Canada Bill Jones, the famous card sharp who coined the phrase "It's the only game in town." Canada Bill's specialty was fleecing suckers on railways and river boats, posing as a bumpkin. On one occasion he offered a rail company a share of his take in exchange for the right to operate undisturbed. When the offer was declined, he made a more attractive one which was also turned down. His friends described Canada Bill as the most gifted card cheat ever to riffle a deck. He had weaseled his way out of so many apparently fatal situations that a former partner remarked at his funeral, "I've seen Bill get out of tighter spots that this."

Ben Thompson, born in either Nova Scotia or England, but certainly raised in Nova Scotia, son of a hard-drinking English sailor, was one of the toughest gunfighters in the business. During the War Between the States he enlisted in the Confederate army and later fought as a mercenary for the Emperor Maximilian of Mexico. After Maximilian was defeated and shot by a firing squad, Ben Thompson fled to the United States and became a professional gunslinger, selling his services on either side of the law impartially, sometimes as an outlaw, sometimes as a sheriff or a deputy. In Ellsworth, Kansas, he single-handedly held off a lynch mob, enabling his young brother, Billy, who had just killed the sheriff, to escape.

In Abilene, Kansas, Thompson and another hired gun, Wild Bill Hickok, operated rival gambling halls. Not eager to face Thompson in a duel, Hickok waited until he was out of town and then killed his partner, Phil Coe, a gambler more skilled in dealing cards than in gunfighting. Marshal Hickok, after killing one of his own deputies by mistake, went berserk, shooting up the whole town. A friend wrote to Thompson, "Only one man could have faced him, Ben, and you weren't there."

Thompson was never bested in a gun duel. He was finally killed by a hidden assassin in a San Antonio theatre in March 1884, after a violent career that had spanned more than thirty years. Over that period he had disposed of an average of more than one rival a year. At his death another Canadian-born gunfighter, Bat Masterson, eulogized him in the following words: "It is doubtful if in his time there was another man living who equalled him with a pistol in a life and death struggle...his aim was as true as his nerves were strong and steady."

Flat Nose George Curry came from Prince Edward Island and made his mark as a bank and train robber in the American west. He was a partner with Butch Cassidy and the Sundance Kid in their wild career across the western states in the 1890s. He finally fell before a hail of bullets when cornered by a posse in Utah in 1900.

Compared to all this, Ontario had little to show except for the Campbell gang, a band of minor outlaws that flourished in the 1850s along the border between Grey and Bruce counties, about thirty miles east of Lake Huron and thirty miles south of Owen Sound, in what was then regarded as Upper Canada's far west.

The Campbells arrived in Grey County about 1850 and settled in Bentinck Township. John and Colin Campbell built a tavern at a crossroads a few miles east of the village of Hanover, near a bridge on the Saugeen River which empties into Lake Huron, north of Port Elgin. The site, now inside the municipality of Hanover, was known as Campbell's Corners.

The tavern quickly became a hangout for drunkards, thieves, and rowdies, known far and wide as a centre of lawlessness and violence. Principal members of the gang who used it as their headquarters, in addition to the two Campbells, were Andrew McFarlane, William McMahon, and three brothers named Bailey. It was a place which honest local farmers avoided and which travellers visited at their peril.

For several years the Campbell gang terrorized their neighbours in Grey and Bruce counties, respecting no law, doing as they pleased on the edge of civilization where there was little restraint on anarchy and people had to live by their own rules. But this situation changed late in the decade with the appointment of magistrates and the swearing-in of police constables to bring some semblance of the rule of law to the wilder part of the colony. The constables were mostly part-time men, usually with no training in police work, but they had the authority of the government behind them and they did their best, often with the help of their neighbours who knew the old common-law custom of hue and cry, which had remained part of the British statutes until 1827. If necessary the magistrates could, as a last resort, appeal for help from the colonial government, in which case they might receive a detachment of police from Toronto (as happened later at Michipicoten) or, if severe disorders threatened, an army patrol.

The train of events that led to the downfall of the Campbells began in 1858 when two horses belonging to Andrew McFarlane were seized by a Bruce County bailiff as security for a delinquent debt. The bailiff impounded the horses at Walkerton, a village about eight miles downriver from Hanover. McFarlane went to the Campbell brothers for help, and early in 1859 the gang descended on Walkerton, liberated the horses, and took them back to Campbell's Corners. Bruce County magistrates then issued warrants for the arrest of Andrew McFarlane and the two Campbells. Constables George Simpson and Caleb Huyck set off to cross the Saugeen River at Campbell's Corners to bring the three men to Walkerton to face charges.

On June 7 the two crossed a bridge near Hanover only to find themselves immediately surrounded by a band of armed men. In addition to the three for whom they had warrants, the gang included William McMahon and the Baileys.

Colin Campbell, spokesman for the gang, demanded that the strangers identify themselves. Huyck replied that they were constables from Walkerton and that they were there to serve warrants for the arrest of Colin and John Campbell and Andrew McFarlane.

Colin Campbell asked to see the warrant and when it was produced, ordered the constable to tear it up. Huyck refused. Campbell then raised his gun and threatened to kill him and

Simpson. At gunpoint Huyck tore the paper into small pieces.

"Bruce County warrant ain't no good in this county," Campbell told the constable. "Now you eat that paper."

Huyck hesitated and Campbell fired a blast into the ground. In fear of his life Huyck began swallowing the scraps of the torn warrant while the Campbells and their friends roared with laughter and asked him how he was enjoying his meal. Huyck did manage to conceal the last few bits of the warrant in his hand and drop them into his pocket in order to produce them later in court.

"Now git," Campbell told the two constables, "back to where ye come from. If ye ever show your noses around here again ye'll be shot."

Meekly the two agents of the law set off downriver to Walkerton, but they had no intention of leaving Grey County in charge of the Campbell gang. They went to Magistrate Jamieson and with his help they organized a large posse of armed men, crossed the Saugeen River, and laid siege to Campbell's Corners.

The seven bandits were all holed up in the log tavern. Magistrate Jamieson called on them to surrender peaceably. Colin Campbell replied that the strangers were trespassing on his land and that anyone who tried to enter the tavern would be shot.

The posse took cover in the nearby woods which surrounded the building and began sniping at its doors and windows. Members of the gang returned the fire. Realizing that they could not flush the Campbells out of the heavy log building by gunfire alone, they tried to sneak up and set it ablaze but were driven back by the outlaws' bullets. There was no approach to the tavern that was not open to fire from one or more of its small windows.

Jamieson then again called on the gang to surrender and was answered by a volley of bullets, several of which splintered bark from the tree he was using for cover. He then ordered another attempt to set fire to the tavern, this time using a portable shield.

They secured a heavy barn door from a nearby farm, and the two constables crept forward behind it until they were near enough to pile dry kindling against the tavern and toss a flaming torch into the midst. The tinder-dry logs cinched with moss quickly began to burn, and the building filled with suffocating smoke. The outlaws had no choice but to get out. However, they came out fighting. John and Colin Campbell emerged back to back, guns at the ready. Then the whole gang discovered that they could make a break for the woods under cover of the thick pall of smoke.

The members of the posse fired at them as they ran, but did not pursue them. McMahon was wounded slightly in one leg. Colin Campbell was struck in the back—not by a bullet which would have disabled him immediately, but by buckshot from the gun of a farmer who lacked a rifle. He stumbled, but ran on, seemingly not seriously wounded. The other five escaped without a scratch. All seven made it successfully to the woods and disappeared. The members of the posse considered the outlaws far too dangerous to be pursued through thick woods, so they left armed constables in Hanover and retired to Walkerton to await developments.

Campbell, it turned out, was wounded badly enough to be forced out of hiding. After several days the lead pellets embedded in his back began to fester, and he had to make his way to Hanover to seek treatment for his wounds. As soon as he entered the town the constables seized him. After treatment he was sent to Goderich for trial, probably because the big Huron County jail in that town was more secure than any lockup in Grey or Bruce counties.

A little later, John and James Bailey and William McMahon were also arrested. There is no record that the other members of the gang were ever caught.

Colin Campbell and his three friends went on trial in Goderich on September 30, 1859, charged with horse stealing and with assaulting the police. More serious charges might have been laid, but they were not. The outlaws were all treated with astonishing leniency, and, in spite of the gun battle and the attempts to carry out threats of murder, the sentences were exceedingly light. They were all found guilty, but only Colin Campbell went to prison. The Baileys and McMahon were fined and bound to keep the peace.

With the infamous tavern reduced to ashes and his welcome in Grey County obviously worn out, John Campbell left for regions more to his taste. There is no official record of what happened to him, but the story as told in Hanover has him moving north to Manitoulin Island, west of Georgian Bay, at the northern end of Lake Huron, a place that was probably still wild enough in the 1860s to accommodate his nature.

CHAPTER 13

THE FORT WHOOP-UP BANDITS

NOTHING IN THE HISTORY of border hopping by Canadians seeking their fortunes in America's wild west equalled the mass invasion of the Canadian prairies by the American whiskey traders. Following the end of the War Between the States in 1865, thousands of unemployed soldiers from both North and South, some of them mercenaries, headed west, hoping to grow rich from their training in homicide in a region where their talents would not be hampered by the rule of law.

Many of these adventurers found their way to the Dakotas and Montana, and those that did soon discovered that the best pickings were in Canada where large bands of Indians still roamed free and millions of fur-bearing animals waited to have their pelts exchanged for rotgut whiskey.

Western Canada, at that time, was not policed even by the hired guns who occasionally enforced something that passed for law in American cattle towns. On tribal lands the Indians enforced their own laws. The Métis, descendants of Indians and French *voyageurs*, had their own community laws centring around leaders whose principal job was to organize the buffalo hunts which were the chief economic activity in the region. Those who were not Indian or Métis were, in effect, answerable to no one. Western Canada in the 1860s was a place where a band of traders could build and fortify illegal trading posts, even arming them with cannons if they chose, safe from American calvary patrols, and with little danger from anyone except other outlaws or bands of enraged Indians.

The Piegans, the Bloods, and the Blackfeet, those in closest touch with the whiskey trade, suffered widespread death and demoralization. Canada's sovereignty in the west was greatly threatened. Canadian-American relations sank to a low level. There was real danger that the American government might simply order the cavalry to begin policing this no-man's-land across a border that was not only undefended, but unpatrolled and often undefined.

Though "whiskey traders" has come to be the accepted term for the prairie outlaws of the 1860s and 1870s, their liquid wares scarcely deserved the name of whiskey, as we shall see. They traded many other kinds of goods as well— war-surplus blankets and especially rifles and ammunition. The repeating rifles that were in such vast supply in the United States just then were greatly coveted by the Indians, most of whom were still armed with single-shot muzzle-loaders.

Until 1869 the government of Canada had no jurisdiction over the prairies. The vast country from the Great Lakes west to the Rocky Mountains was all part of Rupert's Land, nominally the property of the Hudson's Bay Company which had been given a grant in the reign of King Charles II to all the land on the watershed of the rivers draining into Hudson Bay. At the time nobody had the least idea what this territory included. It turned out to be something in the order of a million square miles.

Hudson's Bay Company posts were the social and economic centres of this great lone land. Company employees —trappers, traders, and clerks—accounted for most of the "white" population. The rest of the non-Indian population was Métis, mixed with a few freelance fur traders, many of whom fathered numerous halfbreed children.

Company governors held, on paper, far-reaching legal powers, including the right to enforce their orders by gunpoint and the right to flog, shoot, or hang offenders. But making the law was one thing; enforcing it was something else. The Honourable Company of Adventurers had found it necessary, early in the century, to fight an actual guerrilla war with the upstart Northwest Fur Trading Company of Montreal (controlled by Scottish immigrants, not by French Canadians) and with John Astor's American Fur Trading Company. These battles were eventually settled by compromise and by amalgamation. The Hudson's Bay Company took the defeated Northwest Fur Trading Company into partnership. From that time forward the great commercial company confined itself to issues affecting the fur trade and left the land west of the Red River to look after itself. The Indians and Métis got so used to living by their own laws that eventually they attempted to form their own nation, and the young Canadian nation, following its dream of a single country from ocean to ocean, had to fight a war of conquest which is still referred to as the Northwest Rebellion.

Trouble began in 1864 when the powerful American Fur Trading Company disappeared, and dozens of independent traders rushed in to grab a share of the market. From their base in Fort Benton, Montana, a boom town dubbed "the Chicago of the Plains," they spread across the prairies like a plague. In the civilized east the Chicago of the Plains had a different nickname: the Sagebrush Sodom.

Mixed with the few respectable traders were gunmen, outlaws, vagabonds, and soldiers of fortune. The sale of guns, ammunition, and alcohol to Indians was forbidden in Montana. There were marshals, posses, and occasional cavalry patrols. But all this stopped, more or less, at the international line. The occasional posse might pursue a fugitive over the border but not for far, and the U.S. cavalry was scrupulous about staying inside its appointed bounds unless ordered by Washington to do otherwise.

The Hudson's Bay Company had posts on the Upper Churchill River and at Rocky Mountain House, the latter poorly provisioned and ill equipped for large-scale trade. Southward and westward they made no attempt to enforce either the law or their fur monopoly. Rocky Mountain House was virtually inaccessible to the tribes along the border. To reach it they would have to make long journeys through territory held by the hostile Cree. And some of those hostile tribesmen were already armed with the American repeating rifles that were so superior to the muzzle-loaders still supplied in trade by the Hudson's Bay Company.

But the main attraction at the illegal posts was alcohol. For some two hundred years, French, English, American, and Canadian traders had dealt in rum, brandy, and whiskey. In the early days of New France the Church had outlawed the brandy trade, but for once the Church was defeated by the civil power: the government at Quebec legalized it again. It remained, however, a minor trade item until competition between fur-trading companies forced them to pack the most potent goods into the smallest spaces. Then even the Hudson's Bay Company traded as much as 20,000 proof gallons of rum to the Indians each year.

At least the stuff they traded was real rum, made by legal distillers following some kind of quality control. Business-wise merchants soon realized that the trade in legal booze was self-defeating, since in the long run it demoralized the Indians and destroyed their interest in producing fur. David Thompson of the Northwest Company had smashed barrels of rum rather than trade the stuff to the natives. After absorbing the remnants of the rival Northwest Company, the Hudson's Bay Company was able to phase out its rum trade and by 1860 had almost ceased trading in spirits.

The free traders were not only unconcerned about morals or the survival of the Indians, but were also unconcerned about the survival of the trade itself. Their aim was to grab as much as possible in a year or two and make off with the swag. They sold a concoction that made Hudson's Bay Rum (still used on ceremonial occasions) taste like distilled water. To a base of raw alcohol they would add a little molasses for taste and many other things to "give it a kick." Tobacco juice and pain killers were favoured. Jamaica ginger and pepper gave it the right "feel" in the throat. Red ink was added for colour because Indians associated red with the ideas of fire, blood, and power. Laudanum, an infusion of opium in alcohol, was cheap and plentiful, and a little of it went a long way. A dollar's worth of laudanum added to a keg of "whiskey" gave it a knockout power that no legal booze could match. The stuff was usually heated up before serving so the customer could experience the ultimate blast.

The whites called their invention "bug juice" and rarely if ever drank it themselves. The Indians called it "firewater" and drank it avidly. But by any name it was a hellish brew that included fusel oil (a poisonous mixture of alcohols, normally used as a solvent) and other impurities common to bootleg alcohol, as well as the deliberately added poisons. Indians who drank it in too large draughts sometimes died on the spot. Nevertheless, they ran the risk. It was not uncommon for a booze-crazed native trapper to trade away everything he owned—furs, horses, wives, daughters—for a few more drinks of firewater. Fights, knifings, and murders were all common at the trading sessions.

At first the independent traders operated from wagons and horseback. As business increased and experience taught them how dangerous it was to deal with intoxicated Indians, they began to fortify their posts with rifle ports and small cannons. A few of the names suggest the character of these outposts of civilization: Fort Standoff was named for the time a band of smugglers "stood off" an American marshal who had pursued them over the border. Fort Slideout received its name after the occupants "slid out" one night to escape a war party of Blood Indians determined to kill the men who had been poisoning their people. Another fort was simply named Robbers' Roost.

One of the founders of Fort Spitzee was John "Liver Eating" Johnson, an American mountainman whose Indian wife had been murdered by marauding Crow Indians. Johnson declared a private war on the Crow nation and by the time he established a whiskey post in Rupert's Land was alleged to have killed more than twenty of them in hand-to-hand combat. After felling an enemy, Johnson would scalp him, cut out his liver, and eat it raw. The Liver Eater did not tarry long in Rupert's Land, but the fort he built stood for several years, a centre of violence in the whiskey trade.

Of all the whiskey posts the most notorious and successful was Fort Whoop-Up. Built in 1869, just a few miles from what is now the city of Lethbridge, Alberta, at the junction of the St. Mary and Oldman rivers, it was the brainchild of Al Hamilton and Johnny Healy. Hamilton was the nephew of Isaac G. Barker, a wealthy Fort Benton entrepreneur who financed the Whoop-Up venture. Healy was an Irish adventurer who had travelled west with the American army, searched for gold across the Indian country, prospected as far north as Edmonton, and bragged he was ready to "fight anything from a grizzly bear to a circular saw." The efforts of other outlaw traders would pale in comparison with those of the courageous, flamboyant, resourceful, and utterly ruthless Healy.

In its first six months Fort Whoop-Up turned a profit of fifty thousand dollars. Rival traders took quick notice. They loaded up with trade goods, especially guns and bug juice, and set off on "the Whoop-Up Trail."

The first Fort Whoop-Up was destroyed by fire that may have been accidental or may have been started by angry Indians. It was a collection of rough huts surrounded by a flimsy stockade and represented little loss. Healy and Hamilton, with their spectacular trading profit and generous backing from Fort Benton, built a vastly improved model with every consideration to security. The new Fort Whoop-Up had heavy timbers, thick walls loopholed for rifles, and a stockade to give pause to an army. They fitted windows and chimneys with iron bars. As defence against fire they covered the roofs with earth. One bastion housed a cannon and the other a howitzer. Gunmen carrying long poles patrolled the stockade. Any Indian who attempted to scale the wall would be pushed off. If he persisted, he would be shot. While the Indians outside the walls drank, caroused, and fought, the whites stayed inside the safety of their fort, tasting the pleasures of the flesh, including real whiskey.

The only Indians allowed inside were women whose sexual services had been bought and paid for. The traders dealt with the men through three wickets near the gates. The Indian would push his furs through the opening, and the trader would pass out guns, ammunition, and Whoop-Up Wallop made from Healy's own recipe. It was so strong, he bragged, that an Indian who drank it could be shot through the heart and wouldn't die until he sobered up.

The Indians traded pemmican, a staple of the frontier diet, and pelts. The whites were mainly interested in buffalo robes, then in high demand in the east. The tough hides made good belts for industrial machinery at a time when nearly all heavy machines were controlled by belt drives from steam engines rather than gearing which came later. For the sake of profits and whiskey the great herds of the continent's most powerful grazing animal were literally wiped out of existence by hunters of both races. In a single year Fort Benton exported a hundred thousand buffalo skins. The Indians realized too late that the indiscriminate slaughter would destroy the herds on which they depended for practically their whole livelihood and at the same time would destroy the lifestyle of the free nomad. The white man didn't care in the least if he killed the last buffalo, as long as he could sell its hide.

Among Healy's crowd at Fort Whoop-Up were characters bearing such exotic names as Waxy Weatherwax, Spring Heel Jack, Slippery Dick, Toe String Joe, and Blood Chief Joe Healy, John Healy's adopted Indian son. One of the hangers-on at Whoop-Up was François "Crazy" Vielle, Métis scout, local clown, and guide of dubious courage. Once, when leading a pair of Jesuit priests across the prairie, he mistook a dust cloud for a Blackfoot war party and quickly whipped his horse to a gallop, leaving the priests behind. When they called on him to stop, he shouted back, "You trust in God. I trust in my horse."

The whiskey trade soon devastated the Indians. Men who had been proud hunters and warriors became hopeless sots, stripped of property and dignity. Whenever possible Indian women would try to steal back the goods their men had been cheated of. Dependency on trade goods had, over the years, eroded the Indian's culture and self-sufficiency. Dependency on firewater destroyed his soul.

The situation grew far worse in 1869 when a smallpox epidemic swept across the Canadian west killing thousands of Bloods, Piegans, and Blackfeet. The Indians blamed the whiskey traders for the calamity, accusing them of selling infected blankets. Sick men would make suicidal attacks on the whiskey forts, preferring death in battle to the slow wasting of the disease. Some rubbed their sores on the gates of the stockades, hoping to give the disease back to the whites. By the time the epidemic had run its course, approximately half the Indians of the prairies were dead. The tribes were further demoralized and weakened and became all the more susceptible to the predatory traders. There is grim testimony in letters written by witnesses. Reverend John McDougall, a Methodist missionary who packed a gun as well as a Bible, wrote:

Many Indians were killed, and also quite a number of white men. Within a few miles of us, 42 able-bodied men were victims...all slain in drunken rows. Some terrible scenes occurred when whole camps went on the spree, as was frequently the case, shooting, stabbing, killing, freezing, dying. Mothers lost their children. These were either frozen to death, or devoured by the myriad dogs of the camp. The birth rate decreased, and the poor red man was in a fair way toward extinction, just because some white men, coming out of Christian countries, and themselves the evolution of Christian civilization, were now ruled by lust and greed.

A Catholic priest, Father Constantine Scollen, wrote to Lieutenant Governor Laird in Winnipeg concerning the misery of the Blackfeet: "It was pitiful for me to see the state of poverty to which they had been reduced. Formerly they had been the most opulent Indians in the country, now they were clothed in rags, without horses or guns."

Governor Laird sent Captain W. F. Butler to investigate. Butler reported: "The region is without law, order, or security of property; robbery and murder have for years gone unchecked; and all civil and legal institutions are unknown."

Faced with anarchy and the danger of an Indian uprising, the beleaguered Hudson's Bay Company made a deal with Ottawa in 1869 to sell Rupert's Land to the fledgling Dominion of Canada. It was the largest real-estate transaction in the history of the world, bigger than the Louisiana purchase by the United States or the sale of Alaska by Russia.

The company advised the government of John A. Macdonald to send a military force west to clean up the whiskey forts and establish law and order, but Macdonald, whose procrastinating habits had earned him the nickname "Old Tomorrow," was slow to act. Not until the spring of 1873 when news of a major tragedy came out of the west, did

Parliament pass a bill to organize the North-West Mounted Police.

The disaster that finally compelled the Canadian government to do something about the rule of the whiskey traders involved not only the Whoop-Up gang, but another gang of unscrupulous whites, the wolfers. Wolf pelts were valuable, and the wolfers had an easy way of collecting them at little expense. They would shoot a buffalo and poison the carcass with strychnine. One such bait guaranteed a pack of dead wolves. Indians hated the wolfers, not only because they respected the wild predators, but because camp dogs, used as pack animals, were also killed by the poisoned meat. The Indians considered the wolfers fair game and in one year killed over forty of them.

The Indians hated the wolfers and the wolfers in turn hated the whiskey traders who sold the Indians the repeating rifles with which the wolfers were killed. When their complaints about the arms trade fell on deaf ears, they decided to take action. In the summer of 1872 they rode out of their base, Liver Eating Johnson's old Fort Spitzee, calling themselves the Spitzee Cavalry. There were probably no more than ten of them, led by John Evans and Harry Taylor, whose nickname "Kamoose" meant "Squaw Thief."

At several whiskey forts—Standoff, Slideout, Whiskey Gap, and Robbers' Roost among them—the wolfers met no resistance and easily forced the traders to sign a pledge to end the arms trade. Encouraged by such easy victories, the Spitzee Cavalry went after the biggest gun runner in the west, Fort Whoop-Up.

But Healy did not scare as easily as his colleagues. The outlaw boss calmly invited the grim, heavily armed wolfers to dinner and then after the meal inquired what their business was. Kamoose Taylor bluntly stated their determination to end the arms trade and demanded that Healy sign the pledge. Healy refused, calling the wolfers a pack of mad dogs. As they responded with angry accusations, he informed them that one of his men was outside with a cannon trained on the building and orders to open fire if the visitors would not listen to reason. The subdued wolfers listened. By the time Healy finished talking, the hunters agreed that they and the whiskey traders were all in the same business, working for financial interests in Fort Benton, and that they had better co-operate to make as much money as possible out of the Indians.

That's one story. In another version, Healy confronted the wolfers with an open keg of gunpowder and a lighted cigar, roaring that if they didn't clear out he'd blow himself, the fort, and the Spitzee Cavalry straight to hell. Whatever it was that Healy did, he subdued the wolfers. The Spitzee Cavalry was finished, and the effort to stop the gun trade came to nothing. The wolfers went back to staking out poisoned buffalo and collecting dead wolves.

In the spring of 1873 a band of Canadian and American wolfers travelling to Fort Benton after a winter in the north had their horses stolen by Indians. Enraged, they completed their journey to Fort Benton and there outfitted themselves to make war on the culprits. White men did not share the Indian view that stealing horses was an honourable sport. Horse thieves, especially red-skinned horse thieves, deserved to be shot.

The armed band of thirteen men, including John Evans of Spitzee Cavalry fame and a hard case called Thomas Hardwick, "The Green River Renegade," pursued their quarry until they lost the trail in the Cypress Hills of southern Saskatchewan. A few miles from the place where they stopped was a whiskey post on Battle Creek, named for its proprietor Abel Farwell. Hardwick rode in to Fort Farwell to ask if the trader knew of any Indians with stolen horses in the vicinity. A band of Assiniboines led by Chief Little Soldier was camped nearby, and the Green River Renegade enquired of Farwell whether these might be the Indians he was looking for. Farwell didn't think so. The Assiniboines, he said, had very few horses, and since they had wintered in the north, they could not have been stealing livestock in Montana. Hardwick went back to the wolfer camp with this disappointing news and led the entire party into the whiskey post.

When the wolfers rode in with their smouldering anger and frustration, Fort Farwell was already sitting on a powder keg. For more than a month relations between Indians, traders, and a nearby settlement of Métis had been threatening to explode into violence. Indians had run off a herd of thirty horses belonging to Farwell and his men. The theft surprised and angered the trader who had thought himself on friendly terms with the natives. One of the stolen horses belonged to George Hammond, a Canadian described as "unsavoury." The night the wolfers arrived Hammond's horse was returned by an Indian who demanded to be paid for its rescue. Across the creek from Fort Farwell was another whiskey fort run by Moses Solomon, a man thoroughly hated by the Indians because, even more than the other traders, he abused and cheated them. The Indians were probably already planning an attack on Fort Solomon when the wolfers reined in at Fort Farwell. They had warned the Métis to keep out of the way when the shooting started.

The wolfers spent the night at Farwell's and got up the next day, the first Sunday of May, to a breakfast of whiskey. They continued drinking through the noon hour when George Hammond discovered that his horse, so recently recovered, had gone missing again. Swearing he would take two Indian ponies in return, the drunken Hammond grabbed his rifle and headed for Little Soldier's Assiniboine camp. With him went the entire pack of wolfers and some of Farwell's trading crew.

It seems that Abel Farwell tried to prevent a violent confrontation between the armed factions, but both wolfers and Indians were drunk that afternoon and little disposed to listen to reason. Little Soldier told Farwell that Hammond's mount had probably wandered off. Young Indians taunted the whites. Each group nervously asked the other why they were carrying guns. At this point Farwell decided to fetch his interpreter from the fort in an effort to mediate and clear up any misunderstanding, but he had taken just a few steps when the shooting started.

The high-powered repeating rifles of the wolfers were too much for the northern Indians who were armed with ancient muzzle-loaders and some with only bows and arrows. By the time the smoke cleared away, over thirty Indian corpses littered the ground. One wolfer, a Canadian named Ed Grace, was killed. The Assiniboines fled, abandoning their lodges to the whites. The wolfers plundered the camp and found the chief, Little Soldier, too drunk either to fight or to flee. They butchered him and mounted his head on a pole. According to Farwell's evidence, the few women and children in the camp were also mistreated and some of them murdered. The wolfers tore down the Indian camp, buried Ed Grace, and rode on. They never did recover their horses.

In Fort Benton the Cypress Hills Massacre was hailed as a great victory. The local newspaper referred to the pack of wolfers as "thirteen Kit Carsons." In Canada the crime was viewed as a massive raid by American desperadoes into the Canadian west. Politicians in Ottawa and newspaper editors in Toronto published lurid, exaggerated tales of American violations of Canada's newly acquired sovereignty over the prairies. Alexander Morris, Lieutenant Governor of Manitoba and the Northwest Territories, telegraphed Prime Minister Macdonald: "What have you done as to police force stop their absence may lead to grave disaster."

The white outlaws and the growing unrest among the Indians were not the only factors in Macdonald's belated haste in recruiting and training a body of men to establish Canadian control in what are now the provinces of Saskatchewan and Alberta. Fenian agitators such as John J.

Donnelly of Fort Benton were urging an outright invasion of western Canada. American politicians and speculators were casting greedy eyes on the fertile northern plains, especially the Saskatchewan Valley. They knew from past experience in such places as Texas and New Mexico that an American presence in a coveted land was a major step toward annexation.

For a year the newly formed North-West Mounted Police recruited and drilled. Men from all walks of life lined up to enlist, but most of those accepted had military experience. Former British soldiers and Canadian militiamen made up the bulk of the original company of three hundred, but at least one was a Confederate veteran of the War Between the States. In July of 1874 when the first six divisions set out from Fort Dufferin, Manitoba, Canadians and Americans alike predicted that the redcoats would perish before they ever reached Fort Whoop-Up, their prime objective.

Americans were unhappy about the idea of a Canadian armed force in the west. To placate their suspicions, Macdonald had changed the name of his little army from "Mounted Rifles" to "Mounted Police." Still, many Americans such as Johnny Healy, who now edited a newspaper in Fort Benton, warned their countrymen that the Mounted Police were only a front for British militarism. Healy and others had good reason to object to law enforcement in Whoop-Up country. The whiskey trade had been most important to Montana's economy, and American businessmen were not anxious to see the closure of the wide-open border.

Many Canadians, too, were sure that only death awaited the scarlet riders in the fabled west. In the far more widely settled American west hundreds of soldiers had perished in bloody Indian wars. Gangs of freebooters led by men like Jesse James and Cole Younger still roamed at will. It seemed ridiculous to think that Macdonald's vest-pocket army could pacify hundreds of thousands of square miles of wide-open territory inhabited by Indians driven to desperation and by white outlaws who thought nothing of shooting people by the score.

"No more wildly impossible undertaking was ever staged," wrote Canadian journalist Frank Oliver. The Toronto *Globe* offered a grim little verse to comfort the doomed constables as they rode to their fate:

> Sharp be the blade and sure the blow,
> And short the pang to undergo.

The trek west was, indeed, difficult. Horses died. Men deserted. Guides were so untrustworthy that Commissioner George French suspected them of being spies for "the Whoop Up-villains." By the time the little force reached the Bow River in what is now southern Alberta, the police realized that they were lost. French took a small escort and headed south to Fort Benton to purchase supplies and hire a dependable guide. Perhaps to his own surprise, he got both.

Showing remarkable shrewdness, the Fort Benton merchants had decided there was more money to be made selling supplies to the Mounted Police and to the flood of settlers they were sure would follow than in cheating Indians for the hides of the rapidly dwindling buffalo. So French had no trouble filling out his shopping list. He found an excellent guide in Jerry Potts, a tough, laconic halfbreed descended from a Scottish trader and a Métis woman who was herself born in the Blood Indian tribe. Potts was not terribly fond of the whiskey traders, though he had a taste for firewater. His mother and his half brother had both been murdered in a drunken brawl at a whiskey post. Potts had tracked down and killed the murderer.

Freshly provisioned and guided by a scout who knew the country, the Mounted Police continued their journey. On October 4, 1874, a detachment under Assistant Commissioner James Macleod came within gunshot of Fort Whoop-Up.

The redcoats took up positions well beyond rifle range of the notorious fort and trained the field guns they had brought with them on its fireproof rooftops. Potts and Macdonald rode toward the gates while the men watched the loopholes for the expected flashes of gunfire. This was the moment they had prepared for, a pitched battle with the most hardened criminals in the west.

The gate opened to an eerie silence. The lone occupant, Dave Akers, Healy's old crony, explained to the astonished policemen that his employer, D.W. Davis (a Canadian and a future Member of Parliament), was away on business but that he'd be pleased to welcome them to a dinner of buffalo steaks. A thorough search of the fort failed to turn up a single drop of Whoop-Up Wallop. Obviously the whiskey traders had been informed well in advance of the approach of the Mounted Police.

Over supper, Macleod offered to buy Fort Whoop-Up for ten thousand dollars. He thought it would make an excellent police post. Akers insisted the fort was worth twenty-five thousand. So the deal fell through, and the government built its own post, Fort Macleod.

The outlaws had decided that, even in the face of Macdonald's miniscule armed force, to flee was the better part of valour. Almost overnight they were diminished from a major international problem to a small-time nuisance. A few die-hards continued to smuggle rotgut into the region, were caught and fined, and had their stock confiscated. Most of the bootleg booze was poured on the ground, but some of the more potable stuff found its way to the police barracks, where the constables were known to "whoop it up" on occasion.

Most of the whiskey traders found new occupations. Hamilton served in the Montana state legislature. Kamoose Taylor opened a hotel near Fort Macleod, but not before the police had confiscated his stock of whiskey and his ill-gotten buffalo robes (which they needed to make winter coats for the force). John Evans opened the Extradition Saloon in Fort Benton in honour of the wolfers who had committed the Cypress Hills Massacre and whom the Canadian government had been trying, without success, to extradite for trial in Canada. Those of the killers who did eventually stand trial in Fort Benton and Winnipeg were freed without punishment. It was still relatively safe, on either side of the border, to murder Indians.

Johnny Healy's Fort Benton newspaper defended the whiskey traders as true pioneers who had opened up the great western regions for the advance of civilization. He attacked the Mounted Police as heralds of British tyranny and called them "grabbers of the spoil." From 1877 to 1882 the former chief trader of Fort Whoop-Up was sheriff in Fort Benton. Ironically, the adventurous Irishman who is remembered in Canada as a desperate outlaw is remembered in Montana as one of the legendary "lawmen" whose gun helped to civilize the west. But Healy was not the kind of man to rest content with any civilized job, even as a pistol-packin' sheriff. As soon as Montana grew too quiet for his taste, he packed up and left for the Alaskan goldfields.

The coming of the Mounted Police in 1874 marked the end of the wild west in Canada. The force instantly established a reputation for fearlessness, so much so that a lone officer in a red coat could ride into a feuding settlement or an Indian camp on the brink of a rebellion and establish peace by his sole authority. It was as though the "mounties" were part of a ready-made legend from the day they arrived on the prairies. Later, along with the army, they had to deal with real warfare, but almost without firing a shot, they put an end to the age of the outlaw.

In the United States the west continued at least as wild as it had ever been. While Fort Macleod established the rule of law in western Canada, Jesse and Frank James continued to rob banks and trains. Billy the Kid was yet to shoot his first man. The great gunfight at the OK Corral was still several years in the future.

Lawlessness was by no means at an end in Canada, but the prairies were no longer wide open for brigands and bootleggers. The outlaws had left behind them a very much changed country from the one they had entered a mere fifteen years earlier. It was no longer the private hunting ground of the Hudson's Bay Company. The mighty herds of bison had become a memory. Police posts dotted the land, and survey teams were staking out a route for a transcontinental railway. The Indians, once masters of the plains, were being herded, starving, onto reserves. They had borne the brunt of the outlaws' villainy and had come painfully close to going the way of the buffalo. One American whiskey trader, forced reluctantly into retirement, summed up the plight of the Indians with this chilling statement: "If we had been allowed to carry on the business for another two years, there would have been no trouble now as to feeding the Indians, for there would have been none left to feed. Whiskey, pistols, strychnine, and other like processes would have effectively cleaned away those wretched natives."

CHAPTER 14

THE McLEAN GANG

DURING THE LAST THREE or four years of the 1870s the people of the cattle country around Kamloops, British Columbia, were terrorized by four youths, one of them a mere child, who must go on record as Canada's youngest outlaw band. At the time of their arrest only one, Allan McLean, was over seventeen. He was twenty-five and the band leader. The others were his brothers, Charlie, seventeen, and Archie, fifteen, and their partner, Alex Hare. Archie had been an outlaw from the age of twelve.

If ever three boys were doomed from birth, it was the three young McLeans. Their childhood was a nightmare of poverty, violence, and ill-treatment. Donald McLean, father of the three brothers, was a brutal Scottish immigrant, a Hudson's Bay trader who quarrelled and fought with everyone he met, including his colleagues in the Honourable Company of Adventurers. Though he married two successive native wives who bore him eleven children, Donald McLean despised and mistreated Indians. In 1849, after a Hudson's Bay employee was killed by an Indian, McLean joined the posse that went hunting the fugitive and not only gunned down the man in question but also killed the man's old uncle, the man's son-in-law, and a baby who happened to be in the house where the son-in-law had taken refuge.

The Indians made a number of unsuccessful attempts to avenge these murders. McLean was shot at time and again but seemed to lead a charmed life. He was finally hit in the back by a bullet while hunting Indians during the Chilcotin "uprising" in 1864 and killed. Under his tunic at the time of his death he was found to be wearing a steel breastplate, which perhaps explains why he lived as long as he did. Allan was a boy of about nine, Charlie a mere toddler, and Archie a babe in arms when their father was killed. They inherited nothing but poverty and misery. Halfbreeds were not welcome in white society, and the Indians had little love for the sons of the hated white man. Many Métis children looked much like Indians and could easily pass as members of the tribes. The McLean boys did not. They looked white, having inherited their father's pale skin. But this did not help them with the white community. Their mother was an Indian, and they were treated like vermin, living in a frontier limbo where they were outcasts at every turn.

The government allotted tracts of land (poor land that it was) to the Indians but made no provision for halfbreeds. The boys received no education. Only Archie, the youngest, ever learned to write his name. He spent a few days in an Indian school but, perhaps because he was blond and blue-eyed, was never accepted by his schoolmates and left the school as quickly as possible.

With nothing to sustain them but their own wits and a festering hatred of an unfair world, the McLeans became drifters and vagabonds, dealing with life on whatever terms they could. They worked as casual labourers on cattle and sheep ranches and learned, in the meantime, how to hunt, ride, shoot, and drink.

Like their father, the boys were quarrelsome and made enemies easier than they made friends. When the wages they earned from their menial jobs could not be stretched to buy food and whiskey, they began to steal. The McLeans stole from everybody, red or white, rich or poor. They made off with anything that could be used or sold—money, livestock, food, clothing, firearms. They sometimes beat the victims of their robberies. They were tough, feared nothing, and had no sense of pity or compassion; they were as merciless with the world as the world had been with them. But frontier society was used to tough kids whom you had to chase off with a stick or a gun. It did not take the McLeans seriously—at first.

Because the British Columbia government was tight-fisted, the constabulary undermanned, and the courts over-worked, petty criminals such as the McLean boys often went unpunished. It was not until 1877 that one of them, fifteen-year-old Charlie, was arrested. In a brawl he had bitten off the end of another youth's nose. He was sent to the Kamloops jail for three months but did not actually serve more than a few days of the sentence.

Charlie soon discovered that the calaboose was not to his liking and promptly broke out. He then teamed up with his brothers and pal Alex Hare, and the four became regular outlaws, living entirely by what they could seize from the farms and ranches of southern British Columbia, often at gunpoint, leaving fear and outrage in their wake. They rustled cattle along the American border, seized horses from pastures and stables, looted storerooms of guns and provisions. They stole blankets, clothing, and saddles, robbed a Chinese merchant and beat him savagely, took bread and his stock of brandy from a sheepherder named James Kelly.

The magistrates issued warrants for the arrest of the McLeans, but the warrants were never served. When Allan and Archie were caught and charged with a robbery, they easily escaped from the Kamloops jail. The local constable, Johnny Ussher, was only a part-time policeman and was hard-pressed to keep up with the sudden crime wave. The government ignored his requests for help, and he often had to pay his deputies out of his own pocket. After the McLean jail break he asked the government for a hundred dollars to make the jail more secure. He was refused.

Facing a weak police, an unarmed or frightened populace, and with nothing to lose, the McLean gang commited one depredation after another, threatening to kill anyone who opposed them. A special target for their hatred was John Mara, a Kamloops merchant and politician who had taken Annie McLean, the boys' sister, for his mistress. The brothers swore that Mara would die and Kamloops would go up in flames in revenge for the seduction.

Through 1878 and 1879 the McLeans and Alex Hare had their way. Civilians did not dare to stop them, and the government could not be bothered to try. The young bandits behaved as though they could never be captured. But in the end they picked the wrong victim. In December 1879 they rustled a prize stallion belonging to a rancher named William Palmer. The angry Palmer tracked his horse to the McLean camp near Long Lake. He found Allan, Charlie, Alex, and fifteen-year-old Archie all drunk and brandishing rifles and Colt .45 revolvers. Palmer decided to ignore his stolen horse which was tethered in plain view and after a few words retreated from the camp. He later stated that he was sure the outlaws were waiting for him to draw his gun so they would have an excuse to shoot.

Palmer rode straight to Kamloops and swore out a complaint against the McLeans and Alex Hare for horse stealing. The Justice of the Peace gave Johnny Ussher a warrant for the gang's arrest and rewards were posted by the Hudson's Bay Company and the provincial government. A few days later Ussher and Palmer rode out to apprehend the McLeans. En route they enlisted Amni Shumway, a tracker, and John McLeod, a rancher who had lost some stock to the outlaws.

On December 7 they found the gang camped some sixteen miles from Kamloops. As the posse approached, Charlie raised his rifle and fired. The bullet nicked Palmer's beard and smashed into McLeod's cheek. Palmer returned the fire, and the outlaws replied with a fusillade. Another bullet struck McLeod in the knee, and several shots hit his horse. Ussher called on the young bandits to surrender, dismounted, and approached them unarmed. Suddenly Alex Hare jumped from cover, armed with a gun and Bowie knife. Ussher grappled with him, trying to wrest the gun from his hand. Moments later the constable was on the ground and Hare was driving the knife repeatedly into his body. When Ussher cried, "Don't kill me!" Archie McLean fired his pistol from point-blank range and blew his brains out.

During the exchange of gunfire Charlie had been wounded, but the posse, seeing that Ussher was dead, withdrew. They galloped off to Kamloops where McLeod received attention from a doctor (he was not very seriously wounded). They then got together a new posse headed by John Mara, but when they rode out to the McLean campsite they found it abandoned. Ussher's body, stripped of coat and boots, lay frozen in the snow.

The McLean gang then went on a new rampage. They moved toward the Douglas Lake Indian Reserve where they hoped to rouse the Nicola Indians into a war against the whites. On the way they met James Kelly, the sheepherder who had laid charges against them for stealing his brandy and bread. They killed him, took a pistol and silver watch from his body, and looted his cabin of provisions. They then rode to the ranch of Thomas Trapp where they boasted about killing Ussher and displayed the bloodstained handcuffs which they had taken from him as a trophy. They forced Trapp at gunpoint to give them his rifle, pistol, and stock of ammunition. Trapp later told the posse that young Archie McLean, "the devil himself," had urged the others to kill him and that Allen had tossed a coin to decide whether the terrified man should live or die. The fifty-cent coin which fell in Trapp's favour had been taken from the body of Ussher.

The boys continued on to the ranch of John Roberts, where they surprised the owner with drawn guns while he was slaughtering hogs. They bragged and joked about killing Ussher and Kelly and announced that others were soon to die, including William Palmer. They did not rob or attack John Roberts but asked him for information about various people—whites and Indians with whom they had scores to settle. Roberts swore that he had no information about the people concerned, and the outlaws rode away.

Their next stop was the ranch of William Palmer, the man who had brought Ussher out to arrest them and was now riding with the posse. They treated Palmer's wife civilly but told her that they would kill anyone who came after them. They drank Palmer's brandy and took what firearms they could find in the house, then mounted and headed for the Indian reserve.

Allan McLean had married into the Nicola tribe. The chief, Chillitnetza, was his father-in-law. They rode to his lodge, displayed the small arsenal they had collected, and tried to talk the chief into calling a council of war. Chillitnetza had no love for the whites who were colonizing British Columbia and who had forced his people to accept a sorry scrap of land where they could barely scratch a living, but he knew the foolish scheme Allan McLean proposed was doomed to failure and advised the outlaws to run for the American border as quickly as possible before the police reached the Indian village.

Disappointed with the chief's refusal to fight or to give them any other assistance, the gang rode on to an abandoned cabin near Douglas Lake where the wounded Charlie could rest and regain his strength while they planned their next move. Some of the Indians on the reserve may have sympathized with the halfbreed outlaws, but not all of them. One of them offered to reveal to Constable George Caughill, for a reward of one hundred dollars, the location of the gang's hideout. Caughill then sent off a message to John Clapperton, Justice of the Peace in Nicola.

Within a few hours, groups of armed men were moving in on the lonely cabin where the outlaws were holed up. News spread quickly that the McLeans had been cornered. The government mustered men at New Westminster and prepared to transport them to Kamloops. American authorities were warned of a possible Indian uprising, and missionaries were instructed to remind their native congregations that the impending fight was not theirs. As it turned out, a number of Indians, including Chief Chillitnetza, joined the posse.

Meanwhile the cabin was surrounded by local cowboys, ranchers, Indians, and Métis. John Clapperton called on the outlaws to surrender and was answered by a volley of gunfire. The McLeans were well provisioned and prepared to stand off a siege. The log walls of the cabin could stop bullets, and the young outlaws had all the guns and ammunition they could use. The one thing they were short of was water. At times they poked sticks through chinks in the walls, trying to pull snow inside.

The siege lasted for several days, the monotony broken by occasional bursts of shooting. Indian messengers took notes in to the defenders. (Apparently one or more, perhaps Hare, had learned to read if not to write.) The notes had no effect, but the waiting paid off. On the third day the gang made a dash for the outbuilding where their horses were stabled. Heavy fire drove them back inside and killed three of the horses. The boys shot back, wounding three of the besiegers.

Eventually the posse, too, began to be fed up with the endless waiting. On Friday, December 13, members of the posse loaded a wagon with hay, soaked it with kerosene, and ran it toward the cabin, hoping to smoke the defenders out. They were stopped by a hail of bullets, and one more man was wounded. The outlaws whooped with joy at this small victory, but their time had just about run out. After five days of the most stressful confinement in a small cabin that now stank of their own wastes, the McLeans and Alex Hare, all of them suffering from raging thirst, surrendered. One by one they came out of the cabin, fired their rifles into the air until the last round was spent, then tossed them away.

Clapperton's men attacked and mauled the young killers who fought like wildcats before they were hogtied and lugged off to Kamloops. They were then sent to New Westminster in a week-long journey by horseback, canoe, and stage. Bound and poorly dressed they came close to freezing to death in the sub-zero cold. On Christmas Day 1879 they were locked up in the New Westminster Jail.

If the authorities mistreated the prisoners, the prisoners misbehaved just as badly. Their jailers never had to deal with more difficult subjects: they cursed and spat at the guards, threw dishes and buckets, and cell searches turned up hidden knives and other equipment intended for a prison break. When a guard threatened to shoot Allan McLean for refusing to go to his cell, Allan defied him, "Shoot! I'm not afraid of an ounce of lead."

The three McLeans and Alex Hare went on trial together in March 1880. The defence attempted to portray the prisoners as victims of social injustice. They pointed out the discrimination suffered by halfbreeds in general and by the McLean boys in particular—their lack of education, absence of parental guidance, failure of the law to deal with their earlier, minor offences. The lawyers concluded with a plea for mercy based on their clients' youth. But it was all for nothing. The murders of Johnny Ussher and James Kelly weighed heavily with the jurymen. They returned a verdict of guilty with no recommendation for mercy. The judge then sentenced all four to hang. Before leaving the courtroom the prisoners fought with their police escort and apparently tried to reach their old foe William Palmer.

On appeal, the trial was found to have been legally defective, and a new trial was ordered for November. The same witnesses appeared for the prosecution. The same evidence was produced. The same pleas were made once more. The same verdict was pronounced. The death sentences were read once more, and the date of execution set for January 31, 1881.

At this point the fight seems to have gone out of the McLeans. They made no further trouble for their jailers and stoically waited for the end. Allan McLean sent messages to relatives asking his Indian wife to take good care of the child he had fathered and pleading that no revenge be taken against William Palmer.

Archie McLean, who must have reached his sixteenth birthday before he reached the scaffold, remained defiant to the end. He owed nothing to anybody, he said, and didn't care if everyone he knew was hanged. There is a disturbing photograph of Archie in chains and leg irons looking like a child of about thirteen.

At 8:00 A.M. on the appointed day the four convicts were taken to the prison yard for a group hanging. They mounted the scaffold together; a clergyman said, "Courage, mes enfants"; the traps were sprung and they dropped to their deaths. It is the only recorded instance of three Canadian brothers being hanged at the same time.

CHAPTER 15

THE OUTLAWS OF MICHIPICOTEN

EXCEPT FOR THE ROCKY MOUNTAINS, no part of the country was as inhospitable to the builders of the Canadian Pacific Railway as the wilderness north of Lake Superior. The men who worked on that line in the 1880s had to carve a route through thick forests and lay steel across bottomless swamps, bare rock, and countless rivers. They had to tunnel through bedrock in places where they could not lay steel over the hills. They risked death or injury daily and endured the most wretched discomforts. In summer they were tormented by clouds of blackflies. In winter they endured numbing cold. Their diet was so bad that some of them suffered from scurvy.

Not surprisingly, the men turned to the brief comfort of alcohol at every opportunity. To many of them the "grand drunk" was the only escape from frustration, drudgery, and the sordid dreariness of their lives. The CPR did not approve of mixing drink with railroad building. Under the Public Works Act the stern puritans of the railroad hierarchy who got their own enjoyment from money and power forbade the sale or even the possession of spirits within ten miles of the Canadian Pacific route. But they soon learned it was one thing to declare prohibition, something else to enforce it.

Bootleggers—the vanguard of an army of prostitutes, gamblers, conmen, and thieves—quickly moved into the north country, where whiskey purchased in Toronto for fifty cents a gallon could be sold to men in the camps for five dollars a pint.

Sudbury, still a shantytown of boxcars and tents, became the major base for the smugglers, who bribed railway detectives or left them bound and gagged while they transported large shipments of whiskey, gin, brandy, and beer in barrels marked "peas" and "potatoes." The police at Sudbury were not wholly ineffective. In one three-week period they seized two hundred gallons of contraband spirits. Between September 1883 and October 1884 a single Sudbury magistrate handed down over ninety convictions related to bootlegging.

But everyone knew that for each bootlegger caught, three others went free. The trade flourished, and the host of labourers working on the Superior line could get rip-roaring drunk whenever they could spare the time and money.

Because a continuous length of track had not yet been laid, the worksites on the north Superior shore depended for supplies on steamships out of Sault Ste. Marie. Little ports such as Peninsular Harbour and Michipicoten (an old Hudson's Bay Company post on the northeast shore of the lake) became major depots both for the railway contractors and for the bootleggers.

Workmen would go into such centres to get paid, pick up supplies, and get drunk on liquor dispensed from barrels marked "coal oil." One steamer, the *City of Owen Sound*, came close to being impounded when bootleggers on board sold their wares right from the ship's side on the Michipicoten dock.

When men from the work gangs went to town, they often carried guns and knives, and sprees of drunkenness, gambling, and whoring often ended in brawls, shootings, and robberies. In Michipicoten one man was killed in a brawl.

Near Peninsular Harbour another was found murdered. Someone had brained him with a hammer and rifled his pockets. An old-timer who had lived in American cow towns and mining camps described Peninsular Harbour as the "most wicked place I ever saw." Railway officials complained that the greatest obstacle to the building of the line was "not rock, but rye."

In the summer of 1884 James "Bulldog" Commee, a railway contractor, tried to shut off the flow of whiskey. From his headquarters in Michipicoten Commee sent out a force of special constables headed by one Charles E. Wallace to round up the bootleggers. They had thin pickings, but they did arrest one blackmarket operator named Bond, whom they locked in a "root house"—a dugout of logs and earth used for storing potatoes. Commee dumped six hundred dollars' worth of Bond's stock into Lake Superior and sentenced him to six months in the Michipicoten jail—the root house.

Bond's friends appealed the sentence on the grounds that Commee had no authority for all this, and the prisoner was released. But Bond was soon back in jail, charged again with bootlegging. Commee presided over the trial, swearing that he would enforce the Canadian Pacific rules even if it meant "hanging, hamstringing or bastinadoing."

Bond was convicted, but it took the court three days to consider his sentence. Bulldog wanted to search the law books to see if he had authority to order Bond to be flogged. Disappointed that he could not make an example of Bond at a public whipping post, Commee sentenced him to life imprisonment in the Michipicoten root house.

Meanwhile, Commee had learned that his head constable, Charles Wallace, was a leading bootlegger who had been using his position to promote his own interests while making life difficult for his competitors. He fired Wallace and would doubtless have proceeded with harsher measures, but he had to depart from Michipicoten on railway business. Immediately after he left, Bond either broke jail or was released, but he promptly left the territory for good—perhaps at the suggestion of his business rival, Wallace.

Twenty-six-year-old Charles Wallace was a native of England who had come to Canada from Montana and was known in Superior country as Montana Charlie. Not much of his background is on record. He had a wife, somewhere or other, and had once earned his living as a cook—but he must have been a man of considerable talents and guile to have worked his double game with Commee so successfully.

Following his dismissal from the police force Montana Charlie collected about him a gang of the toughest crooks in the country. Among them were Harry Cleland (or Cleveland), a fugitive from the Michigan State Penitentiary, Little Dick Goldsberry, an Irishman, and two Canadians, Gordon Doherty and Arthur Asselin (alias McGillvery), the latter an escapee from Manitoba's Stoney Mountain Prison. All these men were in their early twenties.

By October of 1884, Charlie Wallace, with the help of his gang of outlaws and the complicity of many others who either disliked prohibition or saw in it an opportunity to make money, had virtually taken control of Michipicoten. He bribed constables. Any whom he could not bribe he had beaten up. Booze, previously sold under cover, was now sold openly. The only requirement was that the seller must pay his dues to the Wallace corporation. Hoodlums abandoned Peninsular Harbour, where the police were troublesome, and flocked into Michipicoten which was now ruled exclusively by criminals.

On October 9 someone fired at Canadian Pacific agent Alexander Macdonald and Ontario magistrate Captain Burden, two officials who were vainly trying to halt the bootleg traffic. They escaped unhurt, but next day notices appeared on public walls in the town threatening death to Macdonald, Burden, and anyone else interfering with the whiskey trade. "Lawmen" were ordered out of town by the next steamer, on threat of assassination if they stayed. The notices had been posted "By Order of the Vigilance Committee," a pseudonym for Wallace's gang.

Macdonald and Burden refused to be intimidated and pursued their investigation into the illicit traffic. That night, October 10, thirty-five masked gunmen opened fire on the building they were using as office and living quarters. They riddled it with three hundred bullets but failed to kill or injure either of their two intended victims. A Canadian Pacific employee named John McKenzie was struck by the rifle fire and had to be sent to Port Arthur for treatment.

Next day Michipicoten was in the hands of a rioting mob. One group attacked the jail (apparently the root house had by then been replaced by a more conventional lockup). They wrecked the building and tore off the cell doors. The lone prisoner, a drunk, begged the rioters not to shoot him. Offered his liberty, he refused to leave his cell. At the time of his arrest he had $300 in his pocket. The police had taken it for safekeeping, and he assumed he would forfeit it if he broke jail. So he sat in his doorless cell until next day when he was officially turned loose and had his money restored.

While one mob attacked the jail, another went off hunting constables who had tried to interfere with the whiskey trade. One of them was wounded in the hand, another in the eye.

The following day there were more notices from the Vigilance Committee promising death to magistrates, constables, and informers.

Authorities could get no information out of people who were either afraid of the Wallace gang or in sympathy with them. They sent off an appeal to Crown Attorney J.M. Hamilton in Sault Ste. Marie, saying they needed military aid to restore order in the town. The unarmed, untrained civilian constables of Michipicoten simply could not face the desperadoes alone.

It took a few days to get action, but on October 17, Captain Burden met with Mayor Boswell in Toronto and with Major Draper, Toronto Chief of Police. After a lengthy debate over the Michipicoten riots, they agreed to send an armed force of Toronto policemen to the north shore of Superior to re-establish law and order. For the job they chose ten unmarried volunteers and one sergeant under the command of an inspector named Seymour.

Next morning the men assembled at Union Station fully armed with carbines, bayonets, and revolvers. There was a delay when Inspector Seymour, who had overslept, arrived late, and command was transferred to Inspector Ward. They departed for Owen Sound at 12:40 P.M. Meanwhile Canadian Pacific had offered the unusually generous reward of $1,200 for information leading to the arrest of the Michipicoten hoodlums, and plans were made to send the Rifle Corps of Sault Ste. Marie to the trouble spot if necessary.

At Owen Sound the Toronto police boarded the S.S. *Alberta*. At Sault Ste. Marie they transferred to the S.S. *Magnet*. Storms on the lake forced the small ship to take shelter at Bachawana Bay and again at Gargantua Bay.

Meanwhile, in Michipicoten the bootleggers still had everything their own way. They fired shots at two magistrates named Borden and Boland, Borden missing death by inches when a bullet entered the wall beside his head while he slept. Wallace and his henchmen swore that no force of Toronto police would ever be allowed to land at Michipicoten. In Toronto people speculated that the police would be forced to turn back or would have to await reinforcements from Sault Ste. Marie before moving in on the wild little town. A man familiar with Michipicoten told the Toronto press that a few gunmen on shore could easily pick off the police if they attempted a landing. While the constables were still waiting out the weather and passing the time fishing and shooting partridges on the Lake Superior shore, a rumour circulated in Toronto that there had already been a major gun battle in which several of the policemen were killed.

As it turned out, the delay may well have been just what was needed. It gave the outlaws time to reflect that they could simply not stand off the government forever if it was determined to take control of the town by armed force. When the S.S. *Magnet* arrived off Michipicoten on October 23, a heavy swell kept her offshore. So the men landed from small boats. They would indeed have been sitting ducks for snipers, but the only volleys directed at them were volleys of verbal abuse from a hostile crowd assembled on the town dock.

The police ignored the welcome, set up barracks in the magistrates' quarters, and set about the task of cleaning up the town. Not an easy job, since most of the residents objected to their presence. Resentment increased when they mistakenly arrested two innocent men. Despite the bad start, by the end of their first day they were holding a number of hoodlums on minor charges, but Montana Charlie Wallace and his gang had fled into the bush.

That night the police barracks were attacked by a band of masked gunmen estimated to number between thirty and forty. One policeman was shot in the hand. One had his head grazed by a bullet. Their cook, a local man, was wounded in the side. Inspector Ward later reported: "We at once took our revolvers and turned out, taking up positions on a little bluff, and under the best shelter we could get. As soon as we came out the firing ceased, and after waiting for a time and seeing no persons about but those who were peaceably disposed, we returned to the boarding house."

However, a Mr. E. Friendly said that the shooting lasted from 9:30 P.M. till midnight, and that he slept the night on the floor of the store he happened to be in, rather than risk going outside.

After the gunplay, Ward heard that the gang intended to rescue the prisoners he had locked up, so he sent men to stand guard at the jail and at the Canadian Pacific office. But no attempts were made on those buildings.

Next morning another death threat was posted, and the police learned that Wallace and his men were hiding in an Indian village about a mile out of town. Ward sent nine men after them, but the outlaws who, he claimed, had "regular Indian training" eluded his force and got away.

On October 25 the police made their first important arrest when they captured Harry Cleland in the North Star Hotel. Cleland, who had sworn not to be taken alive, was in bed with his gun out of reach when the police broke into his room. The arresting policemen, John Cuddy and David McKee, were in civilian clothes and took the outlaw by surprise. Cleland told Ward: "You've got me now and I won't squeal. But if your men who arrested me had been in uniform there would have been some shooting.... I haven't done any shooting yet, but I would have, if I'd had the chance...."

A day or two after their arrest of Cleland, Cuddy and McKee had a less glorious adventure. Acting on a tip (which turned out to be false) that some of the outlaws were on board the steamer *Francis Smith*, they boarded the vessel and began a search, only to discover when they came back on deck that she had sailed from Michipicoten a few minutes after they had boarded her. The captain set them ashore the next morning, and they arrived back in Michipicoten after a long and exhausting walk.

But the presence of the police was gradually having an effect. A band of thirty prostitutes, en route from Penisular Harbour to Michipicoten, decided to continue on to Port Arthur. Montana Charlie sent Captain Burden a message offering to surrender in return for a promise of leniency. Burden would make no deals and sent back a message demanding unconditional surrender. Wallace flew into a rage and again threatened to shoot "the bastards from Toronto."

The police dismasted a small ship that had been used in the whiskey trade, destroyed a hundred and twenty gallons of rye, and decided that the whiskey ring was broken. Leaving most of the outlaws at large, they sailed away on October 30, left Harry Cleland to stand trial in Sault Ste. Marie, and continued on to Toronto. Arrangements had been made to establish a strong body of armed police in Michipicoten and in the meantime to police the town with a large force of special constables ordered to arrest any member of the Wallace gang on sight.

The day after the departure of the Toronto police, Arthur Asselin, Little Dick Goldsberry, Gordon Doherty, and Montana Charlie Wallace all emerged from the woods and paraded heavily armed through the town. Wallace was decked out in what witnesses described as true bandit style with a repeating Winchester rifle, four revolvers, and a Bowie knife. None of the special constables dared to lift a hand against him.

But they had not come to renew their reign of terror in the town. Their destination was the S.S. *Steinhoff* which was docked next to the *City of Owen Sound*. They had decided to take advantage of the premature withdrawal of the Toronto police to clear out before another strong police force arrived. They might get well have made a clean escape from the Superior country, except for Wallace's decision to have one last laugh at the expense of the CPR.

He and his men took possession of the main deck of the ship, shouted to those on shore to stand out of the way, and opened fire on the railway offices. Wallace said he only wanted to kill Macdonald, the CPR agent. Macdonald had taken cover in a safe place, but the gunmen riddled his office with bullets, destroyed some of the papers, and killed a contractor's horse.

When over a hundred rounds had been fired in what one crew member called "a parting salute to the town," the outlaws decided that they'd had enough fun and ordered the *Steinhoff* to cast off. She arrived at Sault Ste. Marie, where they forced the captain to make a landing on the American side. They left their guns on board and went ashore in the small Michigan frontier town to make the rounds of the saloons and boast of their deeds in Michipicoten. This was a crucial mistake. Sheriff Lazars, a native of Belleville, Ontario, learned of the gang's presence, telegraphed the Canadian side of Sault Ste. Marie for more information, and then promptly arrested Wallace and his men and deported them to Canada. The prisoners protested that they had broken no laws in the United States. Some American officials argued that Sheriff Lazars had acted far beyond his legal authority and demanded that the Canadian police release the four men. Lazars' response to his critics might not have had much legal force but was one that American citizens would understand: he simply didn't want characters like those in his town, he said.

That settled it. Wallace and his gang stood trial in Sault Ste. Marie in November. Algoma District court records for that period have been lost, but the register for the Central Prison in Toronto shows that Asselin, Doherty, and Goldsberry each received a one-year sentence for "rioting." Asselin and Goldsberry had their own little joke on being admitted to jail. They gave their occupations as bartender and waiter. Harry Cleland's name does not appear; he may have been turned over as a prison fugitive to American police.

Remarkably, the gang leader, Charlie Wallace, was acquitted. In the absence of documentary evidence, the reasons for his release are unknown. His lucky break in court must have made Montana Charlie contemptuous of the law for soon after the trial he loaded a dog-sled with whiskey and headed for his old territory.

When police in Michipicoten heard that Wallace was doing business on the road between the town and the railway work camp, they sent two constables and a pair of Indian guides to bring him in. The police, tramping through frozen woods on snowshoes, came across the whiskey trader's post at a site seven miles from Michipicoten on January 29, 1885. Owners of the camp were absent, but the officers found two dog teams and a large stock of liquor. They hitched up one of the teams, packed the booze onto the sled, and headed back for town. As they crossed an open area not far from the camp, they were ambushed.

From the cover of a copse of trees Wallace and some other men opened fire with revolvers, wounding Constable Costley in the groin. His companions laid him on the sled, urged the team to full speed, and dashed for cover at the other side of the clearing. Bullets whistled overhead and sent splinters of ice flying at their heels, but they made it into the trees without further casualties and ran for home.

It was almost two weeks before Michipicoten police could organize a manhunt for Wallace. They went out with orders from police chief Joseph McKinnon to shoot to kill if Wallace resisted arrest. For a week the posse scoured the woods finding no clues, and it seemed the outlaw had departed into the frigid wilderness. And then one evening at a remote camp sixty-five miles from Michipicoten they accidentally stumbled across the desperado as he was chopping firewood. Before Wallace could reach for his gun, a constable levelled a pistol at his heart and shouted, "Throw up your thumbs!"

Wallace surrendered. He was a difficult prisoner. He refused to walk and had to be hauled on a sled all the way to Michipicoten, cursing and abusing his captors as they travelled.

Again, missing records leave gaps in the story. Why Wallace was not charged with attempted murder is a mystery. He was tried in Michipicoten on a minor charge and sentenced to eighteen months in jail for giving liquor to Indians. There seems to have been speculation that he would be charged with shooting a policeman when his bootlegging sentence expired. But that was not to be.

Wallace was escorted to Toronto by Costley, the man he had shot, and he entered the Central Prison on February 21, 1885, as prisoner number 7108. He had scarcely reacquainted himself with his old lieutenants, Asselin, Doherty, and

Goldsberry, when on March 3 he was released. Wallace's file in the prison register ends with the words: "Conviction Quashed Special."

Why Wallace escaped punishment while his gang members served sentences for lesser offences remains a mystery. What was "Special" about his case? Why was he able to flout the law not only with impunity but to repeat his offences and still walk away as a free man? Perhaps the answer lies in the missing records.

Upon his release after serving ten days in prison, Montana Charlie disappears from history. Michipicoten was certainly quieter without him. Bootleggers continued to sell their wares to thirsty navvies, but without the accompanying gun battles. Within a year the last spike was driven in the transcontinental railway and the booze market in the northern Ontario wilderness dried up.

Twelve years later a minor gold rush brought a new wave of adventurers to Michipicoten and to the new boom town of Wawa. For a glorious moment it seemed that the strike in northern Ontario might rival that of the distant Klondike. An optimistic whiskey runner set up shop in the district, but, like most of the gold hunters, he was doomed to disappointment. After a few weeks he packed up and left. Michipicoten, no longer a rip-roaring frontier town, returned to being a quiet little supply centre for Indians, woodsmen, and trappers.

CHAPTER 16

ALMIGHTY VOICE

THE FINAL BATTLE of the four hundred years of war between white men and red men in North America was not fought by a great chief or a renowned warrior. The last "renegade" Indian to defy the white man in arms and to enlist his own small war party in a last stand for freedom was a young Cree who, until one reckless moment, was ordinary in everything but name. Circumstance and his own impulsive nature transformed Almighty Voice from lowly labourer to Canada's most legendary Indian outlaw. Beside him in the rifle pit on the last morning of his life was a fourteen-year-old boy with the equally legendary name of Going-up-to-Sky. Another follower, nineteen-year-old Tupean (sometimes called "Dublin"), lay where he had been shot dead many hours before.

Almighty Voice, who died such a redemptive death, had lived a life as drab and colourless as the other poverty-stricken Indians who were reduced to penury and dependence by the triumphal march of white civilization across western Canada in the last quarter of the nineteenth century. Born in Saskatchewan around 1874, he was the son of Sounding Sky and the grandson of the Swampy Cree chief One Arrow. From the day in 1876 when One Arrow reluctantly led his people to a wretched reserve a few miles east of Batoche on the South Saskatchewan River, the once-proud Cree had lived in poverty and humiliation. They hunted what game they could find (the buffalo were gone) and raised a few cattle. Their meagre diet was supplemented by the few crops a people with no agricultural tradition could coax from the poor soil and by scanty government rations of flour, sugar, and beans. Sometimes the former buffalo hunters lived on field mice and roots. Whiskey, malnutrition, disease, and apathy steadily reduced their numbers.

In 1885, when the Métis and Indians joined in a last attempt to save themselves from Imperial Canada and invited the exile Louis Riel home to lead them, One Arrow, and perhaps Sounding Sky, fought beside the Métis general Gabriel Dumont at Batoche, where the rebels were crushed by an overwhelming force from eastern Canada. For his part in the uprising, One Arrow was sentenced to three years in prison. Almighty Voice, a boy of eleven or twelve when his grandfather was hauled off to jail and Riel was hanged in Regina, grew to manhood in a Saskatchewan haunted by memories of battles at Fish Creek, Duck Lake, and Batoche. The Swampy Cree continued to suffer the old indignities, were closely watched by the North-West Mounted Police, and were considered a nuisance by a government eager to populate the unploughed prairies with immigrant farmers.

As a youngster Almighty Voice (registered in agency files under the name Jean Baptiste) was not unlike other youths of the One Arrow Reserve. He was a crack shot with a rifle and a good hunter, when there was anything to hunt. He did odd jobs for local whites, cut hay which the reservation Indians sold to white ranchers, and hung around the police post at Batoche where he ran errands in exchange for being fed. The police did not consider him a troublemaker, but inside his own tribe he made enemies by marrying and abandoning a succession of young wives, a process quite within the laws and customs of the Swampy Cree but hardly calculated to endear him to the girls' relatives.

After Almighty Voice had married and dismissed three wives, the Indian Agent tried to make him take back his first wife and marry her according to the white man's law which would have made the union virtually indissoluble. Almighty Voice refused. He would take as many wives as he wanted, as his ancestors had done, and it is said he even threatened to kill the Indian Agent if he interfered, but this seems unlikely and is probably a later invention.

Almighty Voice was living with his fourth wife, thirteen-year-old Pale Face, when the incident which brought down on him the unrealized weight of the white man's law and launched him into outlawry and legend occurred. In June 1895 Almighty Voice butchered a cow without the agent's permission. One story says that he did it because his young wife was sick and starving and the agency had refused to give him food. Another story says he killed the cow to make broth for his brother's starving child. Perhaps he slaughtered it to fill his own empty belly. Ownership of the cow was and still is disputed. It has been described as the property of the government on loan to the Indians for breeding, as a straggler from a nearby ranch, and as a mere stray owned by nobody.

It can hardly have been an important government breeder, because nobody seems to have missed the cow. Its death went unnoticed for more than four months until a brother of one of the discarded wives brought its demise to the attention of the police. When Almighty Voice went to Duck Lake on October 22 to collect his treaty money, the police seized him and his companion and locked them in jail. Three days earlier Sounding Sky, his father, had been arrested on a charge of theft. The former chief's son had been sent to Prince Albert to serve a six months' sentence hauling manure for the Mounties. Almighty Voice wanted no part of this kind of humiliation. Instead of waiting around to be sent to the manure pile, he slipped out of jail under the nose of a careless guard and headed for the depths of the reserve. There is a legend that a sadistic guard frightened the young man into jumping jail by telling him that he would be hanged for stealing the cow, but there is probably no truth in this story. His companion, who did not run away, was released the next morning with a stern warning to behave himself.

Almighty Voice ran six miles to the South Saskatchewan River. The stream was half a mile wide and the water, at the end of October, was frigid, but he swam to the far shore and hurried another fourteen miles to the house of his mother, Spotted Calf, on the One Arrow Reserve. He rested there briefly, then took his rifle and headed for the Fort La Corne Reserve to pick up his wife.

Breaking jail was considered a serious offence. Indians, above all else, were required to be docile, and when it was discovered that Almighty Voice had disappeared, Sergeant Colin Colebrook, a veteran policeman, went in pursuit of him. Colebrook had no trouble getting information from the relatives of the young man's jilted wives on the One Arrow Reserve. A week after the jailbreak Colebrook, accompanied by the Métis guide and interpreter François Dumont, caught up with his quarry a few miles south of Kinistino.

Almighty Voice had just shot a prairie chicken for his wife to cook when the policeman and the guide approached his camp. Colebrook, riding ahead, ordered Dumont to tell Almighty Voice to surrender. The Indian levelled his rifle and told Dumont that if the officer didn't turn back he'd shoot. Dumont translated the threat and warned Colebrook that the young Cree was serious. But Colebrook had no intention of turning back. He could not report to his superiors that he had retreated just because a lone savage waved a rifle at him. With one hand raised in a gesture of peace and the other in a pocket where he carried a pistol, he slowly rode closer to the fugitive.

Three times Almighty Voice gave his warning, and three times Dumont pleaded with Colebrook to turn back. The young Indian wife was weeping. Almighty Voice was slow to carry out his threat. He backed into the trees. Colebrook got to within a few yards of his man. "Come on, old boy," he said as the Indian backed up. Then the stillness of the autumn morning was shattered by a blast from the Cree's rifle and Sergeant Colin Colebrook fell from the saddle, shot cleanly through the heart.

François Dumont turned his horse and galloped off to get help. Almighty Voice mounted Colebrook's horse and rode away leaving Pale Face and the slain officer behind.

"Now indeed they won't leave me alone for what I have done," he cried to his wife as he galloped away.

Almighty Voice, who had taken women as he pleased, killed a cow when he was in need of meat, and walked out of jail as an act of defiance, was now a murderer. If he had killed another Indian he might have hoped to live. Having killed a white man, especially a policeman, he knew very well that if they ever caught him he'd die at the end of a rope.

Colebrook's body, untouched by the Indians, was located by the police and taken to Prince Albert for burial under a monument stating that he had died in the line of duty. Pale Face returned to her reserve. News of the murder spread rapidly, and in homesteads, settlements, and police posts grim-faced men loaded guns in anticipation of new "Injun trouble." The killer was a son and grandson of Indians who had followed Riel, and the dead man was one of those who had helped defeat Riel's ally, the great Cree Chief Big Bear. A renewal of the violence that had swept over the prairies only a decade before did not seem a remote possibility.

But except for Almighty Voice and a couple of his younger relatives, there was little fight left in the Cree. There was no stirring of insurrection. Neither was there any sign of Almighty Voice. The twenty-one-year-old Indian had vanished into the great empty land. His physical appearance—

five feet ten inches tall, slim build, shoulder-length black hair, "feminine" features—was advertised far and wide. Armies of men, hampered by bad weather and difficult terrain, searched the woods, the marshes, the coulees, and the poplar and willow bluffs which rose like islands from the sea of grass. Among the Indians the searchers met a wall of silence. Even the relatives of the cast-off wives were hostile. They might have tattled to whites who wanted to send him to jail for theft, but they were not about to betray one of their own people into the hands of the white hangman.

Rumours, some of them no doubt deliberately planted to mislead the police, sent the manhunters on lengthy chases. The police arranged for the release of Sounding Sky, hoping the old warrior would lead them to his son. That plan failed. Six months after the killing of Colebrook the federal government posted a reward of five hundred dollars for information leading to the arrest and conviction of "an Indian known as Jean Baptiste or Almighty Voice." There were no takers.

A year passed, and still the outlaw remained at large. Some officials, including Broncho Jack Allan, the police inspector in charge of the search, believed that Almighty Voice had quit Saskatchewan altogether and had probably fled to the United States.

Such speculation was not good enough for whites who still lived with an "Indian scare" or for a government whose much-vaunted police force was receiving criticism and ridicule. Tension increased in November 1896 when a Blood Indian named Charcoal shot and killed police sergeant W.B. Wilde in the Alberta foothills. Newspapers thundered against a police force that could not protect it own officers, let alone the public, from bloodthirsty redskins and taunted a government whose incompetence allowed known killers to run free. After a furious chase Charcoal was betrayed by his own people, captured and hanged. But in Saskatchewan Almighty Voice remained a phantom. News of Charcoal's fate doubtless strengthened the Cree's resolve never to be taken alive.

The rumours persisted. He was in Montana. He was north of Lesser Slave Lake. He had died on the prairie. The police investigated lead after lead, always coming away empty handed. Their reputation was hitting rock bottom when, on May 26, 1897, they got a lucky break.

That day Napoleon Venne, a Métis rancher, saw three Indians slaughtering one of his steers near the One Arrow Reserve. Two of them he identified as Tupean, brother-in-law of Almighty Voice, and a lad named Going-up-to-Sky, the fugitive's fourteen-year-old cousin. The eldest of the three he did not recognize but suspected to be the Indian the Mounties had been chasing for more than a year and a half. Venne rode to Batoche and reported what he had seen to the police.

All the time the Mounties had been combing thousands of square miles searching for him, Almighty Voice had been living right under their noses in the vicinity of the One Arrow Reserve. Several times when they had made surprise visits to the house owned by his mother, Spotted Calf, Almighty Voice had hidden in the root cellar. He had been on a trapping expedition. He had even visited white settlements. None of the improverished Cree, all of whom knew of his presence on the reserve, had chosen to turn him in for the bounty money.

On the morning of May 27 Napoleon Venne returned to the scene of his steer's slaughter with Corporal J.W. Bowridge of the North-West Mounted Police. They searched for some sign of the rustlers and asked a band of nearby Indians about the elusive Almighty Voice. The Indians professed to know nothing. When asked why Sounding Sky had been seen in their company, they merely shrugged. Then Venne saw two Indians dashing for the cover of a poplar bluff. The policeman and the Métis rode toward the tangle of trees and underbrush. There was the sharp crack of a rifle, and a bullet struck Venne in the shoulder. The two turned their horses and dashed for safety. A second bullet passed through Venne's hat.

Bowridge sent for help. The following day Broncho Jack Allan and his posse of policemen and civilians cut off the three Indians as they tried to catch mounts from a herd of ponies driven toward them by an Indian boy. The trio, Almighty Voice, Tupean, and Going-up-to-Sky, retreated to a bluff and prepared to fight it out. The posse encircled the five-acre stand of wood then tried to flush the fugitives from the cover of the trees.

Sergeant C.C. Raven had penetrated some fifty yards into the underbrush when the Indians opened fire. Raven was hit twice, in the thigh and the groin. Nevertheless he returned the fire and shouted for Allan. Broncho Jack galloped toward the sound of the rifle fire and was shot off his horse by Almighty Voice, the bone of his upper right arm shattered by the bullet. Almighty Voice stood a few yards from the wounded officer and pointed to Allan's gunbelt, indicating that he wanted it. Allan refused, but before Almighty Voice could shoot the Inspector again, some of Allan's men saw the Indian and drove him back into the trees with gunfire. The police then withdrew, carrying their two wounded men.

With Allan and Raven out of action, command fell to Corporal C.H.S. Hockin, who sent a Métis scout to tell the outlaws that unless they would surrender he would set fire to the bush. The trapped Indians were defiant. They knew the vegetation was too green to burn. Meanwhile Indians from the One Arrow Reserve arrived and, ignoring orders from the police to leave, lined the ridges to watch the showdown from a distance. Spotted Calf was with them, but Sounding Sky was back in jail, charged with aiding and abetting his fugitive son.

The outlaws in the bluff were without food, water, or horses and had a limited supply of ammunition. Using a knife tied to a stick, they dug a rifle pit in the southwest corner where the growth was thickest. From time to time they fired a round from their dwindling supply of bullets to keep the attackers back.

When a handful of civilian volunteers from Duck Lake arrived to boost Hockin's force from twenty-one to twenty-six, the corporal made a foolhardy decision to launch another assault on the bluff. A few days without food or water would have forced the Indians to surrender, but Hockin may have been afraid that Almighty Voice, who had escaped on two previous occasions so successfully and remained on the run for nineteen months, might slip through the cordon and have the last laugh on them yet.

Leading an assault group of nine men while others patrolled the perimeter, Hockin made two sweeps through the bluff without encountering the enemy. The third sweep brought his party into the outlaws' gunsights. There was a burst of rifle fire from the pit, and Hockin fell, mortally wounded. Constable J.R. Kerr and Ernest Grundy, Duck Lake postmaster and a former member of the force, were killed instantly by the same volley. Once again the attackers withdrew, dragging Hockin and abandoning the bodies of Kerr and Grundy. The outlaws relieved the corpses of guns and coats as they exchanged fire with the retreating Mounties. It is possible that Tupean was killed at this point. There is evidence that he died early in the battle.

Night fell, Hockin died, and the besiegers awaited more reinforcements. From the bluff Almighty Voice called to them, "Brothers, we've had a good fight. I am starving. Send me food. We will finish the fight tomorrow." His answer was a volley of gunfire.

The following day militiamen, veterans of the Riel rebellion, came from Duck Lake, Batoche, and Prince Albert. They brought along a seven-pound field gun and seven rounds of ammunition for it—all the shells available in Prince Albert. That evening Assistant Commissioner John

McIllree arrived from Regina with twenty-four Mounties and a nine-pound gun. The posse now numbered over a hundred heavily armed men. Their quarry, three Indians (or two if Tupean was already dead) were counting their bullets, eating crows which they shot out of the sky, and stripping bark from trees so they could suck out the moisture. From time to time they sniped at the posse, but without further effect.

Late in the afternoon of May 30 the police began to bombard the bluff with cannon fire. The outlaws shot back with rifles and pistols, and Almighty Voice hurled insults at the attackers in the best tradition of the defiant Indian facing certain death. The Cree from the One Arrow Reserve watched in grim silence. Spotted Calf lifted her voice in a traditional chant. She was singing the Cree death song for her son.

The bombardment continued into the night, and between the bursting of shells and the scream of shrapnel the outlaws and the Mounties duelled with small arms.

At dawn on Sunday, May 31, the battle was still going on. The bombardment resumed with round after round from the nine-pounder. (The seven-pounder had long since fired its last available shell.) For four hours of what McIllree called "most excellent practice" they saturated the bluff with cannonballs and canister shot.

At ten o'clock the bombardment stopped. During the four hours of shelling and the following four hours of waiting, no firing came from the battered woods. At two o'clock the police cautiously approached the island of trees and brush.

This time there was no gunfire from the rifle pit. First they found Tupean lying near the edge of the trees. He had been dead a long time. He had been shot in the head, either by one of Hockin's men during the early sweep into the bluff or by a sentry who cut him down as he tried to escape during the night.

Going-up-to-Sky was found sprawled across the body of Almighty Voice in the rifle pit. They had both been killed by the cannon fire. Shrapnel had shattered the knee of the elder Indian, and he had tried to escape the bluff by means of a makeshift crutch. That failing, he had crawled back to the pit where another shell blew off a piece of his skull which is now preserved in a glass case in a Prince Albert museum. The boy, Going-Up-To-Sky, had died at about the same time, taking a cannon shot in his body.

A Métis named Henry Smith took the remains of Almighty Voice from the rifle pit in the bluff and carried them to his mother, Spotted Calf, for burial. There is no official record of where the last defiant Indian was laid to rest. Although the Saskatchewan Archives preserves a photograph of a cross above a common grave in which the three Cree outlaws were allegedly interred, it is quite likely that the bodies of Almighty Voice and his companions were buried in secrecy.

CHAPTER 17

BILL MINER

ON A FOGGY SEPTEMBER EVENING in 1904 three masked men quietly boarded the Canadian Pacific Railway's Transcontinental Express while it took on water near Mission, British Columbia. As the train began moving away westward, the trio scrambled over cars until they reached the engine, where they ordered the engineer, Nat Scott, at gunpoint, to stop the train. The train squealed to a halt a few miles from Mission, and there the masked bandits ordered the crew to uncouple the passenger cars.

Leaving the passengers behind, they continued down the track for about a mile and stopped again. The three gunmen, threatening to use dynamite if they were not obeyed, then ordered the doors of the express and mail cars to be opened. While one of them kept a wary eye on the crew, the others went through the cars and scooped up seven thousand dollars in cash and gold dust.

They then had the engine uncoupled and ordered Scott to drive them another two miles down the line where they jumped from the cab and disappeared into the night. Despite an intense search and rewards posted by the CPR and the British Columbia government, the bandits made a clean getaway.

Canadian police had no ideas about the identity of the train robbers. Nat Scott and his crew reported that two of the men were young and seemed to be quite nervous, but the third man, the leader, was in his fifties or sixties and displayed the cool precision of a professional. They described him as silver-haired, slightly built, soft-spoken, and polite.

It might have seemed unlikely to CPR officials that a middle-aged gentleman could be responsible for the unprecedented robbery of one of their trains, but American police searching the country on their side of the border for signs of the robbers were not in the least surprised. The description of the leading bandit was that of a man whose crimes had made him a legend. He was the gentleman bandit Bill Miner, one of the most notorious highwaymen of the American west.

Contrary to popular belief, this was not the first train robbery in Canada. Five unknown thieves disguised in the robes of the Ku Klux Klan had boarded the express car of the Great Western Railway between Toronto and Port Credit on November 13, 1874, and carried off forty-five thousand dollars. Bill Miner was, however, the first to take on the mighty Canadian Pacific. By so doing he became an outlaw hero to many thousands of railroad-hating Canadians who regarded the CPR as an instrument of invasion and exploitation serving a clique of powerful businessmen. He was one of those desperadoes whose exploits, daring enough in fact, were further romanticized in fiction. Between robberies and jail breaks in the United States he was said to have smuggled beautiful slave girls into Turkey and cargoes of guns into Latin America. In the Nicola Valley of British Columbia he was said to have given money to a poor widow who was about to lose her home to a heartless banker and then stolen the cash back from the ruthless capitalist when the good woman had made her payment. This endearing yarn is a favourite of people who like their outlaws to be noble and has been told of Jesse James, Butch Cassidy, and

Robin Hood, among others. If the people of British Columbia transferred this legend to Bill Miner, it indicates that they admired him, and they admired him only because his chosen victim was the CPR.

There were even those who tried to make him a native Canadian, returned home after his American adventures, but in fact Miner was a native of Kentucky who had drifted west trying his hand at such jobs as cowboy, mule driver, and express rider. When just a boy of sixteen he had decided that honest labour was not his calling and began robbing stage coaches in California.

In April 1866 the nineteen-year-old Miner was caught, convicted on two charges of robbery, and sentenced to five years in the state's hellhole at San Quentin, where he tasted all the horrors of a nineteenth-century prison—overcrowding, primitive sanitation, bad water, rotten food, beatings and tortures inflicted by guards who were more inhuman than the prisoners themselves.

In July 1870 Miner was released, a hardened criminal determined to live the life of a road agent. Within a year he was back at San Quentin, sentenced to serve twelve years in prison for holding up stagecoaches. Two years later Miner escaped, but he was caught within a few hours and taken back to San Quentin where he was stripped, lashed, and thrown into a dark, foul dungeon. There he was fed on bread and water and forced to breath the fumes of quicklime, a punishment reserved for prisoners classed as "difficult." Hauled out of the hole, Miner was fitted with the Oregon Boot, an iron shackle designed to make escape impossible.

In July 1880, after spending more than thirteen of the previous fourteen years in jail, Miner was once more released. He went to Colorado, changed his name, teamed up with another outlaw, Billy Leroy, and resumed his career as a highwayman. When Leroy was caught by a sheriff and lynched by a mob, Miner changed his name again and travelled far east to Onondaga, Michigan, by way of Chicago, posing as a gentleman with an inherited fortune.

Made independent by his accumulated loot, he lived a respectable life for a while, almost got married, and became a popular figure in Onondaga society. When the time came for him to move on, the local citizens honoured him with a farewell banquet at which the mayor presided as master of ceremonies.

Miner had been forced to give up his pleasant and respectable life in Michigan because his "inheritance" was running low. To replenish it he returned to Colorado, recruited a pair of ne'er-do-wells as his assistants, and robbed another stage.

By now the authorities in Colorado and California were becoming familiar with Miner's style. Courtesy was his trademark, and he was already known as "the Gentleman Bandit." Most highwaymen intimidated their victims with abuse and threats, and those slow to respond to their demands might be beaten or shot. Miner's robberies were like bizarre exercises in etiquette. He carried a gun but rarely used it. He spoke politely, apologizing to his victims for the inconvenience he caused them while relieving them of their valuables. He would sometimes let passengers keep their personal property and content himself with looting the freight company's strongbox. It was his habit, as he rode away, to bid a friendly goodbye to the people he had robbed.

A Colorado posse set out after Miner and his accomplices, caught up with them, and subdued them in a gunfight, but on the way to jail Miner untied himself, got hold of a gun, wounded his three guards, and escaped with his two partners. One of the outlaws was soon recaptured, but the other stuck with Miner and helped him in a series of daring robberies in California and Arizona. He was caught again in December 1881 and sentenced to twenty-five years in his old homestead, San Quentin.

He made one attempt to escape but failed and again suffered the sadistic punishments of the fiendish guards. A fellow convict stabbed him, but Miner survived both the wound and the prison's medical facilities. After serving twenty years he emerged old, wrinkled, suffering from ulcers, and ready to pick up where he had left off.

Miner was now an anachronism, a nineteenth-century highwayman in a twentieth-century world. The stagecoaches that he had relied upon for his daily bread were gone. Trains—huge, fast, hard to rob—had replaced them everywhere. Policemen now had the telegraph, the telephone, a whole new world of technology to make life difficult for gentlemen of fortune. The old-time outlaws had either abandoned their trade or died with their boots on. By the time Miner left San Quentin after his third term there, he had outlived most of his colleagues. Jesse James, Sam Bass, Bill Doolin, the Renos, the Daltons were all dead. The surviving outlaws were pale shadows of the wild men who had terrorized the west in the previous century. Cole Younger, after a twenty-five year stretch in Stillwater, Minnesota, was selling tombstones for a living. Frank James was charging tourists fifty cents a head to look at his brother's grave. Prospects like these did not interest Bill Miner. Since his beloved stagecoaches were a thing of the past, he decided to upgrade his skills and take on the trains.

He travelled north from California to Puget Sound, where he took a temporary job working on an oyster bed while he assembled a gang, one of whom was Jimmie James, a distant cousin of the infamous Jesse. On September 23, 1903, the outlaws held up a train of the Great Northern Railroad near Portland, Oregon. They bungled the robbery. One of the bandits was killed, another wounded, and Miner rode away empty handed. He wandered across the United States and Mexico, and then, some time in 1904, arrived in Canada.

Going by the name of George Edwards, the aging man with the outdated cavalryman's moustache settled in the Nicola Valley of British Columbia. He presented himself as a semi-retired rancher who wanted to raise a few cattle and do a bit of prospecting. His courtesy and polished manners made him popular, especially with children, to whom he was a sort of universal grandfather. The parents of the children accepted him as a kindly old gentleman. No one questioned his periods of absence or the strangers from south of the border who sometimes stayed at his house. When the unbelievable robbery of the Canadian Pacific Transcontinental Express happened in September 1904, no one dreamed of suspecting kindly old George Edwards who happened to be away on business at the time. Nor did they connect him with the robbery of the Great Northern Express in November 1905. In that job he and his partners stopped the train near Ballard, Washington, and got away with thirty thousand dollars. American police never officially charged Miner with that robbery, but it had all the marks of one of his slickest jobs.

As George Edwards he thoroughly enjoyed his stay in British Columbia. He travelled, attended dances, and charmed people wherever he went. Then, either for want of action or because his retirement fund was running low, he decided to try the CPR a second time. Accompanied by Thomas "Shorty" Dunn, a Montana gunman on the run from the American police, and Lewis Colquon, a small-time thief from Ontario, Miner stopped the Transcontinental Express on May 8, 1906, near a place called Duck's Station, about seventeen miles from Kamloops.

The operation was almost a duplicate of Miner's first Canadian train robbery. He ordered the engine and mail car uncoupled and moved a mile down the track, where the bandits entered the car and learned to their disgust that a safe containing thirty-five thousand dollars in gold—the main reason for stopping the train—had been left in a second express car which was still attached to the passenger cars whose occupants might already be telegraphing for help. They could not risk returning to the coaches. They rummaged through mail sacks, took a few letters containing a grand total of fifteen dollars, and overlooked a bag with forty thousand dollars in cash. Then they ordered the engine uncoupled and were driven to the place where their horses were waiting. Miner bade the engineer a pleasant farewell and galloped off into the darkness.

The robbery had been a fiasco, but the ensuing manhunt was perhaps the biggest in British Columbia history. It was obviously a repeat performance by the same gang that had successfully robbed the CPR two years earlier, and such daring, persistent bandits could not be allowed to remain at large. In Canada, where great commercial institutions were sacred, ordinary people did not meddle with the CPR which was owned by the greatest financiers in the country and generously subsidized by the government. Hatred, yes; armed robbery, no.

The Canadian Pacific and the government pursued the outlaws with every available resource. To the railway's five thousand dollar reward for the bandits dead or alive, the provincial and federal governments added equal sums. It added up to a fortune for anyone who could turn them in. A dollar in 1906 was still a pretty good day's pay. Railway police joined the provincial police and the Royal North-West Mounted. They swore in cowboys as special constables, hired Siwash Indians as trackers, brought bloodhounds from Calgary and Spokane, and hired American detectives to join the hunt on both sides of the border. A special CPR train shuttled back and forth carrying men, horses, dogs, and supplies.

The search went on for weeks as the outlaws, who had given up their horses, trudged through swamps and forests and across rocky ground trying to give the immense posse the slip. Old Bill was suffering from sore feet as well as stomach and liver ailments. At abandoned campsites the searchers found his empty medicine bottles. Near Douglas Lake provincial constable W.L. Fernie stumbled on three men who told him they were prospectors. He chatted briefly with the old-timer who seemed to be the leader of the group, then rode away, but he wasn't satisfied with their credentials.

Fernie passed word to a party of Royal North-West Mounted Police, who located the men as they were cooking a meal over a campfire. As the old man spoke with the Mounties, trying to convince them that he was indeed a sourdough searching for ore, Shorty Dunn let his nerves get the better of him. He drew his gun, crying that the game was up, and made a dash for the bush. A few moments and a few shots later Dunn surrendered with a bullet in his leg. Miner and Colquon gave up without a fight.

The police took their captives to Kamloops, where the leader was identified as Bill Miner, a genuine desperado whose armed robberies had spanned nearly half a century (thirty-four years of which he had spent in jail). The community was thrilled to have such a celebrity in their midst and could hardly have been more pleased had they discovered that the pleasant neighbour they had been admiring for the past two years was a prince in disguise. They continued to praise his courage and deportment and seemed not to mind in the least if he robbed a train occasionally. The press loudly disagreed. It took no courage to rob trains; one editor proclaimed, "any tramp can do the same."

All the while Miner insisted that his name was George Edwards and that he knew nothing about bandits. He stuck to his story even when an old acquaintance, the warden of San Quentin, came to Kamloops to identify him.

During the first trial, which dragged on for three days in a stifling courtroom, Miner remained calm and aloof while Lewis Colquon and Shorty Dunn sweated out the ordeal; Dunn actually displayed symptoms of a nervous breakdown. The first trial ended in a hung jury, but a second jury lost no time in reaching a verdict of guilty. Miner and Dunn received life sentences and Colquon twenty-five years. As he was escorted from the courtroom, the old man seemed unconcerned. He still denied being Bill Miner.

The New Westminster penitentiary was a far cry from San Quentin, and Miner seemed, from all appearances, resigned to spending his last years there as a model prisoner. He began, for the first time in his life, to show an interest in religion and became friendly with the daughter of the deputy warden, an evangelist dedicated to saving the souls of convicts for Christ. When he asked to be transferred from his inside job to the prison brickyard so he could work in the open air for the good of his health, Miner's request was granted.

After casing the yard carefully, he found a spot near the fence which could not be observed from the guard tower. Helped by three younger convicts, he burrowed under the fence and escaped over the wall on August 8, 1907, a little more than a year after his imprisonment.

Again the chase was on, and Miner's accomplices were recaptured. But the old fox himself was gone. The daughter of the deputy warden was quite upset. She described Bill's ungrateful escape as "horrid...after we had done so much to make life easier for him." The guard on duty in the tower at the time of the prison break was fired. Questions were raised in Parliament, and Prime Minister Wilfrid Laurier delivered a speech expressing his anger that such a "dangerous criminal ... thinking to play with impunity in this country the pranks he had been playing on the other side of the line ...had been allowed to escape from the penitentiary."

There were rumours that Miner had received outside help, that he had used promises of real or pretended money to bribe prison officials. But those were just rumours. The whole thing was too embarrassing for officials at any level to risk the publicity of a proper investigation.

While posses hunted for Miner, the people of British Columbia once again gave him their moral support. They told the police and the press that they hoped Miner would get away. Residents in Nicola Valley declared publicly that Bill Miner, George Edwards, or whatever he cared to call himself, was welcome to live in their community no matter what he had done. They would, if necessary, hide the old bandit and protect him from the police. The newspapers again denounced all this and dismissed his sympathizers as "anarchists of a weak and watery sort."

Miner never accepted the hospitable offer of his Nicola Valley friends. He left Canada and was next heard of as a suspect in a bank robbery at Portland, Oregon, in July 1909.

Almost two years later the state of Georgia experienced its first train robbery when in February 1911 Bill Miner and company held up the Southern Pacific. It was his last act of banditry. He was captured, identified, and sentenced to twenty years, denying all the while that he had ever heard of a man named Miner.

A few months after being locked up, Miner and another convict once again broke out of jail. A posse tracked them down and cornered them in an old boxcar. They tried to shoot it out. Miner's partner was killed. He then surrendered and was taken back to prison. Less than a year later he broke out again.

For a few days after this last of so many prison breaks, Miner wandered through a disease-ridden, snake-infested Georgia swamp. The country in which he was hiding was hard enough to tax the resources of a strong young man. For old Bill, worn out in body if not in spirit, it was fatal. When the authorities finally caught up with him, he was sick, exhausted, and not far from dead. They took him to the prison hospital, and he died there in September 1913, the last surviving old-time highwayman.

CHAPTER 18

THE MAD TRAPPER

IT WAS NOON, DECEMBER 31, 1931, with the brief daylight of the arctic winter, as constables Alfred King and R.G. McDowell and special constables Joe Bernard and Lazarus Sittichinli of the Royal Canadian Mounted Police approached the isolated cabin of a strange man known to them as Albert Johnson. The cabin was located on the banks of the Rat River, a small tributary of the great Mackenzie, near the border between the Northwest Territories and the Yukon, some hundred miles or so inland from the shores of the Beaufort Sea.

Local Indians reported that Johnson, a newcomer to the Northwest, had been springing their traps and hanging them on trees. At that time trapline disputes were common in the Canadian north because laws and licences did not clearly define their boundaries.

The policemen had spent a day and a half travelling in weather where the temperature hovered around forty below zero. They had left camp without eating breakfast, were anxious to take care of what they hoped would be a routine call, and then planned to be on their way to a New Year's party in Fort McPherson.

King, the officer in charge, urged caution. He knew from experience that Johnson was not an average trapper and had already lied when questioned about his movements. This in itself was not unusual in a frontier community where men had to be secretive about gold strikes or the location of their best trapping grounds, but in addition Johnson was an unsociable recluse who came and went like a phantom, spoke to no one, and avoided human contact when possible. Loneliness and the brutal arctic environment had driven many men to eccentric behaviour, but even among the tough individualists of the north Albert Johnson was regarded as an oddball.

Three days earlier King and Bernard had visited Johnson's eight foot by ten foot cabin to question him about the Indians' complaint. Not only had Johnson refused to open the door, he had not even answered when King called to him identifying himself as an RCMP officer. Johnson had peered at King through the one window in his tiny cabin but otherwise had ignored him. This was strange behaviour in a land where doors were never barred and visitors, including policemen, were always welcomed.

Lacking a warrant, King had left the cabin and trekked eighty miles to Aklavik. There Inspector A.N. Eames had issued a warrant to enter and search the cabin and had provided two extra men.

Now, while his companions waited by the river, King walked toward Johnson's cabin. Smoke rose from the chimney and snowshoes leaned against the wall beside the door, so he knew Johnson was inside. He called out, identifying himself, and informed the trapper that he had a warrant and would, if necessary, force the door open. Johnson made no reply.

King shouted, "Are you there, Mr. Johnson?" Again the answer was silence. He knocked on the door. Instantly the sound of an explosion shattered the silence. Splinters flew from the cabin door, and King, his chest pierced by a bullet, sprawled in the snow.

While the wounded policeman crawled to cover, the other three poured a fusillade of bullets into the cabin. Johnson replied with the occasional shot—enough to discourage an attack.

The police dragged King out of range and lashed him to a dogsled. For the moment they ignored the gunman in the cabin. They had to get King to Aklavik before his wound and the arctic cold combined to kill him. They completed the journey in a record-breaking twenty hours, even though they made frequent stops to rub King's face and limbs to prevent frostbite.

In the tiny Aklavik hospital Dr. J.A. Urquhart saved King's life. While a new posse prepared to make the journey upcountry to Rat River, the police studied what little information they had on Albert Johnson. It wasn't much.

On July 7, 1931, two Indian brothers, William and Edward Snowshoes, had met a stranger on the bank of the Peel River near Fort McPherson. They mistook the stranger for a man named Albert Johnson and called to him. The man responded to that name but otherwise had little to say to them. The two Indians reported his presence on the Peel, and the name Albert Johnson stuck, although the man's real name was unknown.

Several times during July "Johnson" had gone into Fort McPherson to buy supplies. Those who met him described him as nervous, taciturn, and shy. He walked with a stoop and had "cold blue eyes." Merchants noted that he always had ready cash to pay for what he bought. He asked a few questions about the surrounding country but otherwise kept to himself. Some people thought he had a slight Scandinavian accent.

On July 21 Constable Edgar Millen had met Johnson in Fort McPherson, asked him where he was from, and enquired what he planned to do in the north. There was good reason for such enquiries. The Great Depression had begun, and in the provinces and states to the south millions of unemployed men were looking for something to do. Many of them, out of desperation, were heading north believing that they could hunt, trap, prospect, and live cheaply. Few had even the most basic training for survival, especially in the Arctic. The police wished to discourage greenhorns from going into the bush unprepared. It was also their job to keep count of people for the census.

Millen noted inconsistencies in Johnson's answers. For example, the man said he had come into the north by way of the Mackenzie River. Millen knew he had been on the Peel, which flows out of the Ogilvie Mountains far to the west of the Mackenzie and does not even approach the larger river until it passes Fort McPherson. But they were minor matters and Millen did not press any questions. Johnson seemed to be a strong, healthy man of 35 or 40 who obviously knew how to take care of himself in the bush. Millen advised him to buy a trapper's licence then left him alone.

A week later Johnson had set out in a canoe for the Rat River. There were three water routes to Destruction City, the shantytown for which Johnson was heading. Each route was difficult and perilous. Countless small craft had been wrecked in the dangerous waters, their flotsam washing ashore and giving the camp its name. Time and again experienced rivermen had turned back rather than risk their lives on the barely navigable Rat. But somehow Johnson made the run singlehanded. It would not be the last time he astounded seasoned northerners with his stamina and remarkable woodsmanship. He built his cabin on a site overlooking a trail eight miles from Destruction City and settled in for the winter.

The police in Aklavik knew no more than this about him. Even his identity was uncertain. They could only guess at his reasons for shooting King. Perhaps he had "cabin fever." If so, he would be dangerous, perhaps murderously insane. Perhaps he was a fugitive from the United States. Perhaps he had committed some crime they had not yet discovered and assumed they had come to arrest him. There could be no answers until the man was brought in and questioned.

On the morning of January 9, 1932, a nine-man party of police, civilian volunteers, and an Indian guide moved in a half circle toward Johnson's cabin. Among them were Inspector Eames and Constable Millen.

Eames wanted to get the job done as quickly as possible. The posse had suffered delays on the trail, and supplies were running low. With temperatures again around forty degrees below zero his men could not remain in the field for long. In the severe cold, men and dogs had to be constantly on the move and had to consume large amounts of food to keep up their body heat.

Eames called on Johnson to surrender. He said that King was alive, so there would be no murder charge. Johnson didn't say a word. He answered with his guns. He had knocked moss out of chinks in all four walls of the cabin so that he had loopholes through which he could fire in all directions. He had also dug a rifle pit in the floor, giving him maximum protection in a good shooting position.

Because his cabin was small, he could command every approach, while its thick logs absorbed bullets and his fire warded off the cold that was biting through the heavy coats of his foes. He apparently knew that at this point he enjoyed a temporary advantage, that the posse would not be able to conduct a prolonged siege but would have to retire in a day or so.

Every rush on the cabin was driven back by gunfire. At one point two policemen, risking their lives, managed to jar the door open. They saw Johnson firing what they thought were two handguns. They later learned that the weapons were a sawed-off shotgun and a .22 calibre rifle with the stock shortened.

Nine hours passed with no success against Johnson's carefully prepared defences. The police lit flares, hoping to blind the lone gunman. That failed. The night grew dark, the cold increased, and the besiegers had to leave their positions to warm themselves beside campfires.

Around midnight Eames decided to use dynamite. Thawing the explosives over an open fire was a treacherous task, but soon the police were hurling the lethal sticks at the cabin, trying to blow open the door or knock down a wall. The sturdy little building, recently built from green logs, held up.

One of the men, Knut Lang, got in close enough to toss a stick of dynamite onto the roof. It blew a hole and knocked down the part of the chimney rising above the roofline but did not really breach the trapper's defences. Within seconds of the explosion Lang was running for the riverbank with Johnson's bullets whistling around him.

At 3:00 A.M. Eames decided on one final all-or-nothing effort. He made a four-pound dynamite bomb by tying the remaining sticks together, lit the fuse, and hurled it at the cabin. The explosion lifted the roof off the cabin and partially caved in the walls. Expecting that Johnson would be killed, or at least stunned, by the blast, the posse rushed forward. One of them, Karl Gardlund, carried a flashlight. No sooner had he reached the ruined pile of logs than the flashlight was shot out of his hand.

Its dynamite exhausted, the posse fled, and Eames ordered his half-frozen men back to Aklavik. It was a humiliating defeat for a force that, according to legend, always got its man. On January 14 Constable Millen and Karl Gardlund returned to the scene of the battle to find Johnson gone.

By radio the outside world had heard of the shooting of King and the subsequent gunfight. The press had promptly dubbed Johnson "The Mad Trapper of Rat River," a title by which he has been known ever since. It was a sensational story that sold newspapers and kept people tuning their radio sets, eager for the next development in the far-off Arctic. It was the sort of story that caught the popular imagination—a lone wolf in a tiny cabin standing off highly trained policemen who outnumbered him nine to one.

This was the Dirty Thirties when honest folk who had lost their jobs or their farms made heroes out of such criminals as John Dillinger and Bonnie and Clyde. They saw in Johnson an underdog, a victim pursued by authority. Johnson never knew it, but his stubborn fight with the Mounties was making headlines around the world, and people from Dawson City to New York were sitting glued to their radios, waiting for his next move.

Inspector Eames wrote to his superiors: "I note in press reports that Johnson is referred to as 'the demented trapper.' On the contrary, he showed himself to be an extremely shrewd and resolute man, capable of quick thought and action, a tough and desperate character."

By January 16 another posse was ready to take up the chase. The RCMP officers were joined by white and Indian trappers and by volunteers from the Royal Canadian Corps of Signals at Aklavik. They took along homemade bombs and a portable radio.

A search of the wrecked cabin revealed no clue to Johnson's identity. A heavy snow had buried any trail that he might have left. A blizzard hampered the progress of the manhunters. For days they searched the countryside around Rat River and found nothing. On January 21, again faced with a shortage of supplies, Eames was forced to retreat. He left Constable Millen with three other men to continue the search.

For a week Millen's party tramped back and forth through the timberland of the Rat River country without success. Once they came upon a cache of food and watched it for many hours, hoping to trap Johnson when he returned to it. But the outlaw never appeared. By January 28 they were almost out of supplies and were ready to turn back when Sergeant R.F. Riddell of the Signals Corps discovered the faint, two-day-old marks of Johnson's trail.

Encouraged, the four-man posse continued the hunt. As they lost the trail, then found it again, they realized that their quarry was a woodsman of uncanny skill, possessed of incredible stamina. He walked a zigzag pattern so that at times he could spy on the posse, coming in from the side or from behind. This meant that he had to cover perhaps twice the distance, on snowshoes and carrying a heavy pack, that they covered by dogsled. In temperatures that dropped to fifty degrees below zero, Johnson could build only small fires under the shelter of snowbanks. Since he could not risk using his rifle, he had to snare small game for food. He worked his way across country which experienced trackers had thought impenetrable and left a thoroughly confusing trail while doing it.

The searchers were on the banks of the Rat River, unsure which way to go, when an Indian came into their camp and told them he had heard a shot in the Bear River area. Going on the slim hope that Johnson had been forced to shoot a large animal, Millen decided to investigate. The posse picked up a trail near the Bear River and followed it back to the Rat. They came across the remains of a caribou and finally, on January 30, located Johnson's camp near a creek that fed into the river.

Millen was sure Johnson would not escape this time. The fugitive had camped in a canyon with a cliff at his back. As the police crept into the canyon, they could hear him whistling cheerfully although they could not see him. The quarry, like the fox of fable, was apparently enjoying the chase. Then one of the men slipped, making a noise. In a split second Johnson stopped whistling, grabbed his rifle, a .30-.30 Savage, and began shooting.

As the police fired back, Johnson leaped across his campfire and hurled himself behind a fallen tree. He seemed to collapse, and the police thought he might have been hit. Millen called to Johnson to surrender but got no reply.

The men did not dare to leave their cover. For two hours they waited, not sure if Johnson was dead, wounded, or planning a new trick. Surely, they thought, he couldn't just lie there in the bitter cold. They could feel their own sweat freezing inside their clothing.

As night approached Millen decided, against the advice of the others, to move in. They moved forward together but had advanced only a few steps when Johnson sprang up and opened fire. Sergeant Riddell dived for cover as a bullet whistled over his head. Constable Millen dropped to one knee and fired two shots. Suddenly he stood up, spun around, dropped his rifle, and collapsed.

While the other two men kept Johnson pinned down with rifle fire, Gardlund crawled to Millen, tied his bootlaces together, and dragged him to cover. He was dead, with a bullet through his heart.

The surviving possemen retreated to a base camp where they found Sergeant Earl Hersey of the Signals Corps. Hersey had brought in a sled-load of supplies. The next day they returned to the site of the gun battle and found that Johnson had escaped by scaling the sheer cliff behind his camp. With Millen's frozen corpse lashed to the sled, they grimly admitted that Albert Johnson, whoever he was, had beaten them again and they started back toward their headquarters.

In Aklavik Inspector Eames realized that he was hunting a most extraordinary man and would have to take extraordinary measures. Not only was a killer on the loose, but the reputation of the RCMP was clearly at stake, with the whole world watching their failure to outshoot a lone gunman who had been on the run for a month in the middle of the arctic winter.

Eames sent out a call for volunteers to help bring the trapper to bay and also requested the use of a search plane. It would be the first time in the history of the force that they had conducted a search from the air. Not only could an airplane cover more ground in an hour than a search party could cover in a week, it could also carry more supplies than a dogsled and move them long distances quickly.

On February 7, while Eames led a search party through the rugged country between the Rat and the Barrier rivers, a Bellanca monoplane lifted a load of supplies to the men in the field. Flying it was W.R. "Wop" May, one of the great pioneer bush pilots in the early days of aviation and the man who had been the target of the Red Baron during the First World War dogfight in which another Canadian flyer, Roy Brown, had shot down the famous German ace.

For the duration of the manhunt, May shuttled supplies and men and watched from the air for signs of the trapper. He spotted blind trails the wily Johnson had left to confuse the police. He risked his life by flying in bad weather. Had it not been for Wop May's work in the Bellanca, Johnson might well have escaped.

For several days following the death of Millen, search parties roamed across the arctic wilderness. Albert Johnson seemed to have vanished. He'd been on the run for thirty-nine days, living on scanty rations, tramping across a hostile country through blizzards that kept some of the toughest men indoors. As one northern trapper put it, "'Tis rough enough just staying alive under those conditions, let alone having to be on the run."

Yet the Mad Trapper remained at large. The police finally got a lead on him on February 12, and what they heard was incredible. Snowshoe tracks, believed to be Johnson's, had been seen near La Pierre House on the Yukon side of the Richardson Mountains.

The Richardsons, a northeastern extension of the Rockies, rise to 6,500 feet. Beyond the limit of trees, they are bare, windswept rock. The passes are dangerous and are generally considered impossible to cross in winter. Indians who knew the region said no man could do it alone in wintertime, and yet, somehow Johnson had done it, not only alone but after an exhausting five weeks of relentless wilderness travel with a pack of manhunters on his trail.

On February 13 Wop May flew some of the police to La Pierre House, while others fitted out an expedition to cross the range by dogteam through Rat Pass (the same route the trapper had probably taken). May soon spotted Johnson's track from the air but lost it again in the trail left by a herd of caribou. The clever outlaw was still using every advantage nature offered. Next day, after a series of zigzag sweeps over the country, May found Johnson's track again, twenty miles up the Eagle River from its confluence with the Bell. He might have been heading for another pass to the southwest which would take him to a tributary of the Yukon River, and so across the border into Alaska.

For the next two days the Bellanca was grounded by heavy fog, but men travelling by dogsled and on snowshoes stuck to Johnson's trail. On February 17 May was able to take his plane aloft again. He followed markers left by the search party and so had a bird's eye view of the final confrontation between the Mad Trapper and his pursuers from the RCMP and the Signals Corps.

Johnson had been moving up the Eagle River and had backtracked, probably hoping to come in behind the trackers as he had done several times before. For once, he misjudged and came face to face with them on a hairpin turn of the Eagle. Sergeant Hersey of the Signals was in the lead. He grabbed his rifle and began firing. Two other officers also took shots at the fugitive.

Johnson ran a few yards, then turned and fired one shot. The bullet struck Hersey, who was kneeling, in the left elbow, deflected to his knee, then deflected again into his chest. Hersey was not dead but seriously wounded and out of action.

As the posse moved to outflank him, Johnson threw himself into the snow, pulled off his pack, and pushed it in front of himself for cover. From this semi-exposed position he tried to shoot it out with his assailants, twelve men including Eames and Gardlund.

Three times the police ordered Johnson to surrender and each time he answered with gunfire. But at last the Mad Trapper with the miraculously accurate aim was at a fatal disadvantage. The police had him in a three-way crossfire.

Six bullets struck his body, one of them exploding some ammunition in his pocket and blowing off a piece of his thigh. Even after that he continued to fire. Then another bullet smashed through his spine, and the Mad Trapper was suddenly dead. Wop May in his Bellanca zoomed low over the prone figure and then signalled to the posse that the fight was indeed finished.

It had been the most difficult chase in the history of Canada's Finest. The Mad Trapper had been run down at enormous expense and effort, but the mystery of why it all happened remained unsolved. There were no papers on the dead man's body, nothing whatever to identify him. The police sent fingerprints to Ottawa and Washington, but there was nothing to match them in any police file on the continent. Whatever Johnson may have been, he was not an ex-convict.

Months later a magazine published a photograph of Johnson taken as he lay dead in an arctic police post, and a number of people thought they recognized him, even though the face was emaciated and frozen into a leering grimace. They wrote to say that he resembled a man they knew as Arthur Nelson. There is considerable, though not conclusive, evidence that "Nelson" and "Johnson" were the same man.

Nelson was a trapper of either Swedish or Danish background who suddenly appeared in northern British Columbia during the gold rush of 1924. He was a strange, withdrawn man who usually avoided people. He was also an excellent woodsman and a renowned marksman.

Nelson had wandered across the north, trapping and prospecting. Some people suspected that he was looking for one of the "lost" gold mines of the Yukon. Indians called him "the Bushman," a sort of bogeyman of native folklore. Nelson had been last seen in May 1931 heading in a direction that might well have taken him to Fort McPherson in the

Northwest Territories. Weeks later the Snowshoes brothers met the man they called Johnson on the Peel River.

Motive is perhaps the greatest mystery of the Mad Trapper. Why did he kill one officer and almost kill two others while running a tortuous arctic gauntlet of rifle fire and dynamite? The initial complaint of tampering with traplines was relatively minor, certainly not enough to provoke that desperate last stand in the murderous arctic winter.

It has been suggested that Johnson was a true madman with a psychotic hatred for the police, paranoid, in fact. But he seemed not to show any sign of this when interviewed by Constable Millen. A man driven to violence by RCMP harassment? A fugitive from the law elsewhere? None of these theories seems to fit. Had he been a fugitive, he would most likely have been identified after his death.

If the theory that Johnson and Nelson were the same man is correct, then the Mad Trapper may well have been an undetected killer long before he took his first shot at a policeman. In some of the areas Nelson had visited, men had disappeared without explanation. It was not unusual, of course, for trappers and prospectors to die in the bush. But one man had apparently been killed in a struggle before his cabin had burned down. In Headless Valley on the South Nahanni River several bodies had been found with heads missing.

Such findings have led to conjecture that Arthur Nelson, alias Albert Johnson, was a thief and murderer of long standing, a man who robbed and murdered whenever an opportunity for profit presented itself and there was little danger of detection. Nelson was known to have travelled a long distance to sell furs, passing a nearby trading post to trade at a more distant one. This would make sense if the furs were stolen, and he did not want a local trader to recognize another man's marks on the pelts.

Among Albert Johnson's possessions when he was killed were $2,410 in Canadian notes, $20 in American notes, five pearls valued at $15, a jar containing alluvial gold, and five pieces of gold dental work. If the gold fillings did not come from Johnson's own teeth, where did he get them?

To date, no one has been able to identify Albert Johnson with certainty or explain his forty-eight day duel with the RCMP and the Signals Corps. In spite of patient research by police, historians, and detectives, the mystery of the Mad Trapper remains unsolved.

AFTERWORD

IF THERE IS ANYTHING to be learned from the lives of the outlaws by land and by sea, it is that crime often pays handsomely—not for everyone, of course, only for those who can perform on a grand scale. We have seen pirates who became noblemen and admirals, one who not only founded a landed family but also became a judge. Some of the outlaws took their winnings and became Members of Parliament or of American legislatures. The monsters who built Fort Whoop-Up and committed the Cyprus Hills Massacre not only got clean away with vast fortunes, but also became respected members of the nineteenth-century bourgeoisie.

Pirates and outlaws often ended their lives on the gallows or in a final shoot-out with the police. We have seen one die in battle on the deck of his ship and another with an axe buried in his skull. But the danger of such mishaps was no greater than the risks run by any soldier of fortune. The prospect of possible but unlikely retribution deterred none but the timid.

By the end of the nineteenth century the pirate and bandit were almost a thing of the past, confined to the Red Sea and the Gulf of Siam, to the Arabian deserts and the mountains of Asia. And then, as western civilization began to break

down, the well-policed world ceased to have such a comfortable appearance. By the late twentieth century, with the
resurgence of the drug trade, piracy was common once more,
not only in distant and perilous seas, but right on the door-
steps of North America in the shipping lanes of the Pacific
and the Atlantic.

The kind of piracy practised by drug smugglers is quite
different from that practised by Easton or Roberts. It usually
involves a sneak attack on a private yacht which is then
converted to a drug runner. Wholesale murder is not always
necessary in piracy of this sort. Sometimes a pirate may
have to dispose of some unlucky yachtsmen by dumping
their bodies at sea. Usually, the ship is simply stolen without
violence from some anchorage among the tropical islands.
Hijacking of drug cargoes is another form of modern-day
piracy. Rivalries involving motorcycle gangs on land and
smugglers at sea have resulted in sporadic underworld warfare, but violence has not reached the levels that enlivened
the liquor trade in the days of prohibition.

As for land-based outlaws, they, too, are with us once
again, perhaps more common than at any time in recent
centuries. Most of them are members of political organizations attempting to seize power or to achieve social change
by terrorism, bank robbery, kidnapping, and other forms of
violence. Europe, Africa, Asia, South and Central America
are all scenes of such outlaw activity on a very large scale.
Even the relatively stable society of the United States was
subject to terrorism by outlaw organizations of the "left"
and "right" during the 1970s.

Canada has escaped almost entirely. Only the *Front de
Liberation de Québec,* briefly and in a minor way, committed acts of brigandage in the 1960s. The recent bombing of
an arms manufacturer and even more recent attacks on
sellers of pornography have scarcely deserved to be called
outlaw activity. The acts were directed entirely against
property, not against human life, and were really no more

than headline-grabbing forms of political demonstration. Canada is one of the few countries where terrorists do their level best not to kill anyone.

Perhaps the whitewash of Canadian history has reversed the social process which in other countries turned pirates and outlaws into national celebrities. Indeed, the greatest myth to come out of Canada's outlaw lore is that of the incorruptible Mountie, the red-coated guardian of the law who always gets his man.

For nearly three hundred and fifty years the regions of North America which now make up Canada bred or played host to a succession of sea dogs, bandits, renegades, and lone-wolf killers. An occasional monument and a handful of blue and gold plaques scattered across the country recall their exploits. A few novelists, playwrights, and filmmakers have dramatized versions of their stories, and in certain areas where the oral tradition has not totally died away, brave and evil men live on in local yarns and legends. Their names, unlike those of English and American desperadoes, have not become so familiar to the public that they are used as gimmicks in advertising campaigns.

The pirates and outlaws of Canada remain, as no doubt they should, haunting shadows in our nation's past.

BIBLIOGRAPHY

Abernethy, Thomas. *Western Lands and the American Revolution.* New York: Russel and Russel, 1959.

Anderson, Frank. *Bill Miner, Train Robber.* Calgary, Alta.: Frontier Books, 1968.

Atkin, Ronald. *Maintain the Right.* Toronto: Macmillan of Canada, 1973.

Berton, Pierre. *The Last Spike.* Toronto: McClelland and Stewart, 1971.

_____. *My Country.* Toronto: McClelland and Stewart, 1976.

_____. *The Wild Frontier.* Toronto: McClelland and Stewart, 1978.

Bird, Isabella. *A Lady's Life in the Rocky Mountains.* New York: G. P. Putnam's Sons, 1890.

Boatner, Mark, ed. *Encyclopedia of the American Revolution.* New York: McKay, 1966.

Boyd, Thomas. *Simon Girty, The White Savage.* New York: Minton, Balch, and Co., 1928.

Bradlee, Francis B. C. *Piracy in the West Indies and its Suppression.* Salem, Mass.: The Essex Institute, 1923.

Brown, William McEnery. *The Queen's Bush. A tale of the early days of Bruce County.* London: J. Bale and Co., 1932.

Butterfield, Consul Willshire. *History of the Girtys: being a concise account of the Girty brothers....* Cincinatti: R. Clarke and Co., 1890.

———. *History of Brûlé's Discoveries and Explorations.* Cleveland: Helman-Taylor Co., 1898.

Champlain Society. *Works of Samuel de Champlain.* Toronto: Champlain Society, 1936.

Chevalier, Jean. *Journal du Jean Chevalier.* Edited by J.A. Messervy. St. Hellier, Channel Islands: Société Jersiaise, 1914.

Cranston, J. Herbert. *Étienne Brûlé, Immortal Scoundrel.* Toronto: Ryerson, 1949.

Davidson, T. A. *A New History of Grey County.* Owen Sound, Ont.: Grey Historical Society, 1972.

Dawson, George. "The Toronto Police and the Michipitcoten Riots." Unpublished Ms. Toronto Police Museum, n.d.

Defoe, Daniel (Captain Charles Johnson). *A General History of the Pirates.* Edited by Phillip Gosse. London: Printed by P. Sainsbury at the Cayne Press, 1724.

Drago, Harry S. *Road Agents and Train Robbers.* New York: Dodd Mead and Co., 1973.

Dupuy, Trevor, and Hammerman, Gay, eds. *People and Events of the American Revolution.* New York: R.R. Bowker, 1974.

Fuller, R. M. *Windsor Heritage.* Windsor, Ont.: Herald Press, 1972.

Gosse, Phillip. *The History of Piracy.* New York: Longmans, Green and Co., 1932.

Goulson, C. F. *Seventeenth Century Canada Source Studies.* Toronto: Macmillan of Canada, 1970.

Hakluyt, Richard. *The Principall navigations, voiages and discoveries of the English nation, made by sea or ouer land....* London: Imprinted by George Bishop, Ralph Newberie, and Christopher Barker, 1598-1600.

Heckewelder, John. *A narrative of the mission of the United Brethren among the Delaware and Mohegan Indians....* Philadelphia: M'Carty and Davis, 1820.

Horan, James D. *The Outlaws.* The Authentic Wild West, Vol. 1. New York: Crown Publishers, 1976.

_____. *The Gunfighters.* The Authentic Wild West, Vol. 2. New York: Crown Publishers, 1977.

_____. *The Lawmen.* The Authentic Wild West, Vol. 3. New York: Crown Publishers, 1980.

Horwood, Harold. *Pirates in Newfoundland in the 17th, 18th, and 19th Centuries.* St. John's: Newfoundland Historical Society, 1967.

Kelly, L. V. *The Range Men.* New York: Argonaut Press, 1965.

Kirke, Henry. *The first English conquest of Canada, with some account of the earliest settlements in Nova Scotia and Newfoundland.* London: S. Low, Marston and Co., 1908.

Mainwaring, Sir Henry. "Of the Beginnings, Practices, and Suppression of Pirates." Unpublished Ms. British Museum, London (c. 1620).

_____. *The Life and Works of Sir Henry Mainwaring.* Edited by G. E. Mainwaring. London: Navy Records Society, 1920-1922.

Mason, John. *A brief discourse of Newfoundland.* Edinburgh: Andro Hart, 1620.

Nash, J. R. *Bloodletters and Badmen,* Vols. 1 and 2. New York: Warner Books, 1975.

North, Dick. *The Mad Trapper of Rat River.* Toronto: Macmillan of Canada, 1972.

Nute, Grace Lee. *Caesars of the Wilderness.* St. Paul: Minnesota Historical Society, 1978.

O'Neill, Paul. *The Frontiersmen.* Old West Series. Alexandria, Va.: Time-Life Books, 1977.

Ormsby, W. ed. *The Grey Journals and Letters: Crisis in the Canadas 1838-1839.* London: Macmillan U.K., 1965.

Paterson, T. W. *Canadian Battles and Massacres.* Langley, B.C.: Stagecoach Publishing, 1977.

————. *Outlaws of Western Canada.* Langley, B.C.: Stagecoach Publishing, 1977.

Paterson, T. W. ed. *Ontario: The Pioneer Years.* Langley B.C.: Sunfire Publishing 1983.

Pipping, Ella. *Soldier of Fortune.* Toronto: Macmillan of Canada, 1971.

Prowse, D. W. *A History of Newfoundland.* London: Macmillan U.K., 1895.

Radisson, Pierre Esprit. *Voyages of Pierre Esprit Radisson.* Edited by Gideon D. Scull. Boston: Print Society of Boston, 1885.

Rasky, Frank. *The Taming of the Canadian West.* Toronto: McClelland and Stewart, 1967.

Robin, Martin. *The Bad and the Lonely.* Toronto: James Lorimer, 1976.

————. *The Saga of Red Ryan.* Saskatoon: Western Producer Prairie Books, 1982.

Roosevelt, T. *The Winning of the West,* Vols. 1-5. New York: G. P. Putnam's Sons, 1900.

Rothenberger, M. *We've Killed Johnny Ussher.* Vancouver: Mitchell Press, 1973.

Sharp, P. F. *Whoop Up Country.* Helena: Montana Historical Society, 1955.

Shortis, H. T. "Historical Sketches: Harbour Grace." Unpublished Ms. Gosling Memorial Library, St. John's, Nfld. (c. 1910).

Smallwood, Joseph R., ed. *The Book of Newfoundland,* Vol. 2. St. John's: Newfoundland Book Publishers, 1937.

_____. *The Encyclopedia of Newfoundland and Labrador,* Vol. 1. St. John's: Newfoundland Book Publishers (1967) Ltd., 1981.

_____. "The Encyclopedia of Newfoundland and Labrador," Vols. 2-4. As yet unpublished. Newfoundland Book Publishers (1967) Ltd.

Steele, S. B. *Forty Years in Canada.* Toronto: McClelland, Goodchild, and Stewart, 1915.

Stoddard, Anna M. *The Life of Isabella Bird.* London: John Murray, 1906.

Tanner, O. *The Canadians.* Old West series. Alexandria, Va.: Time-Life Books, 1977.

Thwaites, R. G., ed. *Jesuit Relations and Allied Documents.* New York: Pageant, 1959.

Van Every, Dale. *A Company of Heroes: The American Frontier.* New York: Arno Press, 1977.

Vaughn, Sir William (Orpheus, junior) *The golden fleece diuided into three parts, under which are discouered the errours of religion, the vices and decayes of the kingdome, and lastly the wayes to get wealth, and to restore trading so much complyned of....* London: Printed for Francis Williams, 1626.

Wheeler, K. *The Chroniclers.* Old West Series. Alexandria, Va.: Time-Life Books, 1976.

Whitbourne, Sir R. *A Discourse and Discovery of the New-Found-Land.* London: F. Kyngston for W. Barret, 1620.

INDEX

Ships' names are in italics. Some names and place names, noted only in passing, are not indexed.